Systems

Volume 9

Creating, Analysing and Sustaining Smarter Cities

A Systems Perspective

Volume 6
Architecting Systems. Concepts, Principles and Practice
Hillary Sillitto

Volume 7
Software Engineering in the Systems Context
Ivar Jacobson and Harold "Bud" Lawson, eds.

Volume 8
Using Systems Thinking to Solve Real-World Problems
Jamie P. Monat and Thomas F. Gannon

Volume 9
Creating, Analysing and Sustaining Smarter Cities. A Systems Perspective
Ian Abbott-Donnelly and Harold "Bud" Lawson, eds.

Creating, Analysing and Sustaining Smarter Cities

A Systems Perspective

Edited by

Ian Abbott-Donnelly

and

Harold "Bud" Lawson

ISBN 978-1-84890-209-1

College Publications
Scientific Director: Dov Gabbay
Managing Director: Jane Spurr

http://www.collegepublications.co.uk

Printed by printondemand-worldwide.com

The Systems series publishes books related to Systems Science, Systems Thinking, Systems Engineering and Software Engineering that address trans-disciplinary Frontiers, Practice and Education

Systems Science having its contemporary roots in the first half of the 20th century is today made up of a diversity of approaches that have entered different fields of investigation. Systems Science explores how common features manifest in natural and social systems of varying complexity in order to provide scientific foundations for describing, understanding and designing systems.

Systems Thinking has grown during the latter part of the 20th century into highly useful discipline independent methods, languages and practices. Systems Thinking focuses upon applying concepts, principles, and paradigms in the analysis of the holistic structural and behavioral properties of complex systems – in particular the patterns of relationships that arise in the interactions of multiple systems.

Systems and Software Engineering.   Systems Engineering has gained momentum during the latter part of the 20th century and has led to engineering related practices and standards that can be used in the life cycle management of complex systems. Software Engineering has continued to grow in importance as the software content of most complex systems has steadily increased and in many cases have become the dominant elements. Both Systems and Software Engineering focus upon transforming the need for a system into products and services that meet the need in an effective, reliable and cost effective manner. While there are similarities between Systems and Software Engineering, the unique properties of software often requires special expertise and approaches to life cycle management.

Systems Science, Systems Thinking, as well as Systems and Software Engineering can, and need to, be considered complementary in establishing the capability to individually and collectively "think" and "act" in terms of systems in order to face the complex challenges of modern systems.

This series is a cooperative enterprise between College Publications, the School of Systems and Enterprises at Stevens Institute of Technology and the Bertalanffy Centre for the Study of Systems Science (BCSSS).

For further information concerning the Systems Series see
http://www.collegepublications.co.uk/systems/

CONTENTS

Chapter 1

TOWARDS SMARTER CITIES: ESTABLISHING A SYSTEMS PERSPECTIVE
Harold "Bud" Lawson

Chapter 2

WHY SMART INFRASTRUCTURE WON'T BUILD SMART COMMUNITIES WITHOUT A SYSTEMS PERSPECTIVE
Dr. Rick Robinson

Chapter 3

A RESILIENCE FRAMEWORK FOR SMART CITIES
Dr Roland Kupers,
Hsi Ching Song,

Chapter 4

IoT SYSTEMS -
SYSTEMS SEAMS & SYSTEMS SOCIALIZATION
Chuck Benson

Chapter 5

MANAGING CYBER RISKS IN SMART CITY SYSTEM OF SYSTEMS

Abhik Chaudhuri

Chapter 6

TIPPSS -
TRUST, IDENTITY, PRIVACY, PROTECTION, SAFETY AND SECURITY FOR SMART CITIES

Florence D. Hudson & Mark Cather

Chapter 7

IT STANDARDIZATION FOR SMART CITIES
François Coallier

Chapter 8

THE *INTELLIGENTER* ACTIONABLE FUTURE LIVING
AN UPDATE ON THE THEORY OF HUMAN MOTIVATION
FROM A SMART CITY SYSTEM-OF-SYSTEMS PERSPECTIVE
Lluïsa Marsal

Chapter 9

SORG ALGORITHM
(SUSTAINABLE ORGANISATION ALGORITHM)
HOW DOES IT GIVE US INSIGHT INTO BECOMING A SMART CITY?
Miguel Reynolds

Chapter 10

THE MEASUREMENT LADDER:
EXPLORING A 4-STEP LADDER ON METRICS FOR SMART CITIES
Hisakazu Okamura

Chapter 11

WHAT DOES IT TAKE?
MODELLING THE TRANSFORMATION OF THE HAMMARBY SJÖSTAD ENERGY SYSTEMS, EXPLORING POTENTIALS FOR INCREASED EFFICIENCY AND REDUCED IMPACTS
Örjan Svane

Chapter 12

PORTLAND, OREGON:
A SMART CITY PROTOTYPE
Charles Kelley,

Chapter 13

SEVEN IDEAS THAT MATTER FOR CREATING AND SUSTAINING SMART CITIES
Ian Abbott-Donnelly

ABOUT THE AUTHORS:

PREFACE

This book has been created to bring together the wide range of systems perspectives to enable a viable 'Smart City to be created, understood and operated for long-term sustainability. It strives to be a pioneering book, a first of a kind. It looks across the many systems that make up a city, and at the hidden dynamics of what it takes to enable people, technology and environment to co-exist well.

To whom are we speaking?

- People who operate city systems e.g. energy, water, transport, food, culture, ecosystems.
- People who design policy that aims to improve the performance of cities.
- People who's livelihoods, quality of life and future depend on how cities unfold
- People who provide products and services to cities

The developments in technology that operate at the city-scale have opened up many new opportunities and associated risks. This change may be the new thing that enables smart cities, however fundamentally the smartness of a city is a function of its people, its ability to create a collective intelligence and the quality of its governance.

A specific aim of this book is to help in creating and sustaining Smarter Cities by:

- Collecting evidence of the importance of systems for the aspiration of Smart Cities
- Exploring city dynamics
- Creating systems understanding to underpin city development and city resilience
- Inspiring readers about what is possible

Each of the chapters looks at the ideas, aspirations and challenges of a Smart City from a different systems perspective. Cities are obviously complex systems and so there is by definition no ideal solution to making them smart. Instead, city leaders, policy makers and citizens need to understand more about how city systems work and design them to be adaptable to the unfolding future.

The insights, methods and recommendations explained in each chapter will give you new ways of understanding how the city operates, new options to develop the city to make it smarter and explore new risks that need to be addressed to prevent cities from failing to adapt.

Increasingly cities are the places where the human population chooses to live. However, the rate of change in cities is dramatic because of the pressures of technology use, resource use and climate change. Cities and the people who run them and live in them need to match this rate of change discovering new ways of living that smarter. Not just technologically smart, but smart in in a way that creates and sustains places that are worth living in. Taking a systems perspective to cities is a vital first step to understanding how they work and an essential ingredient to be able to create the future of our cities.

CHAPTER SUMMARIES

Chapter 1 Attaining a System Perspective - Harold "Bud" Lawson

This chapter presents a proven approach to attaining a system perspective and is based upon the College Publications Systems Series book A Journey Through the Systems Landscape. The aim is to promote the ability to "think" and "act" in terms of systems. Developing this ability is a vital step for all of the actors involved in the multiple aspects of making cities smarter.

Chapter 2 Why smart infrastructure won't build smart communities without a systems perspective – Dr. Rick Robinson

This chapter explores the origins of the ideas of smart cities, communities and infrastructure and technology, economics and social science, and examines the limited progress that has been made putting them into practise today. It identifies challenges and inhibitors to doing so that can only be addressed by the more thorough, holistic understanding of social, political, environmental, economic, infrastructural and technological systems that Systems Thinking provides.

Chapter 3 A Resilience Framework for Smart Cities - Dr Roland Kupers, Hsi Ching Song

Resilience is a necessary ingredient for making cities smart. Viewing cities as complex adaptive systems, we introduce a nine-box resilience framework that cities can use to improve their capacity to respond to the variety of challenges they face. Several examples where it has been applied are described.

Chapter 4 IOT Systems - Systems Seams & Systems Socialization - Chuck Benson

This chapter discusses the notion of seams between Internet of Things (IoT) system components to include interfaces between technology systems, seams between city and vendors, seams between departments in the city implementing the IoT system, and the need to actively manage seams in order to see IoT system implementations succeed. This chapter also discusses the need to socialize IoT systems amongst city IoT system users, system implementers, and maintainers as a requirement for implementation success.

Chapter 5 **Managing Cyber Risks in Smart City System of Systems** - Abhik Chaudhuri

This chapter discusses the dependent and interdependent components of a smart city system of systems, and the opportunities and risks of the interdependent systems. It stresses on effective cyber risk assessment and management of the interconnected systems. It also explores governance and policies to build resilient interdependent systems in smart cities.

Chapter 6 **TIPPSS – Trust, Identity, Privacy, Protection, Safety and Security for Smart Cities** - Florence D. Hudson & Mark Cather

The deployment of Internet of Things (IoT) technologies to enable smart cities provides great opportunities to leverage information to improve city operations, enable process efficiencies, develop new services and enhance the citizen experience. At the same time, the monumental increase in digital connections to physical devices, due to the wide deployment of IoT technologies in a smart city, creates great risk. This chapter will provide an introduction and address future considerations for Trust, Identity, Privacy, Protection, Safety and Security (TIPPSS) when designing and deploying Internet of Things enabled systems in a smart and connected city environment.

Chapter 7 **IT standardization for Smart Cities** -François Coallier

An IT-intensive Smart City is a complex system of systems (SoS) that integrates processes, people, applications, technologies, and standards to promote valuable city interactions. This chapter explores how IT standards enable the integration of useful systems to create smart systems. The Smart City system of systems (SoS) is constantly evolving and relies on strong integrated governance at both a managerial and a technical level to make integration possible and reliable. The chapter explores both an overview of IT standards and an integrated model of de Jure standards mapped to the smart city.

Chapter 8 **The Intelligenter Actionable Future Living - An update on the theory of human motivation from a smart city system-of-systems perspective** - Lluïsa Marsal

This chapter dissertates on the current technological harnessing to help us solve today's big challenges and how this technological reliance might have changed our human priorities and needs. This is analysed within the complexity of urban systems, taking sustainability as a challenge and UN's New Urban Agenda as a use case.

Chapter 9 **SORG ALGORITHM (Sustainable Organisation Algorithm) How Does it give us insight into becoming a Smart City?** -Miguel Reynolds

Cities should be built to instil collaboration and happiness among human beings. The way cities are designed might provoke collaboration and peace or isolation and conflict. It's our choice. The SORG index is a simple, accessible and transparent algorithm that helps to predict sustainability in any organisation. By running a sustainability test using the SORG index before deciding the creation or development of any city structure, we can ensure that it is built to empower collaboration, ingenuity and peace. This is the ultimate goal of the SORG organisation model and the SORG index algorithm.

Chapter 10 **The Measurement Ladder: Exploring a 4-Step Ladder on Metrics for Smart Cities** -Hisakazu Okamura

In the first place, smart city projects should proceed towards a clear goal, however, in real-world projects this sometimes doesn't always go to plan.. The theory says it should starts by (1) discovering the purpose of the smart city, then (2) clarifying the focus of measurement in the assessment phase, then (3) carefully measuring progress, and lastly (4) judging the outcomes of the smart city.

Execution of these 4 steps often comes with difficulties. Among the companies that promote smart cities there are many different approaches and policies. Even the definition of what is a smart city has many meanings. In my experience with IBM while participating and reviewing various types of smart city project across many geographies, I have found this 4-step ladder to be a highly effective way of designing and implementing smart city projects.

Chapter 11 **What Does it Take: Modelling the transformation of the Hammarby Sjöstad energy systems, exploring potentials for increased efficiency and reduced impacts** - Örjan Svane

In the Stockholm district of Hammarby Sjöstad, the local energy management initiative 'ElectriCITY' coordinates the efficiency transformation, but only residents, enterprises and real estate owners influence energy use directly. The chapter explores what other organizations need to be involved in order to bridge the gap between the primary agents of change and ElectriCITY. We are using a soft systems approach, modelling the transformation of the energy systems and their use as a sociotechnical system.

Chapter 12 **Portland, Oregon: A Smart City Prototype** - Charles Kelley

Portland, Oregon has radically changed how citizens use the city to produce better places that amplify health, community cohesion, and wellbeing. This chapter explores the real-world experience developing Smart City ideas in Portland and their application to Japan's signature Smart City Kashiwa-no-ha. It reveals important openspace systems and placemaking ideas complementary to technology to create healthier and better performing communities. By innovating through the use of ideas such as: Transit Oriented Development, Placemaking, Ecodistricts, and small lifestyle interventions the City of Portland demonstrates how community activism and local policy making encourages the exchange of ideas and good lifestyle choices supplemental to Smart Cities.

Chapter 13 **Seven Ideas that Matter for Creating and Sustaining Smart Cities** - Ian Abbott-Donnelly

This chapter gathers together a small collection of ideas that I have found to be useful when applying a systems perspective to challenges of helping cities become Smarter. The complexities of cities mean that there are no simple solutions. However by being able to see the city as a system, from multiple perspectives, it is possible to apply technology, social insights and environmental aspirations in ways that makes cities more liveable, more resilient and more in balance with the environment on which they depend.

ACKNOWLEDGEMENTS

The editors would like to acknowledge and thank all of the authors that have contributed thought provoking insights to make this book possible. Their collective intelligence and practical experience is a role model for what it takes to make our cities smarter.

In addition a special thanks go to Colin Harrison, Juri Paraszczak and Peter Williams for guidance, probing questions and positive critique that have steered the direction of this book.

Abhik Chaudhuri: I would like to dedicate this effort to Ian Abbott-Donnelly, Harold "Bud" Lawson and my daughter Sree

Dr Rick Robinson: I'd like to thank Tom Baker, Dave Smith, Margaret Elliott and Conn Crawford who inspired my initial understanding of cities and communities in Sunderland, and Steve Peel and Richard Snell who went on the journey there with me. I'd also like to thank Alan Penn of UCL and Tim Stonor of Space Syntax for introducing me to the work of Jane Jacobs and beginning my intellectual appreciation of their system of systems, and Rashik Parmar, David Cohn, Peter Coldicott, Colin Davidson and Tony Carrato for inviting me into the heart of IBM's Smarter Cities thinking.

FOREWORD

by Colin Harrison

When we look at city, the first thing we see is the people. But beyond this what we see is overwhelmingly technology, albeit technology enriched with the fruits of art, architecture and human culture, supported by the natural environment. While cities are the most complex creation of humanity, enabling millions of us to live in close proximity and mutual support, they depend and always have depended on the use of technology to build, to operate, and to facilitate the myriad interactions among their inhabitants.

Technology is the focal fact of modern life (Hans Jonas). We live in a technological age and cities are where technology is invented, developed, and applied. Every new technology is tested for its potential role in cities. Technologies that are found by the inhabitants to meet some important need are embraced and, for a time, thrive. This combination of people, technologies, and nature forms the complex system of systems that is the life of the city.

In this book we view the city as the complex of systems encompassing the natural and built environments and the social environment founded on these. Together we call these urban systems. The built environment of the city and the multitude of public and private services and affordances supported by these environments are what enable large numbers of people to live closely together. The natural environment is both the source and the sink for the basic necessities of the life of the city - air, water, raw food materials, construction materials, minerals, fossil and renewable energy as well as solid and liquid waste, atmospheric pollution. The long-term stability of the city depends on the cautious consumption and renewal of these sources and sinks and on the ability of the built environment to protect the city against the risks of the natural environment such as flooding, hurricanes, earthquakes, and so forth.

Technologies that offer great value become incorporated in the life of the city - electricity, subways, motor vehicles, passenger and goods lifts, telephones, and many more - and this changes the life of the city. Water and sewage systems sustain public health. Electricity makes streets safer at night and reduces fire risks from oil or gaslights. Subways and buses enable people to live in one neighourhood and have occupations elsewhere. Lifts enable skyscrapers and thereby increase the population density. Telephones enable the rapid exchange of information. Technology emerges to meet perceived needs and human needs evolve to exploit technology. We invent technology and then technology returns the favour by re-inventing how we live.

But cities have unique personalities - Vienna is not Berlin, New York is not Miami. The notion that standardised technologies can be applied to urban systems is anathema to some. A central lesson to date from technology trials is that people come first and the technology must fit to their needs and values. To find the basis for repeatability and standards we must look beyond, for example, predicting the arrival times of buses, and understand the principles of the urban systems that support life in the city.

Cities are and always have been computers. That is, they are social computers. We are drawn to cities to join the networks of humanity that they support. We desire to share in the many choices and opportunities that these networks offer compared to life on the land. By taking part in these networks or urban systems we become part of the Information Ecology that is constantly producing, disseminating, accumulating, and analysing information and using it to make decisions (Lewis Mumford).

In the last sixty years, we have developed Information and Communication Technology (ICT) and this has had profound impacts on our industries, our culture, and, to a lesser degree, on our governments. It is inevitable that we should ask what roles ICT might play in how cities function. For over fifteen years cities around the world have been experimenting with this in many diverse ways. We call these experiments "Smart Cities" to give them a rather ambiguous name. If we view the city as being *ab initio* a computer, then Smart Cities serve first and foremost to augment these systems of social computation. Importantly this is about augmenting and not about replacing this social computation.

This view of the city as a system of systems is relatively modern and few studies of such systems exist so far. Certainly until we began deploying Smart City technologies, we had few scalable means to study such systems and the behaviours of the inhabitants. The multitudes of sensors deployed in the Internet of Things (IoT) now offer rich sources of data on such systems and individual behaviours, but deploying these technologies, even as Augmentation, may change these systems and behaviours. How can we learn about these in their unaugmented states?

After experimenting with Smart Cities technologies for fifteen years or more, it seems moot to ask: Are these technologies being widely embraced? Many examples exist - Smart Meters, bus tracking and arrival prediction, contactless payment systems for public transportation, free-flow tolling of vehicles, congestion reporting and prediction, pothole reporting, and so forth - but are these repeatable or merely one of a kind?

One of the characteristics of ICT is the power of positive returns to scale, which have lead to exponential reductions in the costs of hardware and software. For example, the cost of municipal street lighting has fallen by factor of 500,000 in the transition from candles to LEDs. Are such gains sufficient to drive broad adoption? Much of such scalability emerges from the development of technical standards and interchangeable parts. Cities are full of standards, codes, and regulations in their built environments. So we ask what standards are emerging and are they being supported by cities and by industry?

The search for answers to such questions, the view of cities as complex systems, and the interactions between people and technologies in cities are the genesis of this book, which is written by Smart City practitioners from around the world. Their work displays a wide range of perspectives from technological systems to social systems and, as Mumford put it: "[How] organic humanism tempers technology".

CHAPTER 1

TOWARDS SMARTER CITIES:
ESTABLISHING A SYSTEMS PERSPECTIVE

Harold "Bud" Lawson

Abstract: Obtaining and utilizing a systems perspective that enables the ability to "think" and "act" in terms of systems is important for all parties involved in the development, establishment, operation, measurement, sustainment, and improvement of the constituent systems of cities. To be able to use concepts and paradigms as common mental models as well as to share a vocabulary of terminology are essential ingredients for understanding and communication amongst the multiple actors involved. In this chapter, a proven approach to attaining a broad common systems perspective based upon systems thinking as well as systems engineering is presented.

1.   INTRODUCTION

"A system is a way of looking at the world...a system, any system, is the point of view of one or several observers."

Gerald Weinberg (Weinberg, 2001)

The British Standards Institute (BSI) defines 'smart city' as *"a term denoting the effective integration of physical, digital and human systems in the built environment to deliver a sustainable, prosperous and inclusive future for its citizens"*.

The National Institute of Standards (NIST) provides the following definition: *"smart cities are complex systems, often called systems of systems," including people, infrastructure, and process components"*.

Viewing cities as systems of systems has become a popular way of categorizing the multitude of services to be provided. The word "system" is likely one of the most utilized words in all of the world's languages. Often it is used in a negative sense – stating that there was a system defect (bug, failure) when rational explanations of a situation do not suffice. However, what lies behind the word system? Can we make some productive usage of the word in the context of smart cities? For example, by being more specific about the meaning and usage of the word system can we improve individual, group, organization understanding and communication about various types of systems and their interrelationships as they form a system of systems.

The perspective presented in this chapter has been utilized productively and has made it possible to teach individuals and groups to "think" and "act" in terms of systems (Lawson, 2010). Attaining a systems perspective has been based upon introducing a limited set of concepts, principles and paradigms that reflect essential aspects of systems and can be applied to both technical and non-technical as well as systems involving both types of elements. For example, a traffic control system for a city involves both technical elements (sensors, actuators, lights, cables, etc.) and elements such as traffic regulations and fines as well as human elements such as parking controllers and police. It is, in fact, a complex system.

Certainly as we move into the age of Internet of Things that will impact multiple aspects of cities and citizens, attaining such a perspective is vital as pointed to by (Hudson and Cather, 2017). They identify the key attributes of Trust, Identity, Privacy, Protection, Safety and Security (TIPPSS) that need to be assessed and addressed for all IoT applications, devices, processes and services.

The need for a holistic systems perspective is definitely required into order to explore and resolve conflicting issues as pointed to by (Robinson, 2017) where he states: "Smart ideas will continue to quickly create arguments between opposing camps rather than constructive progress: infrastructure versus people; top-down versus bottom-up; technology versus urban design; proprietary technology versus open source; public service improvements versus the enablement of open innovation –and so on".

1.1 Systems are Pervasive

"Systems are Everywhere" declared Ludwig von Bertalanffy (von Bertalanffy, 1968). From a technology point of view given the rise of personal computers, mobile telephones, tablets as well as all of the embedded devices in our homes, business, cars, etc. certainly reflects this fact. The world has rapidly become dependent upon complex systems in which software has become a dominant element (Jacobson and Lawson, 2015). This is a two-edged sword. On the one hand, many new and useful products and services have been provided that have changed the fundaments of society. But the vulnerability of software to bugs, viruses, fraud, and hacker attacks has escalated and presents serious safety and security problems in our society. Further the radical changes, due to the wide scale accessibility of information, has created new social, organizational and psychological problems. Consequently the wide spread usage of information technology in the public sector is laden with problems, as well as opportunities, that must be understood and addressed. Here a systems perspective is essential.

Our understanding of complex systems is at best cursory, laying somewhere between mystery and mastery (Flood, 1998). For all but trivial systems achieving complete mastery is a goal that seems to be quite distant. So we are dependent upon diverse knowledge and diverse disciplines to even gain partial understanding.

This chapter considers how deeper knowledge about systems (including Systems Thinking and Systems Engineering) can be utilized by individuals and by organizations like city governments and their administrative departments where IT and in particular software systems have become an essential contributor to successful services as well as the problems that have evolved.

2.   TOWARDS A BROADER VIEW OF SYSTEMS

While there are a variety of definitions of the word system, it is useful to characterize systems by examining the conceptual properties as attributes that are used in building a system perspective.

2.1 Fundamental Properties

"We believe that the essence of a system is togetherness, the drawing together of various parts and the relationships they form in order to produce a new whole..."

John Boardman and Brian Sauser (2008)

This fundamental concept of *togetherness* that implies connectivity between the parts permits us to recognize as von Bertalanffy postulated that systems are everywhere. Consider, for example the togetherness of the technical and non-technical elements of the traffic control system described earlier.

The notion of togetherness leads us to two further related concepts; namely *structure* and *behavior*.

Structures and behaviors are central properties of all man-made systems. The structure of a system is a static property and refers to the constituent elements of the system and their relationship to each other. The behavior is a dynamic property and refers to the effect produced by a system "in operation."

Another related fundamental property that is attributed to system operation is the concept of *emergence*. Emergence arises from both the predictable and unpredictable operational behavior of a system itself and/or in relationship to the environment in which the system resides. This concept is captured in the following quote of Peter Checkland:

"Whole entities exhibit properties which are meaningful only when attributed to the whole, not to its parts…"

Peter Checkland (1999)

2.2 The Role of Man-Made Systems

Why do we create man-made systems? How are they composed? How do "systems" play a significant role in our daily activities? To city governmental institutions these are important questions. (Lawson, 2010) created a paradigm called the Systems Coupling Diagram that answers these questions as portrayed Figure 1.

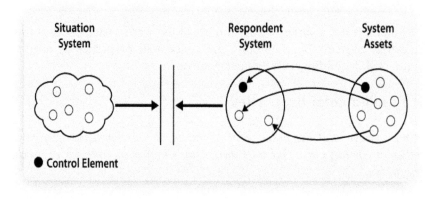

Figure 1 The Systems Coupling Diagram

To the left is a Situation System; that is a situation composed of parts and relationships that is viewed as presenting a problem that needs a response or an opportunity that can be exploited via a response. In the middle is a Respondent System (sometimes called an Intervention System) organized in order to address the problem or opportunity situation. The double bars indicate that there is an interaction between the Respondent and Situation System. The Respondent System receives its inputs from the Situation System and delivers outputs that transform the situation into a new situation. The elements of the Respondent System are taken from instantiations of System Assets that are available, both tangible and non-tangible. One of the instantiated system assets is a control element that directs the Respondent System when it operates.

This diagram should be quite obvious to every reader since we are constantly confronted with problem or opportunity situations in our daily life. We respond to situations based upon the assets that we have available. In a more formal sense we can view that the situation system has a "state" and that by responding, this state is transformed into a new state. For example, given a busy street intersection that continually occurs, a response is needed to utilize various system assets (tangible and non-tangible) that can be instantiated in order to improve the situation (a new state).

A lot of our confusion over systems comes from the fact that we give names to these more generic system aspects, view them as something unique, and forget that they individually and collectively reflect the fundamental system properties that were presented earlier. Typical names that can be associated are as indicated in Table 1

Table 1 Names for Systems

Situation Systems	Respondent Systems	System Assets
Natural	Project	Infrastructure,
Man-Made	Team	Theory, Knowledge,
Mixed	Mission	Standards, Processes,
Thematic	Program	Methods, Practices.
	Task	Frameworks, Tools,
	Sprint	Policies, Guidelines,
	Study	Competencies
	Experiment	

Natural systems are, as they are, as a result of natural substances and forces on earth. Man-made systems are the result of the efforts of man to create and utilize something hard or soft (organizational, social, political, etc.), as well as software. Nowadays, mixed systems involving hard, soft and software elements permeate our everyday life, in the home, at work, leisure time and in transportation. Man-made and mixed systems strive to provide some form of added value. The situation that arises as a problem or opportunity is often in the complex relationships that evolve in respect to their creation, utilization and sustainment.

In order to gain an understanding of situations it is often useful to "simulate" responses to situations based upon the deployment of system assets. Thus, the Situation System may be Thematic (a theme is created). Of course, this is common in amongst others military scenarios, in disaster management and in business games and certainly can be utilized in the context of gaining an understanding of the affect of policies and strategies for smarter cities. For example, since 1997, Singapore has conducted scenario-planning exercises every 3-5 years to refresh the government's thinking on possible futures amidst changing external conditions. This formal process ensures that these National Scenarios are incorporated by different Ministries into their strategic review exercises (Kupers and Song, 2017).

Thus the System Coupling Diagram reflects endeavors (responses) related solely to gaining a deeper understanding of situations by experiments or study and analysis. The diagram also captures the variety of organized efforts aimed towards transforming a situation into a new situation; for example creating a new system service or modifying and existing system to deal with a problem or exploit an opportunity. The response is often called a project, but alternative names such as mission, team, task and sprint or even "iterations" also are viewed as Respondent Systems.

2.3 Surviving in a World of Complex Systems

In addition to the fundamental system properties and the System Coupling Diagram, Lawson (2010) presents further properties of systems that have proved to be useful in building a system perspective. These are presented as a system of system concepts[1] that provide a semantic system context. The system of system concepts together with the System Coupling Diagram and a set of principles based upon the concepts are called the System Survival Kit. Understanding the survival kit assists in forming a system perspective of any type of system. The concepts are categorized and given the specific definitions as follows: fundamental, types, topology, focus, complexity and role as provided in Table 2

Table 1 System of Systems Concepts

Fundamental	
Togetherness	Two or more elements are related resulting in a new whole.
Structure	The constituent elements and their static relationship.
Behavior	The effect produced by the elements and their dynamic element relationships in operation.
Emergence	The predictable or unpredictable behavior occurring as the result of a system in operation.

---

[1] The notion of a system of system concepts was first introduced by Russell Ackoff (Ackoff, 1971).

Table 1. (continued) System of System Concepts.

Types	
Natural System	Origin is in the universe and they are as a result of forces and processes that characterize the universe.
Defined Physical System	Two or more physical elements are integrated together producing a new whole.
Defined Abstract System	Two or more abstract elements are related resulting in a new whole.
Human Activity System	Two or more elements, at least one involving a human activity are integrated resulting in a new whole.

Topology	
Hierarchy	A level-wise structure of systems and system elements that is defined recursively (i.e. lower level elements are systems or terminal elements).
Network	A nodes and links structure of system elements and their interrelationships.

Focus	
Narrow System-of-Interest	The system upon which focus is placed in respect to a view (NSOI).
Wider System-of-Interest	The systems that directly affect (including enabling) the NSOI in respect to a view (WSOI).
Environment	The context that has a direct influence upon the NSOI and WSOI.
Wider Environment	The context that has an indirect influence upon the NSOI and WSOI.

Table 1. (continued) System of System Concepts.

Complexity	
Organized Simplicity	There are a small number of essential factors and large number of less significant and/or insignificant factors.
Organized	The structure is organized in order to be understood and thus be amenable for describing complex behaviors.
Disorganized	There are many variables that exhibit a high level of random behavior. Can be due to not having adequate control over the structure of heterogeneous complex systems (so-called complexity creep).
People Related	Perception of the system fosters a feeling of complexity. Also, rational or irrational behavior of individuals in particular situations.

Role	
Sustained System Asset	A system that is life cycle managed and when instantiated provides system services.
Situation System	Two or more elements become related together resulting in a problem or an opportunity. Alternatively, an objective or end state that defines a desirable situation is established.
Respondent System	A system composed of two or more elements that are assembled in order to respond to a situation.
Thematic System	A system that is composed for the study of possible outcomes of a postulated situation system as well as one or more respondent systems ("what if").

The elements of this system of system concepts build largely upon the contributions of a variety of systems scientists, systems thinkers and systems engineers. The source of the fundamental concept of togetherness and a definition of the emergence concept where identified earlier. Checkland (1993) has provided the categorization of system types.

Concerning the focus category, Ashby (1956) made some important observations about the multiplicity of elements in systems and that selecting subsets of the elements for study is vital in extracting a System-of-Interest. (Flood and Carson, 1988) identified the concepts and relationships of Narrow System-of-Interest, Wider System-of-Interest, Environment and Wider Environment.

(Weaver, 1948) provided an early viewpoint by categorizing complexity into organized simplicity, organized complexity and disorganized complexity. These categories and later reflections by amongst others (Flood and Carson, 1998) and your author provided the impetus for the complexity categorization.

The role category is based upon the System Coupling Diagram. Earlier the focus was placed upon Situation and Respondent systems. However, it is important to note the concept of Sustained System Assets. Our ability to respond to situations is based upon system assets that when instantiated provide the required added value service to the response. In practice this means that the system asset, be it hard, soft or software must be itself properly life cycle managed. Managing system assets is one of the major challenges for the sustainment of smarter cities.

2.4 Systems Thinking

In relationship to the System Coupling Diagram, we are interested in analyzing, building an understanding and communicating about situations be they problems or opportunities. To analyze situations, sometimes coupled with responses as well as the utilization of system assets, the body of knowledge from the various approaches to Systems Thinking provides very useful avenues for achieving understanding that can be communicated. (Senge, et al, 1994) have characterized systems thinking as follows:

"Systems thinking is a process of discovery and diagnosis – an inquiry into the governing processes underlying the problems we face and the opportunities we have."

Note: Your author has added the opportunities aspect.

According to Senge and his colleagues, a good systems thinker, particularly in an organizational setting, is someone who can see four levels operating simultaneously: events, patterns of behavior, systems, and mental models.

Systems thinking evolved during the 20th century, via multiple contributions into a somewhat more understood discipline. Building upon the pioneering contributions of Ludwig von Bertalanffy in the 1920s, Jay Forrester, Russell Ackoff, Ross Ashby, Stafford Beer, Wes Churchman, Peter Checkland, Peter Senge, John Warfield, Barry Richmond, Donella Meadows, John Boardman and others have made important contributions to systems thinking in the latter half of the 20th century.

Checkland (1993), starting from a systems engineering perspective, successively observed the problems in applying systems engineering to the more fuzzy ill-defined problems found in the organizational, social and political arenas. Thus he introduced a distinction between hard systems and soft systems.

2.5 Hard and Soft Systems

Hard systems of the world are characterized by the ability to define purpose, goals and missions that can be addressed via engineering methodologies in attempting to in some sense "optimize" a solution. Soft systems of the world are characterized by extremely complex, problematical and often mysterious phenomenon for which concrete goals cannot be established and which require learning in order to make improvement. Such systems are not limited to the social and political arenas and also exist within and amongst city governments, enterprises, programs, projects, missions, teams, etc. where complex, often ill-defined, patterns of behavior are observed that are limiting the ability to improve. Recognizing this important difference, Checkland points to the fact that a process of inquiry that itself can be organized into a learning system is the most appropriate approach for analyzing and learning about such soft systems in which human activities exist as elements.

Situations, particularly when large quantities of software is involved, are often complex and problematical, thus the need for study and learning should be apparent, but often skipped by the early production of and introduction of solutions. The balance between producing a broader understanding and producing solutions must be taken into account in all approaches to both Software Engineering and Systems Engineering.

2.6 A Variety of Approaches

A number of methodologies, tools, models, languages, and techniques have been developed by systems thinkers that assist in the fundamental aspects of seeing wholes, interrelationships, and patterns of change in hard systems, soft systems and mixtures of the two. This includes such descriptive approaches as the determination of root causes via the Five Why's, Loops, Links and Delay language used to express growth and limiting loops as well as Archetypes of patterns of growth and limits (Senge, et al., 1994), Rich Pictures (Checkland, 1993) and Systemigrams (Boardman and Sauser, 2008). Some approaches are used for both description and simulation such as DYNAMO (Forrester, 1975), Stella and iThink (see www.iseesystems.com) and Gnosis (Collinson, et al, 2012).

Abhik (Chaudhuri, 2017) provides a very useful view of the dependencies and inter-dependencies of the various systems that can be used to provide services to the citizens of smart cities. He also identifies the risks involved and points to various risk mitigation actions. It is clear that in analyzing situations that arise in the planning, implementation and operation of system services that the use of systems thinking tools provide a mechanism for gaining deeper insight into problems and opportunities. Thus, in developing the capability to think in terms of systems, politicians and administrative governmental employees should learn to utilize these tools, methods, languages and techniques as a part of their problem solving and opportunity exploitation arsenal.

A stepwise procedure for applying systems thinking developed by (Monat and Gannon, 2017) identifies key aspects as follows:

Step 1. Develop and articulate a problem statement
Step 2. Identify and delimit the system
Step 3. Identify Events and Patterns
Step 4. Discover the Structures
Step 5. Discover the Mental Models
Step 6. Identify and Address Archetypes
Step 7. Model (if appropriate)
Step 8. Determine the systemic root cause(s)
Step 9. Make recommendations
Step 10. Assess Improvement

A detailed explanation of the multitude of various tools, models, languages, and techniques used in Systems Thinking is outside the scope of this book. For an explanation of these approaches your author recommends his own work (Lawson, 2010), the references provided in the previous paragraph as well as a web search on Systems Thinking or Systemic Thinking will yield an enormous amount of relevant literature. One important source worth specific mentioning is the websites organized by Bellinger (2004 and later).

In respect to learning to think in terms of systems, it is important to point to the usage of analogical reasoning as a means to find parallels that are useful in promoting understanding. One pioneering development that has been successfully applied by a variety of enterprises and individuals is Synectics developed by the late MIT professor W.J.J. Gordon (1961). Abbott-Donnelly (2017) has provided a chapter in this book where he utilizes analogies to substantiate ideas related to creating and sustaining smarter cities.

While the System Survival Kit and the application of Systems Thinking assists in providing a holistic perspective of systems, there are a number of related aspects that should be taken into account in developing the capability to "think" and "act" in terms of systems.

3. THE FUNDAMENTS OF CHANGE

The understanding produced by the application of systems thinking in analyzing situations, regardless of the approach is utilized to make prudent decisions about changes to the systems that are of interest. In (Lawson, 2010) the underlying processes of situation awareness and analysis as well as change action are characterized by coupling together two well-known loops; that is, the paradigm portrayed Figure 2.

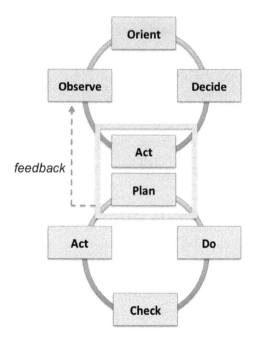

Figure 2 Integrated OODA PDCA Loops

3.1 The OODA Loop (Observe, Orient, Decide, Act)

Col. John Boyd of the U.S. Air Force, a veteran of aircraft combat during the Korean conflict of the 1950s, set out to explain why some pilots succeeded in air combat while others, equally well trained, failed. Over the course of a lifetime, the insights that Boyd gained from studying dogfights grew into a broader description of tactical decision making in dynamic situations (Boyd, 1987). Long taught in military circles especially for command and control, Boyd's ideas gained increasing influence in business and governmental circles. The heart of Boyd's theory is based upon the premise that a tactical decision is the result of activities in a four-step loop.

Observation: Whether observation consists of the visual cues that guide a fighter pilot or the staff papers and briefings presented to a senior administrator, the decision-maker must first perceive and assimilate information about the environment (situation) as a basis for decision.

Orientation: Once the decision-maker has gained information through his/her or others observations, he/she (or a group) must fit those pieces of information into a useful understanding of the situation.

Decision: The decision-maker selects a course of action.

Action: The desired course of action is executed.

OODA activities are highly related to systems thinking and decision-making and are typically executed continuously in leadership and management functions. This "spawning" of problems and opportunities is an integral part of the establishing change actions. For example, when a traffic control system is in operation, problems that arise as a result of congestion illustrate the use of the OODA loop.

3.2 The PDCA Loop (Plan, Do, Check, Act)

The PDCA loop was first introduced by Walter Shewhart in the 1920s as the activities required to achieve successful Statistical Quality Control. The PDCA concept was later popularized by MIT professor W. Edwards Deming as one of the guiding principles of TQM (Total Quality Management). Deming had worked under the mentorship of Shewhart at Bell Telephone Laboratories. While there are some similarities as to the general goals of OODA and PDCA in respect to identifying problems and opportunities, the latter is action based and goes deeper into actually making changes, measuring the effect of changes and taking corrective actions to achieve planned goals. The loop begins with the creation of a Plan.

Plan: Create a plan for accomplishing a goal or set of goals that are related to solving a problem or pursuing an opportunity. The plan will include the definition of the processes and/or activities required to achieve the changes necessary to achieve the goals.

Do: Make the change.

Check: The results of the change are checked (verified) against the goals that were established.

Act: If necessary, corrective actions are taken to adjust the plan, perhaps renegotiate the goals and then to recycle the loop until the goals are achieved or a decision is made to terminate.

Some utilize PDSA (where the S means Study). When used in conjunction with soft systems, the use of study instead of check is quite appropriate.

The application of OODA is always continuous in nature. PDCA in guiding missions, teams, projects, tasks, sprints, etc. is discrete in nature; that is, it is typically applied for achieving specific goals within a specific time frame with provided resources after which the mission or project is terminated. In the traffic control system new technical equipment or changes in traffic regulations may be applied and evaluated to deal with the congestion problem.

The integration of the two loops is realized by coupling the Act activity of the OODA loop to the Plan activity of the PDCA loop. That is, the action to be performed involves the formation of a response such as a mission, project or sprint, the first activity of which is the Plan. As a result of the execution data and information concerning results, problems and opportunities are feed back for Observation in the OODA loop as portrayed in Figure 2

The reader should keep this paradigm in mind as it relates to our mental model System Coupling Diagram. The paradigm can be used to explain most any situation related to thinking and acting in terms of systems and relates directly to Situation Systems and Respondent Systems. Later in the chapter, the use of these two loops as central aspects of Change Management will be described.

4.   A SYSTEMS PERSPECTIVE OF LIFE CYCLES

The methodologies and practices of Systems Engineering provide a controlled means of "acting" where transforming needed capabilities into a product or service has been the traditional goal. Several standards and best practices have evolved in this regard. An important standard that is utilized to describe the essence of the life cycle management of systems via a limited generic set of processes is (ISO/IEC/IEEE 15288, 2002, 2008, 2015). This standard, first released in 2002 was created in order to promote trading in system products and services and has a direct impact upon enterprise and business management as noted by Arnold and Lawson (2004).

The standard concerns those systems that are man-made and may be configured with one or more of the following: hardware, software, data, humans, processes (e.g., processes for providing service to users), procedures (e.g., operator instructions), facilities, materials and naturally occurring entities.   Thus it deals with all types of man-made systems including technical and so-called human activity systems.   See Lawson (2010) for a summary description of the set of processes.

4.1 Generic Life Cycle Model

Let us consider a model illustrating the essence of Systems Engineering as portrayed in Figure 3 (see Pyster and Olwell, 2013). The provisioning of a System-of-Interest is accomplished by creating a System Breakdown Structure and then by managing the Life Cycles of the system as well as the Life Cycles of elements of the system when they are defined systems as well (remember recursion as described earlier).

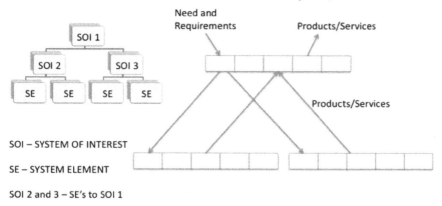

SOI – SYSTEM OF INTEREST

SE – SYSTEM ELEMENT

SOI 2 and 3 – SE's to SOI 1

Figure 3 Fundamental Aspects of Systems Engineering

On the left hand side of the figure observe that there are three Systems

The System-of-Interest identified in the form of a System Breakdown Structure. SOI 1 is decomposed into its elements that in this case are systems as well (SOI 2 and SOI 3). These two systems are composed of System Elements which are not further refined.

On the right hand side of the figure observe that each of the Systems-of-Interest has a corresponding Life Cycle Model composed of stages that are populated with process activities that are used to define the work to be performed. Note that some of the requirements defined to meet the need are distributed in the early stages of the life cycle for SOI 1 to the life cycles of SOI 2, respectively SOI 3. This decomposition of the system illustrates the fundamental concept of Recursion as defined in the ISO/IEC/IEEE 15288 standard. That is the standard is reapplied for each of the Systems-of-Interest.

Note that the system elements are integrated in SOI 2, respectively SOI 3 thus realizing a product or service that is delivered to the life cycle of SOI 1 for integration in realizing the product or service that meets the stated need.

An example that relate to this system need is an embedded system (SOI 1) composed of a hardware system (SOI 2) and a software system (SOI 3) such as a traffic intersection controller composed of a microprocessor and real-time software. Nowadays we can observe this type of controller in many IOT (Internet of Things) products. Another example is a human resource system composed of a recruitment system and a competence management system to be developed and deployed in a public sector organization. In performing the work in stages, most often iteration between stages is required. For example, in the successive refinement of the definition of the system, in providing an update (upgrade or problem solution) of a realized and even delivered product or service.

The work performed during the stages can be performed in a concurrent manner within the life cycle of any of the Systems-of-Interest and concurrent amongst the multiple life cycles.

4.2 Enabling Systems

The work performed during the life cycle of a System-of-Interest always requires the deployment of other systems that enable (support) the work to be done. This is exemplified in Figure 4. These are systems that when instantiated must provide their service; thus, they must also be life cycle managed in a prudent manner. The recognition of this relationship was a great break-through in the ISO/IEC/IEEE 15288 standard. So, the same standard can be re-applied for all of the systems. The Project Design system is worth mentioning since it is often an enterprise related system about how to map of the project(s) that are to be active during the life cycle. The actual life cycle stage structure is not dictated by the standard. You might think about the enabling systems required to develop, install and operate the cities traffic control system.

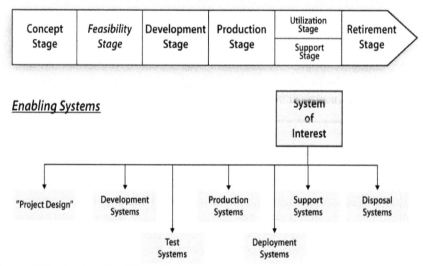

Figure 4 Deploying Enabling Systems

4.3 Life Cycle Transformations

Various results are produced by "executing" processes during the life cycle as the System-of-Interest evolves from need or opportunity to concept

16

and to reality in the form of products and services. To portray these transformations based upon the knowledge that has been provided thus far, consider the life-cycle structure illustrated in Figure 5

Here we observe at the top of the figure that the System-of-Interest is first described as Defined Abstract Systems that are then transformed into concrete Defined Physical and/or Human Activity Systems when they become a product that is instantiated for utilization. An eventual retirement of a System-of-Interest involves disposing of instances and can also involve retirement of the system definition, that is, the Defined Abstract Systems.

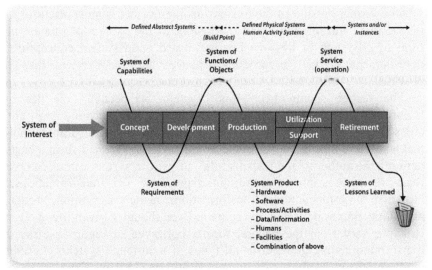

Figure 5 Life Cycle Transformations (System-of-Interest Versions)

It is important to note the perspective portrayed in the figure in naming the various stage and process related results as "systems". We view the various descriptions as well as the eventual product as "versions" of the System-of-Interest. That is from a need, the first version of the System-of-Interest is created as a System of Capabilities. This description meets all of the criteria for a system as defined earlier where the most fundamental aspect is "togetherness".

From this System of Capabilities, the next version of the System-of-Interest is created in the form of a System of Requirements reflecting both the functional as well as non-functional requirements to be placed upon the System-of-Interest. The next version of the System-of-Interest is a System of Functions or Objects that describe the basic transformations that the instantiated System Products are expected to perform when they provide their service. Typically, this involves some type of flow of energy, material, data or information.

In order to provide for orderly development, production and usage, it is important to keep consistency between the various descriptions, that is, traceability between the elements of the various versions of the System-of-Interest.

Based upon the description versions, System Products are produced as the result of the integration of elements that can include hardware, software, processes/activities, data/information, humans, facilities, natural elements or combinations thereof. (Note that the early versions of the system (prototypes) may actually be realized in the Development stage as indicated by the dotted line "build point" that is most always the case for software systems.) When the product is utilized in its final environment, it provides the System Service, that is the behaviors that it has been designed to achieve.

One further version of the System-of-Interest that is most often forgotten is to capture information about the history of the System-of-Interest in the form of a System of Lessons Learned based upon system conception and development as well as product instances and the services they have provided.

The reader should keep this "system perspective" on life cycle transformations in mind, perhaps by considering how it would apply for the cities traffic control system. The various system version transformations that take place during the life cycle as portrayed in Figure 5 form a basis for defining the authority and responsibility of various system actors. In order to focus the discussion of important aspects of the transformations, we introduce three fundamental transformations; namely Definition, Production and Utilization as portrayed in Figure 6. Even though a given life cycle stage structure vary from the general format portrayed in Figure 5 these three transformations are generic for all types of man-made systems. Further, in the figure the utilization of the universal System Coupling Diagram model is provided in order to portray its applicability in the "situations" that is, the transformations that arise during the life cycle management of systems. This planned usage of the System Coupling Diagram illustrates how system assets that are required to do the work in the stage (or iteration) are instantiated in a Respondent System that interacts with the current situation and transforms it into a new situation.

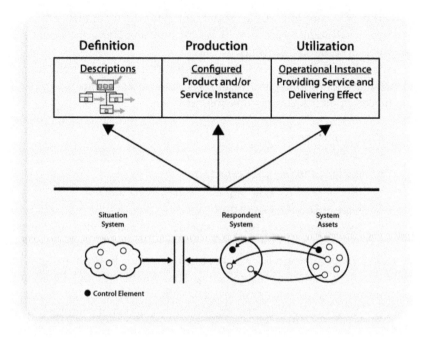

Figure 6 Life Cycle Transformations and the System Coupling Diagram

The Life Cycle structures that have portrayed in Figures 5 and 6 can naturally be refined into activities that are performed in parallel and incrementally. Boehm (2015) has developed the Incremental Commitment Spiral Model (ICSM) where parallel work is done on various aspects, capabilities, requirements, decomposition to functions/objects, etc. in an incremental manner. These increments are identified as Exploration, Valuation, Development and Operation. However the System Coupling Diagram is also an appropriate description of the responses performed in each increment.

5.   THE CENTRAL ROLE OF ARCHITECTURE

One of the primary reasons for system failures (including operational and development failures) is that an appropriate and viable architectural structure of the system has not been established and sustained. While this is the case for all types of hard, soft and mixed systems, it has continually been a specific problem for software systems. Due to the easy to change property of software, solutions are far too often done on a Q&D (quick and dirty) basis leading to enormous bug-laden maintenance problems. Even planned software efforts often fail due to the lack of architectural considerations or

19

due to architectural entropy (identified earlier as complexity creep). Certainly, if lean and agile approaches to development are used, the importance of architecture should be apparent in setting the boundaries and establishing solution directions.

According to Sillitto (2014), the purpose of "systems architecting" is to ensure that the various parts of our systems, when connected to each other and placed in their operating environment:

- fit together
- work together
- achieve the required effect
- do not produce unacceptable side-effects and can be
- kept operational over time
- reconfigured to meet "reasonable unforeseen" circumstances.

Developing appropriate architectures requires holistic insight into the problem or opportunity, establishing the boundaries of the system, the relationship to enabling systems as well as the broader environmental aspects. A key factor is the establishment a small number of driving concepts and principles that all relevant parties can keep in their mind as mental models (Lawson, 1990; Lawson and Martin, 2008). This promotes understanding and communication and provides boundaries for decision-making during the life cycle.

Your author has written several articles about the history of why today's software systems suffer from significant unnecessary complexity as the result of the lack of appropriate balanced hardware and software architectures. Several of the historical events that changed the computing landscape are described in (Lawson, 2002, Lawson, 2012). In "The Mythical Man-Month", Brooks (1975) has documented aspects of this problem in respect to the development of the IBM System 360 operating system in the mid 1960's. In the 1970s, the microprocessor appeared that radically altered hardware economics. However, due to the very primitive facilities provided, too much software is developed in a plethora of low level programming languages, scripts and middleware systems. Middleware while providing a bridge certainly does not remove the unnecessary complexity. There were solutions to building solid hardware-software architectures in the late 1960's and early 70's that disappeared as described in (Lawson, 2002; Lawson, 2012).

Gaining a holistic perspective on describing architectures has come into focus by considering architectural views based upon stakeholder viewpoints. This has resulted, firstly in the software architecture standard IEEE 1471 (2000) that has been superseded by the system standard ISO/IEC/IEEE 42010 (ISO/IEC/IEEE 42010, 2011). These standards provide a useful means promoting understanding and communication amongst stakeholders, developers, testers, operators, maintainers, and so on (Hilliard, 2015).

20

Understanding this standard is highly recommended for those involved in the establishment of new system products and services for the city environment.

6. CYBERNETICS AND CHANGE MANAGEMENT SYSTEMS

The field of cybernetics was developed in the mid to late 1940s by Warren McCulloch and Norbert Weiner as a discipline independent means of explaining complex system interrelationships with regard to control, information, measurement and logic. A generic cybernetic system composed of three system elements and their relationships is portrayed in Figure 7

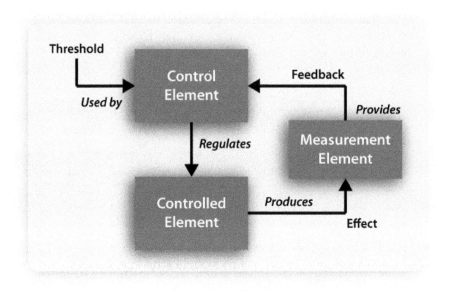

Figure 7 A Generic Cybernetic System

A Control Element regulates a Controlled Element. The Controlled Element produces Effect. A Measurement Element measures the effect and provides Feedback to the Control Element. The Control Element compares the current effect with a Threshold value that it uses in deciding upon further regulation of the Controlled Element.

Cybernetics is applied in physical systems, for example in the regulation of room temperature. In this case, physical regulation sensors are used to measure the current effect which is fed back to a Control Element where the current effect is compared with a threshold setting which can result in activating or deactivating a heating or cooling element. Such regulation operates continuously as long as the Controlled, Control and Measurement

Elements are operational. In a traffic control environment the threshold value can well be the waiting time at an intersection.

In relationship to the System Coupling Diagram in Figure 1, it is useful to note that some form of control element is necessary for Respondent Systems in which case this element controls the other elements as the Respondent System handles the Situation System. Thus, the cybernetic model is directly applicable whether we are regulating room temperatures, traffic lights, the progression of stages in a life cycle, or treatment of a problem or even crisis that has arisen. In fact, control elements should be viewed as system assets that are life cycle managed and instantiated as operative controllers.

While the nature of the control, controlled and measurement elements are different, the principles of cybernetics can be equally applied to non-physical systems; for example a city employees recruitment system. Cybernetics forms, along with the utilization of the OODA and PDCA loops, the basis for the implementation of the Change Management Model introduced by Lawson (2010) and presented here in Figure 8

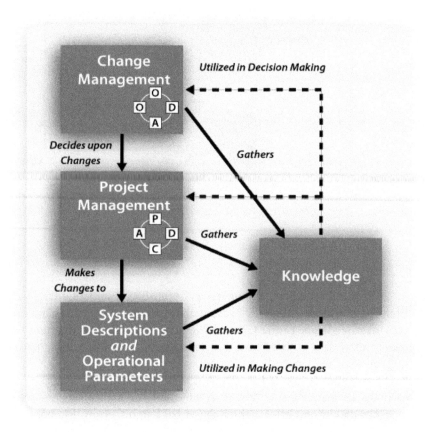

Figure 8 Change Management System

- Change Management functions as the Control Element. It uses Knowledge as Feedback in making decisions. Purpose, Goals, and Missions to be accomplished along with policy, rules and regulations serve as Threshold values.
- When changes are made via Projects, the Project becomes the Controlled Element. When operational parameter changes are made by a line organization, it is the Controlled Element.
- Outputs produced by the execution of Processes produce Effect in respect to changes in System Description and Operational Parameters (for instances of system products or services that are in utilization).
- The Effect (outputs) produced by all of the elements on the left are gathered as data, interpreted as relevant information and when related to other information becomes the Knowledge that is fed back and fed forward (in order to improve actions).

In implementing the model as a system, the Control Element operates continuously according the Observe, Orient, Decide, and Act paradigm. The Controlled Element, be it a project, mission or a line organization operates in a discrete manner; that is, it makes the change within planned time constraints according to the PDCA paradigm.

Several of the concepts and paradigms that are described in (Lawson, 2010) have now been introduced. There are further supporting concepts and paradigms that should be explored in that reference. In addition, an important aspect of attaining a systems perspective is in the definition and operation of organizations and enterprises that certainly encompass governmental organizations (see Gotze and Jensen-Waud, 2013).

7.   A SYSTEMS PERSPECTIVE OF ENTERPRISES

City Managers – See yourself as a system owner and understand your relationship to other City Enterprise relevant systems and, in particular the software elements of the systems. Convey this perspective to all Organizations and the Enterprises they create that are aimed at producing value added products and/or services that are of interest. The provisioning of products and/or services are the primary Systems-of-Interest goals of the Enterprise. However, in organizing the City Enterprise to provide the products and/or services, the Enterprise is dependent upon infrastructure systems that enable the provisioning in an expedient manner. So, as illustrated in Figure 9 the Enterprise must have a systems focus concerning its portfolio of system assets that it utilizes in its responses aimed at achieving its purpose, goals and missions.

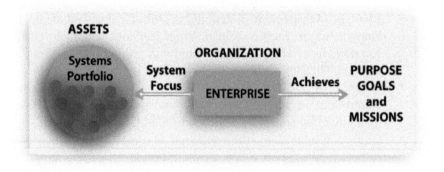

Figure 9 Focusing on Organization/Enterprise Systems

In organizing the efforts, particularly in larger organizations such as city governments, various managers are appointed to manage the provisioning of essential functions that contribute to the Enterprise. By taking a systems perspective, these managers are in fact the owners of the system assets portrayed in Figure 9.

It is a hypothesis of this presentation that when all of the managers view themselves as system owners and are equipped with essential system knowledge that they can understand and communicate with each other in an effective manner. Finally, we can view the systems of an enterprise as an aggregation of systems organized according to enterprise architecture views as portrayed in Figure 10. The reader should observe the parallels with the operation of city governmental services.

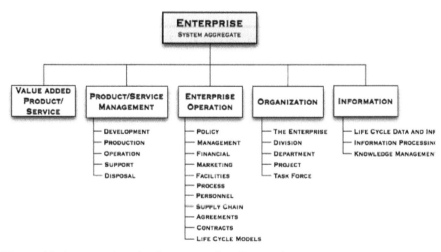

Figure 10 Aggregating the Systems of an Enterprise

The aggregation as a system of systems can, and should be, viewed as the architecture framework of the enterprise where the views of the system owners are expressed via appropriate descriptive models, languages, etc. This is a very different lightweight approach than many of the heavy enterprise architectural frameworks that have become popular in the last decade. It should provide an intelligent basis for dealing with the cascading and propagation of faults and problems that occur within the infrastructure systems of the City Enterprise.

8.   CONCLUSIONS

Attaining a systems perspective resulting in the capability to "think" and "act" in terms of systems is vital for individuals as well as groups. In this chapter, a proven approach to providing a systems perspective has been provided. Certainly as basis for improving understanding and communication a broad systems perspective is an essential aspect of the creation, analysis and sustainment of smarter cities.

REFERENCES

Abbott-Donnelly I. (2017) Seven Ideas That Matter for Creating and Sustaining a Smarter City, appearing in this book.

Ackoff, R. L. (1971) Towards a System of Systems Concepts. Management Science, 17(11).

Arnold, S. and Lawson, H. (2004) Viewing Systems from a Business Management Perspective, Systems Engineering, The Journal of The International Council on Systems Engineering, Vol. 7, No. 3, pp 229-242.

Ashby, W.R. (1956) An Introduction to Cybernetics, Chaptman & Hall, London.

Bellinger, G. (2004) www.systems-thinking.org and http://www.systemswiki.org/

Boardman, J. and Sauser, B. (2008) Systems Thinking – Coping with 21st Century Problems, CRC Press, Boca Raton, FL.

Boehm, B. (2015) Principles and Rationale for Successful Systems and Software Processes, appearing in Software Engineering in the Systems Context, Systems Series, Volume 7, College Publications, Kings College, UK

Brooks, F. (1975) The Mythical Man-Month, Addison Wesley.

Checkland, P. (1993) Systems Thinking, Systems Practice, John Wiley, Chichester, UK.

Checkland, P. (1999) Systems Thinking, Systems Practice – Includes a 30 year Retrospective, JohnWiley, Chichester, UK.

Chaudhuri, A. (2017) Managing Cyber Risks in Smart City System of Systems, appearing in this book.

Collinson, M., et.al. (2012) A Discipline of Mathematical Systems Modelling, Systems Series, Volume 2, College Publications, Kings College, UK.

Flood, R.L. and Carson, E.R. (1988) Dealing with Complexity: An Introduction to the Theory and Application of Systems Science, Second Edition, Plenum Press, London and New York.

Flood, R.L. (1998) Rethinking the Fifth Discipline: Learning within the unknowable, Routledge, London and New York.

Gordon, W.J.J. (1961) Synectics, the Development of Creative Capacity, Harper & Row, New York

Gotze, J. and Jensen-Waud, A. (2013) Beyond Alignment: Applying Systems Thinking in Architecting Enterprises, Systems Series, Volume 3, College Publications, Kings College, UK.

Hilliard, R. (2015) Lessons from the Unity of Architecting, appearing in Software Engineering in the Systems Context, Systems Series, Volume 7, College Publications, Kings College, UK.

Hudson, F. and Cather, M. TIPPSS - Trust, Identity, Privacy, Protection, Safety and Security for Smart Cities, appearing in this book.

IEEE 1471 (2000) Recommended Practice for Architectural Description of Software-Intensive Systems, Institute for Electrical and Electronic Engineering.

ISO/IEC/IEEE 12207 (2008) Systems and Software Engineering - Software life cycle processes, International Standardization Organization/International Electrotechnical Commission, 1, rue de Varembe, CH-1211 Geneve 20, Switzerland.

ISO/IEC/IEEE 15288 (2002, 2008, 2015) Systems and Software Engineering - System life cycle processes, International Standardization Organization/International Electrotechnical Commission, 1, rue de Varembe, CH-1211 Geneve 20, Switzerland.

ISO/IEC/IEEE 42010 (2011) Systems and Software Engineering - Architecture description International Standardization Organization/International Electrotechnical Commission, 1, rue de Varembe, CH-1211 Geneve 20, Switzerland.

Kupers, R. and Song, H.C. (2017) A Resilience Framework for Smart Cities, appearing in this book.

Lawson, H. (1990) Philosophies for Engineering Computer-Based Systems, IEEE Computer, Vol 23, No.12, 1990.

Lawson, H. (2002) Rebirth of the Computer Industry, Communications of the ACM June 2002/Vol. 45, No. 6.

Lawson, H. and Martin, J. (2008) On the Use of Concepts and Principles for Improving Systems Engineering Practice, Proceedings of the INCOSE International Conference, Utrecht.

Lawson, H. (2010) A Journey Through the Systems Landscape, Systems Series, Volume 1, College Publications, Kings College, UK.

Lawson, H. (2012) Experiences and Reflections, appearing in Reflections on the History of Computing – Preserving Memories and Sharing Stories, Springer 2012 IFIP Advances in Information and Communication Technology (Arthur Tatnall, editor).

Monat, J. and Gannon, T. (2017) Using Systems Thinking to Solve Real-World Problems, Systems Series, Volume 8, College Publications, Kings College, UK.

Robinson, R. (2017) Why Smart Infrastructure won't Build Smart Communities without a Systems Perspective, appearing in this book.

Senge, P.M. (1990) The Fifth Discipline: The Art & Practice of The Learning Organization, Currency Doubleday, New York.

Sillitto, H. (2014) Architecting Systems-Concepts, Principles and Practice, Systems Series, Volume 6, College Publications, Kings College, UK.

Weaver, W. (1948) Science and Complexity. American Science, 36 pp 536-544.

Weinberg, G. M. (2001) An Introduction to General Systems Thinking, Dorset House Publishing Company, 1st edition.

CHAPTER 2

WHY SMART INFRASTRUCTURE WON'T BUILD SMART COMMUNITIES WITHOUT A SYSTEMS PERSPECTIVE

Dr Rick Robinson

The futuristic "Emerald City" in the 1939 film "The Wizard of Oz".
The "wizard" who controls the city is a fraud who uses theatrical technology to disguise his lack of real power.
Image: https://clipartfest.com

1.   INTRODUCTION

The idea of "Smart" cities, infrastructure and communities is 20 years old now; but despite some high profile pilot projects and a lot of attention, it has so far had very little impact on its objective, which is to invest in technology in order to create economic, social and environmental improvements.

Many businesses are using "Smart" technology to great, sometimes astonishing effect – the phenomenally rapid growth of "platform" businesses such as Uber and Airbnb is an oft-quoted example. But these are simply "for profit" businesses, and any wider benefits that they create (beyond convenience for their customers) are simply side effects, or externalities as Economists would call them.

I do not mean to be critical of the private sector. it is where I have worked for my entire career. It is the engine of our economy, and without its profits we would not create the jobs needed by a growing global population, or the means to pay the taxes that sustain our public services, or the surplus wealth that creates an ability to invest in our future. But we cannot simply assume that the externalities of private sector business operating in a free market will create the social, economic and environmental outcomes that society needs – that is why we have regulated industries.

For the past ten years, I have been working with cities, communities and Government bodies, mostly in the UK, to secure more direct investments in technology in order to tackle the issues that concern them: the challenge of delivering more effective public services – especially social and healthcare – at a lower cost base; improving the UK's dreadfully poor social mobility; improving economic productivity at both a national and regional level; and ultimately providing their residents with happier, healthier, more productive, and – importantly – fairer lives.

Whilst I am convinced that systems thinking is fundamentally important to shaping those investments and designing the technology solutions they enable – topics that are covered in fabulous breadth and depth throughout this book – I think it is important first to properly understand the nature of the challenge we face in securing investment in the first place. That challenge is a significant one, and it has not yet been solved. We should focus our systems thinking efforts on it first, because it is the most fundamental challenge we face.

The raw truth is that – outside one-off projects funded by research and innovation grants – only a *tiny* amount of investment from sustainable, repeatable, scalable sources has ever been made in "Smart" projects that use technology in innovative ways to directly achieve social, economic and environmental outcomes; and there is little sign that this situation will change rapidly.

That is an economic and political challenge, not a technology trend; and it is an imperative challenge because of the nature and extent of the risks we face as a society today. Whilst the demands created by urbanisation and growth in the global population[1] threaten to outstrip the resources and infrastructure capacity available to us [1], those resources are under threat from man-made climate change [1]; and we live in a world in which many think that access to resources is becoming dangerously unfair [1].

We will only address that challenge if we lift the debate about Smart cities, communities and infrastructure out of the domain of technology and into the domain of economics and policy, because we need politicians and economists to shape the policies and investment vehicles that will enable the emergence of new business models that combine profitability with a direct contribution to social, economic and environmental goals.

And we will only persuade them to do that if we are able to provide them with credible, compelling evidence: the evidence that only systems thinking can provide from the rich, complex – and often downright messy – "systems of systems" that are the only way to properly understand the behaviours of cities, communities and economies.

William Robinson Leigh's 1908 painting "Visionary City" envisaged future cities constructed from mile-long buildings of hundreds of stories connected by gas-lit skyways for trams, pedestrians and horse-drawn carriages. A century later we're starting to realise not only that developments in transport and power technology have eclipsed Leigh's vision, but that we don't want to live in cities constructed from buildings on this scale.

Our problem starts in a very basic way: the lack of a clear definition of what a Smart city or community is. From the earliest days, they have been defined in terms of either smart infrastructure or smart citizens; but rarely both at the same time.

For example, in "City of Bits[1] " in 1996, William Mitchell, Director of the Smart Cities Research Group at MIT's Media Lab, predicted the widespread deployment of digital technology to transform city infrastructures:

"... as the infobahn takes over a widening range of functions, the roles of inhabited structures and transportation systems are shifting once again, fresh urban patterns are forming, and we have the opportunity to rethink received ideas of what buildings and cities are, how they can be made, and what they are really for."

Whilst in their paper "E-Governance and Smart Communities: A Social Learning Challenge[i]", published in the Social Science Computer Review in 2001, Amanda Coe, Gilles Paquet and Jeffrey Roy described the 1997 emergence of the idea of "Smart Communities" in which citizens and communities are given a stronger voice in their own governance by the power of Internet communication technologies:

"A smart community is defined as a geographical area ranging in size from a neighbourhood to a multi-county region within which citizens, organizations and governing institutions deploy and embrace NICT ["New Information and Communication Technologies"] to transform their region in significant and fundamental ways (Eger 1997). In an information age, smart communities are intended to promote job growth, economic development and improve quality of life within the community."

These two ideas are neither the same; nor mutually exclusive or contradictory. But they are cannot be reconciled simply. A systems perspective of communities, infrastructure, technology, economy, society, politics and the environment is needed to bring them into harmony.

Until we create that systems perspective – and I hope this book represents a significant contribution to doing so – discussions about "Smart" ideas will continue to quickly create arguments between opposing camps rather than constructive progress: infrastructure versus people; top-down versus bottom-up; a common understanding of challenges and solutions versus an appreciation of the glorious diversity between and within cities; technology versus urban design; proprietary technology versus open source; public service improvements versus the enablement of open innovation – and so on.

2.   MAKING THE CASE THAT "SMART" IS A COMPELLING ECONOMIC AND POLITICAL CHALLENGE, NOT A TECHNOLOGY TREND

In my discussions with political leaders and their teams at both national and local level, it has become clear that "Smart" ideas will only properly hold their attention if they are convinced that they are of comparable social and economic importance to issues such as education, social care, health, economic growth and social mobility; and if they are convinced that technology is both one of the strongest forces driving change in our society, and one of the most powerful tools to improve it.

I believe there is plenty of high-level evidence to make that case already, as I will explain next; but politicians will not act unless these ideas are supported by robust evidence – the sort of evidence that only systems thinking can provide through the study of complex, interdisciplinary systems.

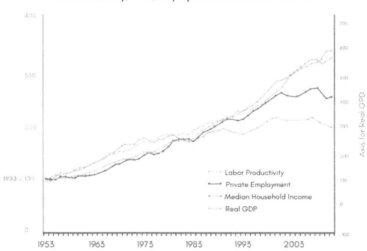

United States GDP plotted against median household income from 1953 to present. Until about 1980, growth in the economy correlated to increases in household wealth. But from 1980 onwards as digital technology has transformed the economy, household income has remained flat despite continuing economic growth. From MIT Economist Andrew McAfee's blog[i], explained in his book "The Second Machine Age[ii]", Erik Brynjolfsson, summarised in this article[iii].

Massive commercial investments are already being made in smart technology at a scale that is transforming our world - $32 billion of venture capital was invested in "Internet of Things" startup companies in the 2nd quarter of 2017 alone, for example[ii]. But these investments in technology primarily support the development of new products and services that consumers want to buy. That's guaranteed to create convenience for consumers and profit for companies; but it's far from guaranteed to create resilient, socially mobile, vibrant and healthy cities and communities. It's just as likely to reduce our life expectancy and social engagement by making it easier to order high-fat, high-sugar takeaway food on our smartphones to be delivered to our couches by drones whilst we immerse ourselves in multiplayer virtual reality games.

That's why whilst technology advocates praise the ingenuity of technology-enabled "sharing economy" business models such as Airbnb and Uber[ii], and the opportunities for employment and business they create, other commentators point out that far from being platforms for "sharing" many are simply profit-seeking transaction brokers[ii]. More fundamentally, some economists are seriously concerned that the economy is becoming dominated by such platform business models and that the majority of the value they create is captured by a small number of platform owners[ii]– world leaders discussed these issues[ii] at the World Economic Forum's 2016 Davos conference. Whilst there are arguments on both sides, there is enough evidence to suggest that we should be concerned that the exploitation of technology by business is contributing to the evolution of the global economy in a way that makes it less equal. For example, Oxfam estimate that whilst the globalised technological economy has lifted a billion people worldwide out of extreme poverty since 1990, it would have lifted 200 million more people out of extreme poverty if it hadn't also created significantly increases in inequality[ii].

Finally, the similarly massive investments continually made in property development and infrastructure are, for the most part, not creating investments in digital technology in the public interest. Sometimes that's because there's no incentive to do so: development investors make their returns by selling the property they construct; they often have no interest in whether the tenants of that property start successful digital businesses, and they receive no income from any connectivity services those tenants might use. In other cases, policy actively inhibits more socially minded developers from providing digital services. One developer of a £1billion regeneration project told me that European Union restrictions on state aid had prevented them making any investment in connectivity. They could only build buildings without connectivity – in an area with no mobile coverage – and attempt to attract people and businesses to move in, thereby creating demand for telecommunications companies to subsequently compete to fulfill.

We'll only build Smart communities when we shape the market for investing in technology for public services and infrastructure in a way that incentivises the outcomes we decide are important.

In her seminal 1961 work "The Death and Life of Great American Cities[iii]", Jane Jacobs wrote that:

"Private investment shapes cities, but social ideas (and laws) shape private investment. First comes the image of what we want, then the machinery is adapted to turn out that image."

Cities, towns, regions and countries around the world have set out their self-images of a Smart future, but we have not adapted the financial, regulatory and economic machinery – the policies, the procurement practices, the development frameworks, the investment models – to incentivise the private sector to create them.

But we cannot simply assume that economic growth driven by private sector investments in technology to improve business performance will create broad social, economic and environmental benefits. There is no guarantee that it will.

Outside philanthropy, charitable donations and social business models, private sector investments are made in order to make a profit, period. In doing so, social, economic and environmental benefits may also be created, but they are side effects that, at best, result from the informed investment choices of conscientious business leaders. At worst, they are simply irrelevant to the imperative of the profit motive.

Some businesses have the scale, vision and stability to make more direct links in their strategies and decision-making to the dependency between their success as businesses and the health of the society in which they operate – Unilever has been a notable and high-profile example[iii]. And all businesses are run by real people whose consciences influence their business decisions (with unfortunate exceptions, of course).

But those examples do not add up to the alignment of private sector investment objectives with the aspirations of city authorities or citizens for their future. As MIT economists Andy McAfee and Erik Brynjolfsson, amongst others, have shown, most current evidence indicates that the technology economy is exacerbating the inequality that exists in our society[iii] (see graph above). That is the opposite of the future aspirations expressed by many cities, communities and their governments.

This leads us to the political and economic imperative represented by the Smart movement: to adapt the machinery of our economy – including the enormous potential for private sector investments and business models to improve society - to influence investments in business, property and infrastructure technology so that they contribute to the social, economic and environmental outcomes that we want.

3.   LEARNING FROM PREVIOUS GENERATIONS OF TECHNOLOGY

Historically, there is plenty of evidence that investments in technology and infrastructure can cause great harm if market forces alone are left to shape them.

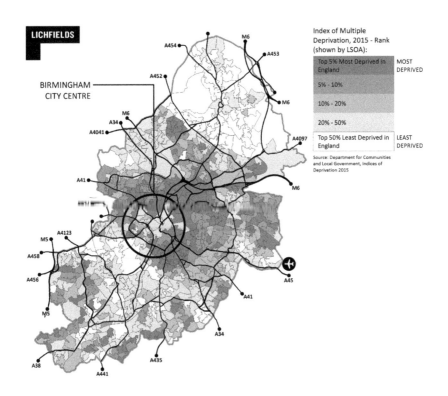

Areas of relative wealth and deprivation in Birmingham
as measured by the Indices of Multiple Deprivation[iii].
Birmingham, like many of the UK's Core Cities, has a ring of persistently deprived areas immediately outside the city centre, co-located with the highest concentration of transport infrastructure allowing traffic to flow in and out of the centre

For example, in the decades after the Second World War, cities in developed countries rebuilt themselves using the technologies of the time – concrete and the internal combustion engine. Networks of urban highways were built into city centres in the interests of connecting city economies with national and international transport links to commerce, and enabling commuters to travel between attractive homes in the suburbs and lucrative jobs in city centres.

Those infrastructures supported economic growth, but they did not provide access to the communities they passed through in areas close to, but just outside, the city centre, and creating pollution, noise and physical danger. UCL's research on the relationship between transport and poverty points out that many residents of these communities are employed in relatively low-income jobs that mean they often have no choice but to live and work in these areas. [iv]

The 2015 Indices of Multiple Deprivation[V] in the UK demonstrate that some of those communities face great challenges as a result. The indices identify neighbourhoods with combinations of low levels of employment and income; poor health; poor access to quality education and training; high levels of crime; poor quality living environments and shortages of quality housing and services. An analysis of these areas in the UK's Core Cities[V] (the eight economically largest cities outside London, plus Glasgow and Cardiff) show that many of them exist in rings surrounding relatively thriving city centres. Whilst clearly the full causes are complex, it is no surprise that those rings feature a concentration of transport infrastructure passing through them, but primarily serving the interests of those passing in and out of the centre. (And this is without taking into account the full health impacts of transport-related pollution, which we're only just starting to appreciate[V]).

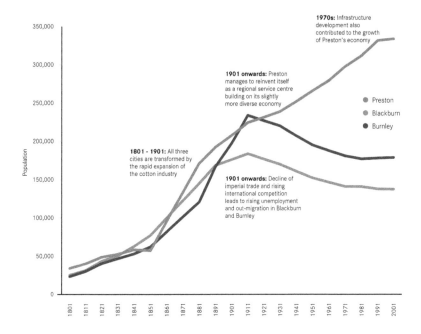

Similar effects can be seen historically. In their report "Cities Outlook 1901[(v)] ", Centre for Cities explored the previous century of urban development in the UK, examining why at various times some cities thrived and some did not. They concluded that the single most important influence on the success of cities was their ability to provide their citizens with the right skills and opportunities to find employment, as the skills required in the economy *changed as technology evolved*. (See the sample graph below). A recent short article in The Economist magazine[(v)] similarly argued that history shows there is no inevitable mechanism that ensures that the benefits of economic growth driven by technology-enabled productivity improvements are broadly distributed. It cites huge investments made in the US education system in the late 19th and early 20th Centuries[v] to ensure that the general population was in a position to benefit from the technological developments of the Industrial Revolution as an example of the efforts that may need to be made.

The relationships between investments in infrastructure, its design, construction and use, and the local and global economic, social and environmental outcomes it creates are complex; far from well understood; and bear all the hallmarks of a challenge requiring systems thinking. And if we attempt to develop policies to address those challenges without using systems thinking to inform them, there is a very real risk that unintended consequences could do more harm than good.

4.   RECONCILING TOP-DOWN POLICIES AND BOTTOM-UP INNOVATION

Population changes in Blackburn, Burnley and Preston from 1901-2001.
In the early part of the century, all three cities grew, supported by successful manufacturing economies. But in the latter half, only Preston continued to grow as it transitioned successfully to a service economy. If cities do not adapt to changes in the economy driven by technology, history shows that they fail. From "Cities Outlook 1901[vi]" by Centre for Cities

So far, I've focused my argument on the role of political leaders developing policies that could promote investment in Smart Cities and communities.

When I discuss this topic, I often encounter a counter-argument that my thinking is too "top-down" and that instead, we should focus on the "bottom-up" creativity that is the richest source of innovation and of practical solutions to problems that are rooted in local context.

My answer to this challenge is that I agree *completely* that it is bottom-up innovation that will create the majority of the answers to our challenges. But bottom-up innovation is already happening everywhere around us – it is what everyone does every day to create a better business, a better community, a better life. The problem with bottom-up innovation doesn't lie in making it happen; it lies in enabling it to have a bigger impact. If bottom-up innovation on its own were the answer, then we wouldn't have the staggering and increasing levels of inequality that we see today, and the economic growth created by the information revolution would be more broadly distributed.

We do not need "top-down" *or*" bottom-up" approaches: we need both to work in harmony; and our challenge is that we do not yet understand how to achieve that harmony.

The systems thinker and architect Kelvin Campbell framed this challenge perfectly when he created the "Massive / Small" movement[vii], which seeks to answer the question: "what are the characteristics of the physical and policy environment that give rise to **massive** amounts of **small**-scale innovation?

That question is the essence of the "Smart" challenge and answering it will depend on a systems approach to cities, communities, infrastructure, the environment and the economy.

Innovation Birmingham's Chief Executive David Hardman
describes the £7m "iCentrum" facility that will open in March 2016 to local stakeholders.
It will offer entrepreneurial companies opportunities to co-develop smart city products and
services with larger organisations such as RWE nPower, the Transport Systems Catapult and
Centro, Birmingham's Public Transport Executive[viii]

5.   LEARNING FROM WHAT'S WORKED

Whilst I've concentrated so far on many of the challenges that have made it very hard to put "Smart" ideas into practice, there are also positive examples in the UK, from Sunderland to London to Norfolk to Birmingham, of initiatives that are supported by sustainable funding sources and investment streams; that are not dependent on research and development grants from national or international innovation funds or technology companies; and that essentially could be applied by any city or community. The means by which these initiatives have been carried out – and they extent to which they have been successful or not – highlight the areas which we should subject to analysis by systems thinking if we want to generalise them to approaches that can be pursued more broadly.

I summarised these repeatable models recently in the article:

"4 ways to get on with building Smart Cities.
And the societal failure that stops us using them[ix]":

5.1 Include "Smart" criteria in the procurement of services by local authorities to encourage competitive innovation from private sector providers

Whilst local authority budgets are under pressure around the world, and have certainly suffered enormous cuts in the UK, local authorities nevertheless spend up to billions of pounds sterling annually on goods, services and staff time. The majority of procurements that direct that spending still procure traditional goods and services through traditional criteria and contracts. By contrast, Sunderland[x], a UK city, and Norfolk[xi], a UK county, have shown that by emphasising city and regional aspirations in procurement scoring criteria it is possible to incentivise suppliers to invest in smart solutions that contribute to local objectives; and the Local Government Association's National Procurement Strategy [xii]encourages such innovations.

5.2 Encourage development opportunities to include "smart" infrastructure

Investors invest in infrastructure and property development because it creates returns for them – to the tune of billions of pounds sterling annually in the UK[xiii]. Those investments are already made in the context of regulations – planning frameworks, building codes and energy performance criteria, for example. Those regulations can be adapted to demand that investments in property and physical infrastructure include investment in digital infrastructure in a way that contributes to local authority and community objectives[xiv]. The East Wick and Sweetwater development in London – a multi-£100million development that is part of the 2012 Olympics legacy, was financed by a pension fund investment and was awarded to it's developer, based in part, on their commitments to invest in this way[xv].

5.3 Commit to entrepreneurial programmes

There are many examples of new urban or public services being delivered by entrepreneurial organisations who develop new business and operating models enabled by technology – I've already cited Uber and Airbnb as examples that contribute to traveller convenience; Casserole Club[xvi], a service that uses social media to connect people who can't provide their own food with neighbours who are happy to cook an extra portion of a meal for someone else, is an example that has more obviously social benefits. Many cities have local investment funds and support services for entrepreneurial businesses, and Sunderland's Software Centre[xvii], Birmingham's iCentrum development[xviii], and Sheffield's Smart Lab[xix] are examples where those investments have been linked to local smart city objectives.

5.4 Enable and support Social Enterprise

The objectives of Smart initiatives are analogous to the "triple bottom line[xx]" objectives of Social Enterprises[xxi] – organisations whose finances are sustained by revenues from the products or services that they provide, but that commit themselves to social, environmental or economic outcomes, rather than to maximising their financial returns to shareholders. A vast number of Smart initiatives are carried out by these organisations when they innovate using technology. Local Authorities that find a way to systematically enable social enterprises to succeed could unlock a reservoir of beneficial innovation, as the Impact Hub network[xxii], a global community of collaborative workspaces, has shown.

5.5 How to lead a Smart community: Commitment, Collaboration, Consistency and Community

Each of the approaches I've described is dependent on both political leadership from a local authority and collaboration with regional stakeholders – businesses, developers, Universities, community groups and so on.

So the first task for political leaders who wish to drive an effective Smart programme is to facilitate the co-creation of regional consensus and an action plan (I'm not going to use the word "roadmap". My experience of Smart roadmaps is that they are, as the name implies, passive documents that don't go anywhere). That action plan should have both short- and long-term objectives and activities, independent of political cycles; clear ownership; and a clear approach to funding and investment.

Doing so successfully requires the demonstration of a particular set of leadership behaviours that are vital to any attempt to create change in a system as complex as a city, community or economy.

I describe them using "four C's":
Commitment, **Collaboration**, **Consistency** and **Community**.

Commitment

A successful approach to a Smart City or community needs the commitment, leadership and active engagement of the most senior local government leaders. Of course, elected Mayors, Council Leaders and Chief Executives are busy people with a multitude of responsibilities and they inevitably delegate; but this is a responsibility that cannot be delegated too far. The vast majority of local authorities that I have seen pursue this agenda with tangible results – through whichever approach, even those authorities who have been successful funding their initiatives through research and innovation grants – have appointed a dedicated Executive officer reporting directly to the Chief Executive, Council Leader or Regional Mayor and with a clear mandate to create, communicate and drive a collaborative smart strategy and programme.

Collaboration

A collaborative, empowered regional stakeholder forum is needed to convene local resources. Whilst a local authority is the only elected body with a mandate to set regional objectives, local authorities directly control only a fraction of regional resources, and do not directly set many local priorities. Most approaches to Smart initiatives require · coordinated activity by a variety of local organisations. That only comes about if those organisations decide to collaborate at the most senior level, mutually agree their objectives for doing so consistent with all of their individual interests, and meet regularly to agree actions to achieve them. The local authority's elected mandate usually makes it the most appropriate organisation to facilitate the formation and chair the proceedings of such fora; but it cannot direct them. This collaboration creates the conditions where a systems perspective becomes possible.

Consistency

In order to collaborate, regional stakeholders need to agree a clear, consistent, specific local vision for their future. Without that, they will lack a context in which to take decisions that reconcile their individual interests with shared regional objectives; and any bids for funding and investments they make, whether individually or jointly, will appear inconsistent and unconvincing.

Community

Finally, the only people who really know what a smart community should look like are the citizens, taxpayers, voters, customers, business owners and employees who form it; who live and work in the same place; and who will ultimately pay for its services and infrastructure either directly or through their taxes or pension contributions. It's their bottom-up innovation that will give rise to the most meaningful and effective initiatives. Their voice – heard through events, consultation exercises, town hall meetings, social media and so on – should lead to the visions and policies to create an environment in which they can flourish.

Birmingham's newly opened city centre trams
are an example of a reversal of 20th-century trends
that prioritised car traffic over the public transport systems
that we have re-discovered to be so important to healthy cities

6.   BEYOND "TOP-DOWN" V "BOTTOM-UP": TRANSLATIONAL LEADERSHIP, SMART DIGITAL URBANISM AND A SYSTEMS PERSPECTIVE

Having established that there's a challenge worth facing, argued that we need political leaders to take action to address it, and explored what that action should be, I'd like finally to return to some of the arguments I explored along the way, and link them to a systems perspective of communities, places and infrastructure.

Action by political leaders is, almost by definition, "top-down"; and, whilst I stand by my argument that it's the most important missing element of the majority of smart initiatives today, it's vitally important that those top-down actions are taken in such a way as to encourage, enable and empower "bottom-up" innovation by the people, communities and businesses from which real places are made. It's not only important that our leaders take the actions that I've argued for; it's important that they act in the right way – to enable others to succeed, rather than to direct change prescriptively. Smart communities are not "business as usual"; and they are also not "behaviour as usual

The smart initiatives that I have been part of or had the privilege to observe, and that have delivered meaningful outcomes, have taken me on an inspirational personal journey that has fundamentally changed my understanding of the world that I live and work in. They have involved meeting with, listening to and working with people, organisations and communities that I would not have previously expected to be part of my working life, and that I was not previously familiar with– from social enterprises to community groups to individual people with unusual ideas.

Writing in "Resilience: Why Things Bounce Back[xxiii]", Andrew Zolli observes that the leaders of initiatives that have created real, lasting and surprising change in communities around the world show a quality that he defines as "Translational Leadership[xxiv]". Translational leaders have the ability to overcome the institutional and cultural barriers to engagement and collaboration between small-scale, informal innovators in communities and large-scale, formal institutions with resources. They naturally understand how to behave in a positive, influential and consensus-building way within a complex system of systems.

This is precisely the ability that any leaders involved in Smart initiatives need in order to properly understand how the powerful "top-down" forces within their influence – policies, procurements and investments – can be adapted to empower and enable real people, real communities and real businesses.

Translational leaders understand that their role is not to direct change, but to create the conditions in which others can be successful.

We can learn how to create those conditions from the decades of experience that town planners and urban designers have acquired in creating "human-scale cities" that don't repeat the mistakes that were made in constructing vast urban highways, tower blocks and housing projects from unforgiving concrete in the past century.

And there is good precedent to do so. It is not just that the experience of town planners and urban designers leads us unmistakably to "design thinking" that focuses on the needs of the individual citizens whose daily experiences collectively create the behaviour of smart communities, from villages to cities to nations. That is surely the only approach that will succeed; and the designers of smart technologies and infrastructures will fail unless they take it. But there is also a long-lasting and profound relationship between the design techniques of town planners and of software engineers[xxv]. The basic architectures of the Internet and mobile applications we use today were designed using those techniques in the last decade of the last millennium and the first decade of this one.

The architect Kelvin Campbell's concept of "massive/small smart urbanism[xxvi]" can teach us how to join the effects of "top-down" investments and policy with the capacity for "bottom-up" innovation that exists in people, businesses and communities everywhere. In the information age, we create the capacity for "massive amounts of small-scale innovation" if digital infrastructures are accessible and adaptable through the provision of open data interfaces, and accessible from open source software on cloud computing platforms – the digital equivalent of accessible public space and human-scale, mixed-used urban environments.

I call this "Smart Digital Urbanism", and many of its principles are already apparent[xxvii] because their value has been demonstrated time and again[xxviii]. These principles should be the starting point for adapting planning frameworks, procurement practices and the other policies that influence spending and investment in cities and public services.

Recent research in economics and in evolutionary social biology – a classic example of cross-discipline systems thinking – may also be yielding prescriptive insights into how we can design business models that are as wildly successful as those of Über, Airbnb and the other "platform businesses" transforming our economy[xxix]; but with models of corporate governance that ensure that the wealth they create is more broadly and fairly distributed.

In conversation with a researcher at Imperial College London a few years ago, I said that I thought we needed to find criteria to distinguish "platform" businesses like Casserole Club whose objective is to create social value, from those like Über that focus principally on the creation of profit for platform owners, and where broader social value is an externality. (Casserole Club uses social media to match people who are unable to provide meals for themselves with neighbours who are happy to cook and share an extra portion of their meal).

The researcher told me I should consult Elinor Ostrom's work in Economics. Ostrom, who won the Nobel prize in 2009, spent her life working with communities around the world who successfully manage shared resources (land, forests, fresh water, fisheries etc.) sustainably[xxx], and writing down the common features of their organisational models. Her Nobel prize was awarded for using this evidence to disprove the "tragedy of the commons[xxxi]"; the doctrine which economists had previously believed for decades proved that sustainable commons management was impossible.

(Elinor Ostrom working with irrigation management in Nepal[xxxii])

Most of Ostrom's principles for organisational design and behaviour are strikingly similar to the models used by platform businesses such as Über and Airbnb. But the principles she discovered that are the most interesting are the ones that Über and Airbnb don't follow – the price of exchange being agreed by all of the participants in a transaction, for example, rather than it being set by the platform owner. Ostrom's work has been continued by David Sloan Wilson who has demonstrated that the principles she discovered follow from evolutionary social biology[xxxiii] – the science that studies the evolution of human social behaviour.

Elinor Ostrom's design principles for commons organisations offer us not only a toolkit for the design of successful, socially responsible platform businesses; they offer us a toolkit for their regulation, too, by specifying the characteristics of businesses that we should preferentially reward through market regulation and tax policy. They are a classic example of systems thinking offering a constructive, practical tool that could reshape our economy to better deliver a truly Smart society.

7.   SMART SYSTEMS THINKING

I have dedicated the last decade of my life to the idea that digital technology can address some of the social, economic and environmental challenges that we face, and that I am personally convinced are becoming severe and acute. At the time of writing I am both encouraged and concerned at the progress being made: I have been a part of some wonderful projects with inspiring people, but I do not yet think we are successfully harnessing the potential of technology as a society, and there is evidence to suggest that it is creating at least as many challenges as it is solving.

Systems thinking has a tremendously important role to play in diagnosing how to improve our ability to harness technology in the complex systems of systems in which we live, work, travel and play. Most of the real and sustainable initiatives I am familiar with have come about through a "leap of faith": through the conviction of a political, business or community leader that the initiative is clearly "the right thing to do" and on this basis driving through a business case containing what would otherwise be seen as too high a level of risk to its outcome.

I have enormous admiration for the people who have taken those leaps of faith; but their leaps will not scale to the level of societal improvements for us all. If their leadership is to be followed more broadly – and in order for more leaders to come forward with confidence – better evidence of the benefits of "Smart" ideas is required. And that will only come from systems thinking.

REFERENCES

[i] "Smart Cities … why they're not working for us yet", Rick Robinson, http://www.slideshare.net/drrickrobinson/smart-cities-why-theyre-not-working-for-us-yet

[ii] "Information and choice: nine reasons our future is in the balance", Rick Robinson, https://theurbantechnologist.com/2013/12/03/information-and-choice-nine-reasons-our-future-is-in-the-balance/#urbanisation

[iii] "Information and choice: nine reasons our future is in the balance", Rick Robinson, https://theurbantechnologist.com/2013/12/03/information-and-choice-nine-reasons-our-future-is-in-the-balance/#climate

[iv] "'Case is made' for anthropocene epoch", BBC News, http://www.bbc.co.uk/news/science-environment-35259194

[v] "Oxfam says wealth of richest 1% equal to other 99%", BBC News, http://www.bbc.co.uk/news/business-35339475

[vi] "City of Bits", William Mitchell, MIT Press, https://mitpress.mit.edu/books/city-bits

[vii] "E-Governance and Smart Communities: A Social Learning Challenge", Amanda Coe, Gilles Paquet and Jeffrey Roy, Social Science Computer Review 2001, http://www.gouvernance.ca/publications/00-53.pdf

[viii] Andrew McAfee's blog http://andrewmcafee.org/blog/

[ix] "The Second Machine Age", Andy McAfee and Erik Brynjolfsson, MIT, http://secondmachineage.com/

[x] "New World Order: Labor, Capital, and Ideas in the Power Law Economy", Erik Brynjolfsson, Andrew McAfee, and Michael Spence, Foreign Affairs, https://www.foreignaffairs.com/articles/united-states/2014-06-04/new-world-order

[xi] "Venture Investing in the Internet of Things (IoT) – Q2 2017", Venture Scanner, https://venturescannerinsights.wordpress.com/category/internet-of-things-iot/

[xii] "Zipcar Founder -- Sharing Economy Is Transforming Capitalism", The Street, https://www.thestreet.com/story/13212294/1/zipcar-founder--sharing-economy-is-transforming-capitalism.html

[xiii] "Never Mind the Sharing Economy: Here's Platform Capitalism", Sebastian Olma, Institute of Network Cultures, http://networkcultures.org/mycreativity/2014/10/16/never-mind-the-sharing-economy-heres-platform-capitalism/

[xiv] "New World Order: Labor, Capital, and Ideas in the Power Law Economy", Erik Brynjolfsson, Andrew McAfee, and Michael Spence, Foreign Affairs,

https://www.foreignaffairs.com/articles/united-states/2014-06-04/new-world-order

xv "Why Robots Mean Interest Rates Could Go Even Lower In The Future", Simon Kennedy, Bloomberg, https://www.bloomberg.com/news/articles/2016-01-25/why-robots-mean-interest-rates-could-go-even-lower-in-the-future

xvi "It's time to demolish the myth of trickle-down economics". World Economic Forum, https://www.weforum.org/agenda/2016/07/it-s-time-to-demolish-the-myth-of-trickle-down-economics?utm_content=buffer26ed8&utm_medium=social&utm_source=twitter.com&utm_campaign=buffer#

xvii "The Death and Life of Great American Cities", Jane Jacobs, https://en.wikipedia.org/wiki/The_Death_and_Life_of_Great_American_Cities

xviii "Unilever Pledges 100% Traceable Palm Oil by End of 2014", Sustainable Brands, http://www.sustainablebrands.com/news_and_views/food_systems/mike-hower/unilever-promises-100-palm-oil-will-be-traceable-known-source

xix "New World Order: Labor, Capital, and Ideas in the Power Law Economy", Erik Brynjolfsson, Andrew McAfee, and Michael Spence, Foreign Affairs, https://www.foreignaffairs.com/articles/united-states/2014-06-04/new-world-order

xx "Transport and Policy: a Review of the Evidence", UCL, https://www.ucl.ac.uk/transport-institute/pdfs/transport-poverty

xxi "Cities and Deprivation", Nathaniel Lichfield and Partners, http://nlpplanning.com/blog/category/imd2015/

xxii "Core Cities", http://www.corecities.com/

xxiii "Dirty diesel death toll hits 60,000", Sunday Times, http://www.thesundaytimes.co.uk/sto/news/uk_news/National/article1489882.ece

xxiv "Cities Outlook 1901", Centre for Cities, http://www.centreforcities.org/publication/cities-outlook-1901/

xxv "On the inevitability of justice", The Economist, http://www.economist.com/blogs/freeexchange/2013/12/economic-growth?fsrc=scn/tw/te/bl/inevitablyjustice

xxvi "The Race between Education and Technology: The Evolution of U.S. Educational Wage Differentials, 1890 to 2005", Claudia Goldin and Lawrence F. Katz, National Bureau of Economic Research, http://www.nber.org/papers/w12984

xxvii "Cities Outlook 1901", Centre for Cities, http://www.centreforcities.org/publication/cities-outlook-1901/

xxviii http://www.massivesmall.org/

xxix "Centro and the Transport Systems Catapult to run Intelligent Mobility incubator", Transport Systems Catapult, https://ts.catapult.org.uk/news-events-gallery/news/centro-and-the-transport-systems-catapult-to-run-intelligent-mobility-incubator/

xxx 4 ways to get on with building Smart Cities. And the societal failure that stops us using them", The Urban Technologist, https://theurbantechnologist.com/2015/10/11/4-ways-to-get-on-with-building-smart-cities-and-the-societal-failure-that-stops-us-using-them/

xxxi "Sunderland cloud implementation points the way for local councils", CloudPro, http://www.cloudpro.co.uk/cloud-essentials/private-cloud/3555/sunderland-cloud-implementation-points-way-local-councils

xxxii "CIO Interview: Norfolk County Council's Tom Baker on using data to improve public services", Computer Weekly, http://www.computerweekly.com/news/2240212771/CIO-Interview-Norfolk-County-Councils-Tom-Baker-on-using-data-to-improve-public-services

xxxiii "National Procurement Strategy", Local Government Association, https://www.local.gov.uk/national-procurement-strategy

xxxiv "How to build a Smarter City: 23 design principles for digital urbanism", the Urban Technologist, https://theurbantechnologist.com/2013/06/17/how-to-build-a-smarter-city-23-design-principles-for-digital-urbanism/

xxxv "Mayor announces 1,500 new homes on the park six years earlier than planned", Queen Elizabeth Olympic Park, http://www.queenelizabetholympicpark.co.uk/news/news-articles/2015/03/mayor-announces-1500-new-homes-on-the-park-six-years-earlier-than-planned

xxxvi Casserole Club: https://www.casseroleclub.com/

xxxvii Sunderland Software City: http://www.sunderlandsoftwarecity.com/

xxxviii "iCentrum to launch 'intelligent mobility' business centre", Birmingham Post, http://www.birminghampost.co.uk/business/commercial-property/icentrum-launch-intelligent-mobility-business-9617729

xxxix Sheffield Smart Lab: http://www.ferrovial.com/en/projects/sheffield-smart-lab/

xl "Triple Bottom Line", Wikipedia, https://en.wikipedia.org/wiki/Triple_bottom_line

xli "Social Enterprise FAQs", Social Enterprise UK, http://www.socialenterprise.org.uk/about/about-social-enterprise

xlii Impact Hub global community: http://www.impacthub.net/

xliii "Resilience: why things bounce back", Andrew Zolli and Ann Marie Healy, http://resiliencethebook.com/

[xliv] "A Tropical Tale Of Tourists, Networks, And A New Kind Of Leadership", Andrew Zolli and Ann Marie Healy, https://www.fastcompany.com/1842367/tropical-tale-tourists-networks-and-new-kind-leadership

[xlv] "Do we need a Pattern Language for Smarter Cities", the Urban Technologist, https://theurbantechnologist.com/2013/02/15/do-we-need-a-pattern-language-for-smarter-cities/

[xlvi] The "Massive / Small" initiative: http://www.massivesmall.com/

[xlvii] "Smart Digital Urbanism: creating the conditions for equitably distributed opportunity in the digital age", the Urban Technologist, https://theurbantechnologist.com/2015/02/01/smart-digital-urbanism-creating-the-conditions-for-equitably-distributed-opportunity-in-the-digital-age/

[xlviii] "12 simple technologies for cities that are Smart, open and fair", the Urban Technologist, https://theurbantechnologist.com/2014/07/01/12-simple-technologies-for-cities-that-are-smart-open-and-fair/

[xliv] "Platform Shift: How New Business Models Are Changing the Shape of Industry", Marshall Van Alstyne, Boston University and MIT, http://www.slideshare.net/InfoEcon/platform-shift-how-new-business-models-are-changing-the-shape-of-industry

[l] "Elinor Ostrom and the solution to the tragedy of the commons", the American Enterprise Institute, http://www.aei.org/publication/elinor-ostrom-and-the-solution-to-the-tragedy-of-the-commons/

[li] "Tragedy of the Commons", Wikipedia, https://en.wikipedia.org/wiki/Tragedy_of_the_commons

[lii] "What This Year's Nobel Prize in Economics Says About the Nobel Prize in Economics", Steven D Levitt, https://luckybogey.wordpress.com/2009/10/15/sveriges-riksbank-prize-nobel-2009one-for-economics-the-other-for-a-political-scientist/

[liii] "The Tragedy of the Commons: How Elinor Ostrom Solved One of Life's Greatest Dilemmas", David Sloan Wilson, http://evonomics.com/tragedy-of-the-commons-elinor-ostrom/

CHAPTER 3

A RESILIENCE FRAMEWORK FOR SMART CITIES

Dr. Roland Kupers, Associate Fellow University of Oxford, Advisor Complexity, Resilience and Energy Transition,

Hsi Ching Song, Senior Researcher, Institute of Governance and Policy, Civil Service College Singapore

Abstract: Resilience is receiving increased attention as a way of better framing the capacity of urban or regional systems to respond the great variety of challenges they face. Inevitably the difficulty lies in bridging from the richness of an abstract concept to the required action on the ground. The ambition should be to achieve this connection between the conceptual and the practical, without compromising either: resilience requires deep systemic understanding, and cities need visible and impactful interventions. In this chapter we present a framework that we believe achieves both these objectives. We illustrate each of the aspects of the framework and describe how it is being applied in concrete cases.

The framework we apply was largely developed over a two year period from 2012-14, when nine multinational companies assembled under the name of Resilience Action Initiative to deepen their understanding of what role they might play in building the resilience of the socio-economic systems they provide goods and services to. Prompted by a series of CEO conversations at the World Economic Forum, the project led to a concluding book (Turbulence AUP 2014). The tools and insights continue to be applied by the companies themselves, but have also been deployed more widely and further evolved.

In particular, we present and discuss the Resilience Garage, a format that emerged from the previous project and has since been used successfully in Garages in Amsterdam, New Delhi, Singapore and Mexico City, in partnership with the Rockefeller Foundation's 100 Resilient Cities and the cities' Chief Resilience Officers.

"Resilience, in short, is largely about learning how to change in order not to be changed. Certainty is impossible. The point is to build systems that will be safe when they fail, not to try to build fail-safe systems."

Brian Walker (2013)

1.   INTRODUCTION

Resilience is receiving growing attention as a tool for improving the capacity of urban or regional systems to respond to the variety of challenges they face. Given the difficulty in translating an abstract concept such as resilience to practical action on the ground, the ambition should be to bridge the conceptual and the practical without overly compromising either: Resilience requires deep systemic understanding, while governments require visible and impactful interventions. In this paper we present a framework that could be used to achieve both these objectives. We illustrate each of the aspects of the framework and describe how it applies in concrete cases.

This framework was developed over two years from 2012-14, when nine multinational companies collaborated to deepen their understanding of what role they might play in building the resilience of the socio-economic systems they provide goods and services to. Would their offerings need to be different? Would the nature of their relationships change? Would this require the acquisition of new competencies? Prompted by a series of CEO conversations at the World Economic Forum, the project led to a final report titled *Turbulence* (Kupers 2014) before dissolving. The tools and insights generated continue to be applied by the companies themselves. They have also been applied more widely, for example by the Rockefeller Foundation's 100 Resilient Cities initiative.

2.   WHAT IS RESILIENCE?

There are varying definitions of resilience but we choose to emphasise two particular aspects. We find this distinction helpful in developing practical interventions.

The first aspect is the ability of a system to bounce back from stress. The stresses a city faces can be different in nature: they may be chronic or acute, exogenous or endogenous, natural or social, knowable or unknowable. The system can be a bungee cord, someone's body, a company or a city, etc. Bouncing back is important, but if it were only that, it would be mere robustness. Robustness is building ever higher dikes to protect cities against floods, like in New Orleans or Amsterdam; or to make buildings earthquake-proof like in Tokyo.

The magic of resilience comes with learning – this is the second aspect. This is when the system becomes smarter and more resistant through friction with the external world; just like a child's immune system which becomes smarter when injected with weakened bacteria. This is crucial to the adaptive capacities of cities. At a resilience workshop in 2014, the chief resilience officer of New York City David Zarilli said that they were trying to understand social resilience by focusing on what was unique about communities that self-organised best in the aftermath of Hurricane Sandy. Boosting the capacity of communities to learn and self-organise is harder, but cheaper, than just building more infrastructure. The former also builds more resilience. This second aspect also holds the key to transformation: learning enables the system to transform and stay in a new state, especially when it is not desirable for the system to return to its original state.

That said, we may not always want to maximise resilience. Some systems are too resilient, such as those of organised crime or even a benign social structure where change is overdue. In those cases resilience must be reduced, so as to create new options and possibilities. In organisations, reducing undesired but resilient cultural norms is frequently done through departmental reorganisation and movement of key personnel. For cities, participatory tools such as open space technology, appreciative inquiry, citizen juries and deliberative polling have been used to frame and structure conversations which seek to break resilient but dysfunctional or outdated structures and mental models.

Resilience is a property of a complex adaptive system. It emerges as a result of many interactions within the system (Colander and Kupers, 2014). As such it is a global property, but it does not equate to the sum of its parts. A collection of very resilient cities does not necessarily make a resilient country, just as a collection of great sports people does not automatically make a great team. Hence we should be cautious when designing resilience metrics. There is natural interest in developing resilience metrics, but it can be counter-productive. This is because "measuring and monitoring a narrow set of indicators or reducing resilience to a single unit of measurement may block the deeper understanding of system dynamics needed to apply resilience thinking and inform management actions" (Quinlan 2015). Focus on achieving one of the metrics may inadvertently lead to suboptimal outcomes at the broader systemic level. In most cases, a qualitative discussion about resilience measures should take priority over a detailed set of quantitative resilience metrics.

Another point to note is that efficiency often comes at the expense of resilience. It is difficult and unpopular to argue against efficiency. Yet many losses in resilience come about through relentless optimisation drives. The reverse does not hold; not all efficiency reduces resilience. Wasting food is clearly inefficient and does nothing to build resilience. On the other hand, the relentless focus on efficiency in agricultural systems has brought great benefits but also reduced resilience with the loss of biodiversity, erosion of soil quality and loss of livelihoods. The trade-offs between resilience and efficiency constitute one of the more challenging and impactful aspects of applying a resilience frame.

3. THE NINE-BOX FRAMEWORK

To help practitioners understand and discuss these aspects of resilience, a nine-box frame has been developed. The frame has been tested through urban and corporate cases in various cities and regions. The resilience aspects are organised in groups of three and described below.

Structural Resilience	Integrative Resilience	Transformative Resilience
Redundancy	Multi-scalar interactions	Distributed governance
Modularity	Thresholds	Foresight capacity
Requisite diversity	Social cohesion	Innovation & experimentation

The Nine-Box Resilience Framework

Figure 1

STRUCTURAL RESILIENCE – the systemic, infrastructure-related aspects of resilience; i.e. redundancy, modularity and requisite diversity.

1 - Redundancy refers to spare capacity or 'fat' in the system. This is often the most straightforward but also most costly way of building resilience. Sometimes it may not be politically or financially feasible. Examples of redundancy include: the spare tyre of a car, additional staff to deal with unexpected peaks, spare capacity in a power grid.

An interesting phenomenon in recent years is the rise of the sharing economy that is challenging the notion that redundancy is costly. Companies such as Airbnb and ridesharing BlaBlaCar have enabled cities to boost their short-term capacity in rooms, cars, courier services etc. relatively quickly and inexpensively. However, when the sharing economy simply translates hidden spare capacity into production, it is increasing the efficiency – but doing nothing for resilience. It is the dynamic tapping of spare capacity that is enabled in the sharing economy that builds resilience.

2 - Modularity refers to loosely coupled components. When one part of the system is affected, the components can be separated and recombined to continue operations. Well-designed modularity means that the system can be re-combined in many ways to respond to changes in the environment. For example, the shipping container is designed with fixings and dimensions that can work well across multiple modes of transport – road, rail and sea. However, one needs to be careful of "fake modularity". The 2008/9 Financial Crisis demonstrated "fake modularity" as financial companies and institutions were much more strongly connected than previously perceived. When the crisis hit, it became clear that they had behaved in a similar fashion, without fundamentally diversified risks.

3 - Requisite diversity: Diversity reduces business risks. Workforce diversity also enables different responses in times of crisis. However, increasing diversity may reduce efficiency in the short term. Rather than diversity for its own sake, it is important to consider what types of diversity are relevant for particular circumstances, hence *requisite* diversity. Examples include the effort by the public service to include more diversity in thinking through mid-career recruitment, secondments and cross-postings. Another example is the mixing of commercial, residential and recreational facilities in urban planning to build neighbourhood character and avoid the problem of deserted streets in the central business district in the evenings.

Singapore's Water Story –

From vulnerability to strategic advantage

While Singapore is surrounded by seawater, it is water-scarce because of its limited land to store rainwater. The World Resources Institute ranks Singapore as an "extremely high water stress" country in its assessment of 180 countries, ahead of Saudi Arabia and Kuwait (Reig et al 2013).

To cope with Singapore's water vulnerability, PUB, Singapore's National Water Agency has been testing and using new water technologies since the 1970s. PUB, which manages the whole water loop in Singapore, pursues three key strategies: It collects every drop of water, reuses water endlessly and desalinates more seawater.

Two-thirds of the city-state serves as water catchment and the rainwater collected is stored in 17 reservoirs. The city-state also imports water from neighbouring Malaysian state Johor under a 1962 water agreement. To further increase its water supply, Singapore desalinates seawater into drinking water. Used water from the system is also reclaimed and purified into high-grade water of drinking-water standards known to Singaporeans as NEWater. The different sources – local catchment water, imported water, NEWater and desalinated water – make up Singapore's **Four National Taps**.

Singapore's diversified supply of water reduces its reliance on any one source of water. In particular, NEWater and desalination build modularity into the system by decoupling water supply from freshwater availability. That said, desalination uses more energy than conventional water treatment and PUB is continually researching ways to improve the energy efficiency of desalination. NEWater creates a multiplier effect in water yield, as the bulk of the water supply is used and re-used. The current NEWater process turns 75% of feed water (i.e. treated used water) into NEWater and PUB is studying ways to improve this water recovery rate. To make the water supply more sustainable, PUB has been relentless in promoting water conservation and minimising water leakage. At 5% of total water production, Singapore's 'unaccounted for water' (or, water lost in the pipelines during transmission) is one of the lowest in the world.

Nevertheless, at 151 litres per day, domestic water consumption per capita remains higher than desired. Recent efforts to reduce water consumption include mandatory submission of water efficiency management plans by large non-domestic water users and the study of behavioural insights to reduce demand for water. Saving water amounts to a 'fifth tap', adding further diversity.

INTEGRATIVE RESILIENCE emphasises the complex interconnections of the system, i.e. multi-scalar interactions, thresholds and social cohesion.

4 - Multi-scalar interactions characterise the relationships of the system under consideration with other systems at different scales around it. Scales can be geographical (e.g. neighbourhood, city, province and nation) or temporal (short, medium and long term). From empirical studies as well as theoretical insights, it appears that the ability to understand a system at multiple scales, both above and below the focal scale which one is operating in, is crucial for building resilience. This is because feedback loops operate across scales and have an impact on the focal scale. It is the quality of the links between the scales that strongly influences the resilience of the system.

5 - Thresholds are often excluded from standard policy narratives. Whether it is the Global Financial Crisis or the sudden almost universal disuse of plastic bags in Ireland in 2009 within three months after introducing a very small tax on bags; these step-changes are often unanticipated. Frequently, a system functions in a stable mode for what seems a long time then once past a threshold the system begins to work in unexpected ways. Examples include shifts in industry competitiveness, neighbourhood attractiveness, transport capacity and the impact of pollution.

Discussions and plans about the future almost always project smooth and gradual change. We rarely anticipate discontinuities that occur as a result of thresholds being crossed. Many threshold events are impossible to forecast, but that does not mean sudden change should not feature in planning. Envisaging thresholds, even unknown thresholds, can build resilience and adaptive capacity to deal with them, when they arise.

6 - Social cohesion can contribute much to resilience. As mentioned above, the city of New York studied how social cohesion helped neighbourhoods self-organise in the aftermath of Hurricane Sandy. Self-organising capabilities, social norms and trust levels within the existing system all have an impact on policy options. A key point of resilience is how to increase the self-organising capacity of societies.

Sidewalks as parks

"Public space is for living, doing business, kissing, and playing. Its value can't be measured with economics or mathematics; it must be felt with the soul."

Enrique Peñalosa, Mayor of Bogotá (1998-2001, 2016-)

Like many developing country metropolises, Bogotá was increasingly grid-locked from a rapid rise in car ownership. Mayor Peñalosa recognised that this was much more than a transportation problem, and that there was also a profound social equity issue. Rather than focusing exclusively on the traffic problem, he spotted an opportunity for addressing a number of other interconnected problems made worse by cars.

His insight is that sidewalks are much more than roads for pedestrians; they are more akin to parks than to transportation. They are a place where people meet and mingle, where social cohesion is built. In practice the few sidewalks that existed were being occupied by parked cars. In addition to the roads, the small minority of Bogotá residents who owned cars thus laid claim to a vastly disproportionate share of public space.

Reclaiming the existing sidewalks from parked cars and vastly expanding sidewalk capacity in poor neighbourhoods was a resounding success. In some neighbourhoods, it contributed to a precipitous decline in crime.

Peñalosa also pioneered the construction of pedestrian and bicycle paths on agricultural land in the immediate surroundings of the city. When the city expanded, it would develop around this new infrastructure. The lock-in to the car infrastructure often creates a huge threshold to change, which doesn't exist in greenfield expansion sites.

SOURCE: 2011 OXFORD LECTURE

TRANSFORMATIVE RESILIENCE examines broader capacity issues and longer time horizons in terms of distributed governance, foresight capacity and innovation & experimentation.

7 - Distributed governance or polycentric governance is the core model for managing resilience. Centralised control is often perceived to be more efficient, but it represents a classic trade-off between resilience and efficiency. While occasionally frustrating, democratic processes, stakeholder consultation or even family meetings are all examples of the ultimate strength of a distributed model of governance. Elinor Ostrom's work (Ostrom 2010) is the most comprehensive and well-known elaboration of this idea, and provides the conceptual foundation for public governance.

In the context of building resilience, it is important to realise that overlapping competence, or what some may perceive as slightly messy forms of governance are valuable.

8 - Foresight capacity is the competence to go beyond a culture of forecasting, to include irreducible uncertainties and the plausibility of multiple futures into the planning culture of the city. Having institutional capacity to engage decision makers and help them be comfortable with multiple possible futures will build adaptive capacity for resilience. Various techniques such as Scenario Planning (Public Service Division 2011, Wilkinson 2014) and futures tools are available, but they all require a sustained effort to influence the governance culture. Since 1997, Singapore has conducted scenario-planning exercises every 3-5 years to refresh the government's thinking on possible futures amidst changing external conditions. A formal process ensures that these National Scenarios are incorporated by different Ministries into their strategic review exercises.

9 - Innovation & experimentation are obviously important for generating new ideas. However, in this context there is an additional purpose, which is to build a culture that systematically explores the edges of the system. Having people who are comfortable with ideas of radical change and experiencing the friction of very diverse concepts increases the adaptive capacity of the system and builds resilience. Google's policy of encouraging employees to dedicate a fixed percentage of their time on personal innovation projects is an example. It may yield some new ideas, but it will certainly deliver a more adaptive employee and corporate culture. Likewise, the US Department of Defence has been sponsoring the Highlands Forum since 1994 to systematically introduce new ideas to the organisation. The forum regularly convenes a wide-ranging, cross-disciplinary group of professionals and experts to discuss emerging issues that may have an impact on the Department's work.

Building transformative resilience: Netherlands flood management

One third of the Netherlands is under sea level, so flood management receives a lot of attention. After the catastrophic floods of 1953, a 50-year project was rolled out to strengthen sea defences, based on a detailed flood risk calculation and the statistical value of human lives. These two parameters allowed engineers to design new infrastructure with sufficient robustness to face down the elements, with great effectiveness.

With the completion of the original plan in the beginning of the 21st century, an extensive participatory evaluation was conducted as to the requirements for the next phase. Foresight studies had identified a shift in the nature of the surrounding system, which required a new policy approach. Risks were no longer readily quantifiable, as they increasingly became heavy-tailed. A resilience framework was adopted, which complemented traditional robustness strategies. River basins were widened, existing dikes were dismantled and flooding reservoirs such as parking garages were built with the express purpose of absorbing events that were no longer avoidable. This was a radical shift from the original strategy which sought to keep out floods entirely.

The roots of the governance of the water system can be traced back to 1120, when various towns assembled to build a dike along the Rhine. This evolved into the current polycentric system, where separate elections are held for the governance of the water boards. These boards have their own taxes, but are intertwined with provincial and city governance in various ways. While these overlapping institutional arrangements may appear messy to the casual observer, it helps to promote accountability towards the smaller communities across the water boards, preserve local knowledge in decision-making, and distribute power among key stakeholders which guards against systems failure from ineffective, top-down control. It is an example of a governance system honed over the centuries for resilience, rather than for efficiency; a well justified trade-off.

4.   APPLYING THE NINE-BOX FRAMEWORK: THE RESILIENCE GARAGE

There are different ways to apply the nine-box resilience framework. For instance, organisations can use it as an internal reference to assess the resilience of their individual projects, or use it as a tool to facilitate discussions with an external group of experts. One method which focuses on the latter is the Resilience Garage. The Resilience Garage was designed as an output of the two-year collaboration of multinational companies (Kupers 2014), which explored how to make resilience actionable in the context of the cities and regions, while at the same time retain a deep systems perspective. The Garage has been adopted by the Rockefeller Foundation's 100 Resilient Cities Initiative as one of its core tools to engage city officials, companies and local NGOs. The first four Garages were held in Amsterdam, Delhi, Singapore and Mexico City in 2014-16. Feedback allowed the Garage to evolve to the process described here and the very positive experiences underscore the relevance and applicability across diverse cultures and challenges.

Figure 2 - Amsterdam Resilience Garage 2014

The essence of the Resilience Garage lies in its facilitated process which creates a safe platform where practitioners and scientists/researchers from across different sectors convene to challenge, learn, and hone their approaches to resilience building. During the Garage, they seek to understand resilience challenges of specific, place-based investment or development opportunities that one or more of the Garage members are considering, and suggest solutions to address these challenges.

In that way, the Resilience Garage is a form of peer review or assurance performed under non-disclosure agreements by trans-disciplinary and cross-sectoral teams of resilience experts. This improves the likelihood of success of the reviewed project. Overall, the purpose of the Resilience Garage is to accelerate the rigorous application of resilience theory in practice and the refinement of resilience theory based on practical experience and empirical evidence.

5.   EPILOGUE

We have presented a resilience framework that can be used to discover and prioritise resilience interventions in the government sector and governance context. The framework provides nine different lenses on the resilience of a particular system. It is not an analytical framework in the sense that it represents an exhaustive list. Indeed that would be at odds with the complex systems perspective, where the interconnected nature of the system determines its behaviour. But it is a pragmatic and tested framework to help policy makers make sense of resilience interventions. As such it can help generate richer conversations in environments where conversations tend to be dominated by efficiency concerns.

Rethinking how governments can enhance the resilience of the systems they manage, is not about implementing a set of prescribed solutions. Rather, the idea here is to encourage policy officers to look beyond their immediate purview to the larger operating environment and think in terms of how their actions can impact other areas. From our perspective, resilience only has meaning in the context of the whole system. This is because resilience is a property of a complex system. Given that our context and operating environments are often different, the use of this framework should generate insights and policy actions that are suited to one's unique context.

REFERENCES

Colander and Kupers (2014), Complexity and the Art of Public Policy: Solving society's problems from the bottom-up. Princeton and Oxford: Princeton University Press.

Kupers (ed) (2014). Turbulence – A Corporate Perspective on Collaborating for Resilience, Amsterdam University Press.

Ostrom, E. (2010), Beyond Markets and States: Polycentric Governance of Complex Economic Systems, American Economic Review 100 (June 2010): 1–33.

Public Service Division, Singapore (2011), Conversations for the Future: Singapore's Experiences with Strategic Planning (1988-2011). Singapore. URL: http://www.csf.gov.sg/docs/default-source/default-document-library/conversations-for-the-future.pdf

Quinlan et al (2015), Measuring and assessing resilience: broadening understanding through multiple disciplinary perspectives, Journal of Applied Ecology, doi: 10.1111/1365-2664.12550.

Reig, P., Maddocks, A. & Gassert, F. (2013, December 12). World's 36 Most Water-Stressed Countries. World Resources Institute. Retrieved on September 23, 2016 from http://www.wri.org.

Walker, B (2013), What Is Resilience?, Project Syndicate editorial, July 5th, retrieved from https://www.project-syndicate.org/commentary/what-is-resilience-by-brian-walker

Wilkinson, A. and Kupers, R. (2014), The Essence of Scenarios: Learning from the Shell experience, Amsterdam University Press

CHAPTER 4

IoT SYSTEMS - SYSTEMS SEAMS & SYSTEMS SOCIALIZATION

Chuck Benson, University of Washington,

Abstract: Internet of Things (IoT) Systems have the potential to bring great value to cities and smart city deployments. However, if the systems are not selected, implemented, and managed thoughtfully, the investment in the system will not be realized and, possibly worse, a city's risk profile can be degraded with a poor implementation.

IoT Systems include energy management systems, public safety systems, building and community space automation systems, as well as others.

IoT Systems risk management topics include articulating and raising expectations of IoT Systems vendor performance, the growing number of proprietary, non-interoperable IoT Systems offered by vendors, the lack of language, conceptual framework, and precedent to discuss IoT Systems risk issues, cultural/organizational changes required in cities and governments required for successful deployments, exposure to online IoT System analysis tools such as shodan.io, and technical issues such as network segmentation management.

Early identification of these issues is required so that the public can realize the value of their investment in smart city technologies. Early failed smart city implementations will discourage the public from supporting future smart city investments.

1.   INTRODUCTION

The technology systems — Internet of Things (IoT) Systems that underpin smart cities institutions are a new and different breed of technology. If these systems are not implemented thoughtfully, 1) the return on investment (ROI) will not be seen, and 2) things can actually be made worse for a city from a cyber-risk (to include privacy, among others) perspective. IoT Systems are different from traditional enterprise systems and there is little precedent for implementing them.

Internet of Things Systems or IoT Systems are those systems that are the technology behind the "smart" in "smart cities" along with other technologies such as big data, cognitive computing, mobile, and social. These systems typically deploy sensors that collect and aggregate data, process that data in some form, and then make it available for some intended use — which could be across several different populations within a city.

IoT Systems in a city or a large institution might include building automation systems controlling local environments (e.g. temperature, humidity, lighting), building access systems such as identification card based door openers, networked surveillance systems, facial recognition systems, vehicle recognition systems, energy management systems, traffic management systems, waste management systems, public safety systems, and others. IoT Systems in specialized institutions such as corporations and Higher Education institutions might also have additional substantial IoT Systems use as a part of their research, manufacturing, production, and teaching/learning systems.

1.1 What is an IoT device? What is an IoT System?

The Internet of Things does or will consist of a feasibly uncountable number of devices (i.e., "things"). The ability to inventory and categorize simply will not be possible, at least in any traditional sense. While there are many definitions for IoT that continue to evolve, IoT devices generally have these attributes. The device:

- Is networked
- Computes (from basic network support to larger scale computation)
- Interacts with the environment in some way by sensing or making local changes (movement, temperature change, etc.)

For example:

- A **FitBit** activity-tracking device computes, is networked, and interacts with the environment (i.e., collects data from the FitBit wearer).
- An **industrial smart grid meter** computes, is networked, and interacts with the environment (i.e., collects power data).
- A **residential Nest[2] meter** computes, is networked, and interacts with the environment (i.e., collects temperature data).
- Devices in **Chicago's Array of Things[3]** compute, are networked, and collect data from the environment (see below)
- **Blood glucose monitors[4]** compute, are networked, and interact with the environment (i.e., collect data from the user).

---

[2] https://nest.com/

[3] https://arrayofthings.github.io/
[4]

https://www.fda.gov/MedicalDevices/ProductsandMedicalProcedures/InVitroDiagnostics/GlucoseTestingDevices/default.htm

An *IoT System* can be considered to be a set of IoT devices that communicate with each other and/or communicate with a central server that aggregates data and/or provides control information.

One example is Chicago's Array of Things where city sensors will sample and collect:

- air temperature
- humidity
- air pressure
- vibration
- sound intensity
- magnetic field strength
- air quality — carbon monoxide, hydrogen sulfide, others
- light intensity
- cloud cover
- surface temperature
- vehicle traffic
- pedestrian traffic
- others

2.   IOT SYSTEMS ARE DIFFERENT

IoT systems are different from traditional enterprise IT and information management systems and require new approaches to achieve investment value as well as to maintain or enhance a city's cyber-risk profile.

At least six factors distinguish IoT systems from other technology systems:

1. the large (and rapidly growing) number of networked, computing devices
2. the high variability of types of devices & subcomponents of devices
3. the lack of language and conceptual frameworks to discuss and easily categorize and classify devices
4. IoT systems span many organizations within an institution
5. out of sight and out of mind - the myriad of devices that are or will be embedded in the physical infrastructure around us tend to be out of sight and out of mind.

6. there is little precedent within city resources for implementation and sustainable management of these systems

Further, many if not most of these IoT information systems will enter the city's domain in new ways for which there is no existing or mature vetting process. Over the past two or three decades, cities have evolved the ability, to varying degrees of effectiveness, to evaluate various enterprise systems being considered for procurement and implementation. IoT Systems, on the other hand, might be procured through an entirely separate department from the central IT department. A hypothetical example might be that the city's department of transportation acquires a distributed road temperature sensing technology in the interest of predicting road maintenance needs in at-risk road areas. That acquired IoT System collects surface temperature data, aggregates it, does some analysis on it, and publishes it in some way. The transportation department sees this as an operational asset, not as an IT asset, but a predictive mechanism that helps it better serve the city. Further complicating the issue is that the boundaries between operational control technology and consumer led information technology can be blurred.

2.1 Large numbers

In 2011, Cisco predicted that 50 billion devices will be connected to the Internet by 2020 [5] and the growth appears to be compounding. There are varying predictions, but most point to compounding IoT device growth in the range of at least tens of billions over the next few years. It can be difficult to wrap one's head around the magnitude of this growth.

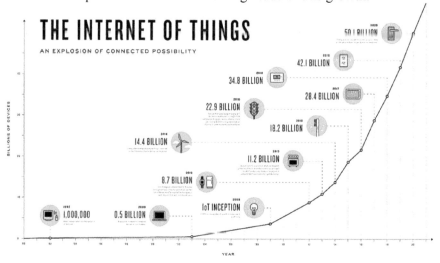

THE INTERNET OF THINGS

AN EXPLOSION OF CONNECTED POSSIBILITY

---

[5] https://www.ncta.com/platform/wp-content/uploads/2014/05/growth-of-internet-of-things-hero-1024x585.jpg

Borrowing the Rule of 72 estimating 'trick' from finance, we can estimate how long it takes a number of devices to double if the growth is displaying compounding behavior. For example, an International Data Corporation (IDC) report [6] suggests an 18.6% annual growth rate in the IoT market in manufacturing operations, starting with a $42 billion market in 2013. Applying the Rule of 72 and dividing the percentage growth rate into the number 72: 72/18.6 = 3.9, meaning the market size will grow from $42 billion to $84 billion by 2017, an estimated 4 years.

2.2 High variability

The variety of types of devices and of the hardware and software components within each device is very high. IoT devices do numerous different tasks, including measuring building energy, video monitoring a space, reading a heart rate, and sensing air quality every few seconds in a research facility. Devices can have many different types of hardware from many different manufacturers as well as many different layers of software, each possibly from a different software company (or person). This huge variability contributes to the challenge of identifying device categories that can be helpful in developing risk management approaches.

Third party software developed for multiple device types deployed in multiple and varied contexts provides another facet to the high variability characteristic. The Shodan web-based service[7] that scans the Internet for IoT and industrial control systems (ICS) not infrequently returns third-party software such as Virata EmWeb[8], Allegro-Software-RomPager[9], GoAhead-Webs[10], and other. These products are web-server software companies that create small web servers specifically for embedded devices for many different product/service lines. Notably, software such as Virata, though

---

[6] http://www.prnewswire.com/news-releases/virata-extends-functionality-of-its-emweb-web-based-network-management-solution-71567012.html

[7] http://shodan.io

[8] http://www.prnewswire.com/news-releases/virata-extends-functionality-of-its-emweb-web-based-network-management-solution-71567012.html

[9] http://www.allegrosoft.com/

[10] https://embedthis.com/goahead/

likely not as feature-rich as similar software today, has been around for some time (early 2000's). This common practice of using third-parties to comprise IoT device components produces many additional potential points of entry to an IoT device or IoT System for those with malicious intent – the practice, driven by economics and competition (driving cost down and time to market) increases the attack surface. Given growth rates discussed earlier, the number of instances of the sort of functionality that Virata and similar companies provide can be expected to be substantially higher, particularly if the device count is compounding as it appears to be, at least at this point in time.

While offering reasonable and understandable valuable economic advantage for IoT Systems developers, a compromise or vulnerability of one of these third-party web developers could ultimately present itself across multiple different products, services, across completely disparate companies, and into institutions with completely different procurement practices.

(Quick note — a new web-scanning tool, though one that uses a different approach, is the Censys web application developed at the University of Michigan). [11]

2.3 Lack of language

We do not have commonly accepted and shared language or conceptual frameworks for talking about IoT. We need language that spans roles and constituencies – from technical support roles, citizens, city leaders, and vendor partners – so that meaningful discussions on planning, operations, and risk management and mitigation can occur. Without a shared, spanning language, discussing the benefits of an IoT system, planning IoT systems implementations, and managing risk around systems is very difficult. It is also challenging to establish standards and vendor contract performance expectations without this language.

---

[11] https://censys.io

The desire is often expressed to develop deep systems taxonomies to attempt to address this complexity. Peter Senge[12], in The Fifth Discipline, addresses an aspect of this and calls this sort of complexity challenge "detail complexity." The problem is that developing a deep taxonomy can rapidly hit the point of diminishing returns. In practice, few have the resources, be it staffing, funds, or time to garner a return on investment of deep taxonomies. In this age of rapid technological change, developing deep taxonomies run the risk of becoming effort that won't be recovered. That said, a broadly shared, consumable, and accepted taxonomy a couple of layers deep can have actionable value to practitioners.

2.4 Spanning many organizations

IoT systems will span multiple organizations within smart cities. For example, a system with deployed sensors and aggregation servers that capture, process, analyze, and publish the results of air quality around a city might involve the:

- city's central IT organization
- the city's facilities management group
- the city's 'digital engagement' group (managing the city's online presence)

---

[12] Senge, Peter M. 1990. *The fifth discipline: the art and practice of the learning organization.* New York: Doubleday/Currency.

- many product/service vendors and subcontractors
- waste water management department
- parks department
- water department
- transportation department
- possibly local IT groups to include contracted support
- libraries (for results publication and reference)
- capital development department
- planning department
- possibly others

Aligning efforts across multiple inter-organizational relationships, in part, involves "problems of understanding" [13] in those same relationships. While it is possible, that city departments will naturally align and collaborate effectively, it is unlikely at least in the near term. (See 'Seams between the departments within the city.')

2.5 Out of sight, out of mind

IoT systems are unique in that many of the technical parts of the IoT system—that is, the computing and networking endpoints—are built into the physical infrastructure such as buildings and shared spaces, out of sight and out of mind. For example, a smart grid/city energy management system can easily have thousands of networked, computing, sensing endpoints that are built into a city's buildings and public spaces. We generally don't think about them because we don't see them, but even embedded and unseen, they are networked (and often reasonably powerful) computers. This is problematic because if we don't that think about them, we can't mitigate risk stemming from these systems and it is difficult to effectively monitor them or service them.

2.6 Precedent for implementation

Because of these factors, implementation and management of these systems is different than the same for traditional enterprise systems and there is generally little precedent for successful implementation and management of city-wide IoT Systems much less multiple city-wide IoT Systems that are possibly interconnected. Attempting to implement these systems without

---

[13] Koschmann, Matthew A. 2016. "The Communicative Accomplishment of Collaboration Failure: Collaboration Failure." Journal of Communication 66 (3): 409–32. doi:10.1111/jcom.12233.

acknowledging their differences from traditional, centrally-focused enterprise systems is a recipe for failure.

While systems involving embedded technologies such as elevators, escalators, and electronic building access systems have been around for some time, the factors above – particularly the large scale of networked computing device deployment that IoT Systems bring and the interdependency between multiple systems – creates implementation and management requirements for which there are few examples much less management patterns, processes, and procedures.

For example, a medium-sized traditional building might have three elevators and two escalators that incorporate some sort of embedded technology and control logic. A modern 'smart' building of similar size will have that along with perhaps hundreds to thousands of energy consumption sensors, additional utility sensors such as water and sewer, occupancy sensors, networked video surveillance, etc. Implementation of these many sensors (and actuators) involves coordination and collaboration across many organizations within a city and can have real privacy implications, require increased and geographically disbursed maintenance support, and require increased coordination and management across multiple departments such as central IT, facilities management, capital development, and planning groups. Because these are not the systems of the past for which these support groups were designed, most, if not all, cities are ill-prepared for the scale and breadth of this new systems management complexity.

Selecting, procuring, implementing, and managing these complex systems are substantial new areas of work and competencies for cities and large institutions. There are opportunities to do these things well and even more opportunities to do them poorly.

We'll look at two areas in particular around IoT Systems implementation — Systems Seams and Systems Socialization.

3. SYSTEMS SEAMS

3.1 Introduction

The interface or set of connection points and processes, social and technical, between two organizations can be thought of as a seam. Seams exist between the city and their multiple technology system providers (vendors/contractors). Seams also exist between organizations/departments within those cities and institutions. Successful IoT Systems implementation requires active management of those seams — both between city/institution and their vendors as well as internal organizations/departments between each other. *Seams are not self-aware and they do not self-manage.* The organizations making up the seam must contribute to managing that seem and doing so entails collaborating with other organizations.

The challenge is that this collaboration and cooperation is non-trivial to successfully implement. Collaboration is often lauded as critical to inter-organizational success, however, there is a delta between theory and practice, "the discrepancy between the promise of collaboration and the reality of persistent failure." [14] Collaboration can be deceptively complex in inter-organizational relations that can include organic departments and vendors because "issues of trust, identity, power relationships, network configurations, boundary spanning, agency, and authority, negotiation … [are magnified]". Further, despite recognition of prevalence and significance of collaboration (or collaboration attempts) in civil society, it is very complex and often fails.

3.2 Seams between the city & the provider

One of the greatest areas of governmental, institutional, and populace risk related to IoT does not necessarily come from the IoT systems themselves but, rather, from the implementation of IoT systems. *A seam forms between the delivery of the system by the vendor/provider and the use of that system by the city*. Seams, in themselves, are not bad. In fact, they're essential for complex systems. They connect and integrate various parts of a system, enabling it to work toward a cohesive whole. However, how a city chooses to approach and manage these seams makes a significant difference.

Seams are where interesting things happen. In 2015, college baseball changed its ball seams to flat instead of raised in order to drive more hits and home runs[15]. Upon implementation, both statistics increased. In American football seam routes, a receiver tries to exploit the gap, the seam, between defenders. And anyone who has ever sat in the window seat by the wing of an airplane knows that there are many more seams in a plane than a passenger would probably care to see. Seams can be where things come apart.

Vendor relationships and vendor management have always been important for cities, firms and institutions. However, the invasive nature of IoT systems makes vendor management particularly critical for successful IoT system implementations and subsequent operation. In addition, the work and staffing required to manage these customer-to-vendor (and vendor-to-vendor) relationships and to provide the oversight needed to operate IoT

[14] Koschman 2016
[15] http://www.espn.com/college-sports/story/_/id/12419383/ncaa-reports-big-jump-home-runs-new-flat-seam-ball

systems safely and effectively often gets obfuscated by the promises and shininess of the new technology.

The implementations of IoT systems differ from traditional deployments of workstations, laptops, and servers. The 'things', the devices, in IoT systems are embedded and usually unseen, in the built environments all around us. Traditional IT systems, on the other hand, with which we are more familiar, are deployed with servers and virtual machines in data centers and the endpoints are visible and touchable workstations, laptops, tablets, and phones. Because the endpoints in IoT systems are typically, and by design, embedded or hidden in the space around us, it can be difficult for the consumer, for example a city's purchasing group, central IT, audit, or other department to perceive a broad-reaching IoT system to be owned, managed, and risk-mitigated.

Complicating the matter is that these differences in traditional enterprise and IoT systems mean that these systems might enter the city's purview without coming through a traditional IT acquisition path. These traditional IT acquisition paths generally have some sort of documented systems requirements or other vetting process. When these IoT systems are procured by other city groups, there are not existing vetting procedures for system selection, implementation, and management so the systems enter the city's portfolio are without systematic review. This is not to suggest that central IT should be doing the vetting (since they typically don't have much IoT systems experience either), but rather *to identify and acknowledge that many IoT systems are probably entering the city without much review, systematic analysis, or clear ownership.*

Cities purchase IoT systems to address various needs in their operations. These IoT systems might be related to environmental monitoring, control, energy efficiency, public safety (e.g., fire, security), biometric authentication, surveillance, and other functions. As a result, IoT devices can be brought into a city's physical space and cyberspace by the hundreds or thousands or more within the confines of a single vendor contract. Partial or poorly-planned configuration of such systems and devices can lead to significant consequences for the city — as can also a lack of planning regarding long-term support, whether local or via a vendor maintenance contract or both.

3.3 Interfacing new IoT systems to existing infrastructure

In most cities, implementing a third-party solution—hardware, software, Software-as-a-Service (SaaS), or hybrid—requires an internal supporting infrastructure for that solution. The customer city must create an interface that allows the vendor solution to interface with appropriate parts of the customer's existing infrastructure. This includes hardware and software –– and most expensively and sometimes disruptively – people and processes. Taking the time and resources to plan, build, and maintain this interface is integral to the operational success of the new IoT system. Doing so also provides the city with an opportunity to manage some of the risk that the new system introduces.

One of the worst-case scenarios for a city is believing that an IoT System seam, that technical-people-process relationship between the city and the vendor, is being managed when it actually is not. At this point in the evolution of IoT deployments, I suspect that this scenario is more often the rule than the exception. Sun Tsu stressed the importance to "know yourself" in warfare, another example of a complex organization, doing complex things, with incomplete information and high levels of uncertainty. Hackers and others continuously explore these seams for weaknesses and gaps. It is not unusual for the hacker to know the qualities, attributes, and functionality of that seam better than the city itself. A framework for continuous review and vulnerability discovery in that seam is worthy of further exploration, but out of scope for this chapter.

Because the rate of computing-networked device acquisition exceeds the ability to manage the same, we need to ask ourselves, *'can we manage what we own?'* The IoT phenomenon will undoubtedly change how we seek to know and characterize our cities and large institutions as a part of the risk management process. A good place to start knowing ourselves is acknowledging, planning for, building, and managing that seam where the interesting things happen.

3.4 Vendor count & complexity

Complicating the management of this seam is the growing number of internal and external system providers that a city must deal with. The vendor count for IoT systems being managed by an institution will only increase in the coming months and years and will likely increase substantially. Some of this increase will be from traditional systems like HVAC, which have been in the space longer than most and are increasingly evolving and extending their IoT developments and deployment. Growth in an institution's vendor count will also come from companies with brand-new products and service lines, particularly cloud services, made possible by IoT innovation and expansion. Many of the benefits of the Internet of Things will result from products and services offered by vendors that interact and exchange information with each other, such as an IoT implementation leveraging the cloud. Regardless of the source, as the number of IoT vendors grows, the number of customer-to-vendor relationships will grow, and because of the increasing interdependencies between systems, the number of vendor-to-vendor relationships will also grow. A somewhat insidious side effect is that the number of relationships to be managed (or left unmanaged) will grow even faster than the vendor count itself.

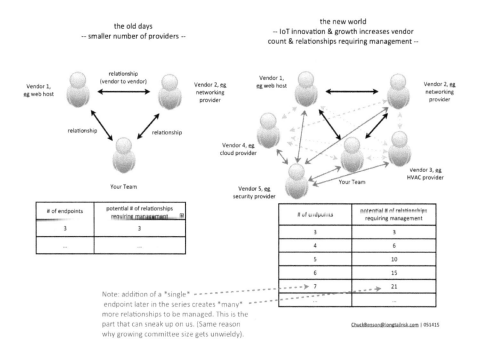

Relationships between business customers and vendors have friction, that is, system loss. And the system has non-infinite resources. There's a limit. This friction comes in the form of day-to-day relationship management overhead such as communication planning and contract management as well as more challenging aspects that include expectation alignment/misalignment and resource allocation problems. This friction can also be thought of as a cost – the relationship uses some amount of resource that was not planned for.

Every system has some friction or unanticipated loss, from Darcy-Weissbach's [16] pressure drop in a pipe, Shannon's channel capacity limitations[17] in information theory, Carnot's limitations of heat engine efficiency[18], to Clausewitz's concept of friction in warfighting.[19] Friction, a type of system loss, also occurs in relationships between individuals and organizations.

[16] https://en.wikipedia.org/wiki/Darcy%E2%80%93Weisbach_equation
[17] http://www.gaussianwaves.com/2008/04/channel-capacity/
[18] https://www.bluffton.edu/homepages/facstaff/bergerd/NSC_111/thermo4.html
[19] https://www.clausewitz.com/readings/OnWar1873/BK1ch07.html

Friction in a business relationship, which is unavoidable to some degree, means that less information gets communicated than expected and less work gets done in practice than what was anticipated. *Both results, the unexpected drop in communication and the unexpected drop in work accomplished, serve to increase uncertainty.* Further, friction in a network of relationships can manifest itself in yet even more uncertainty.

With the increasing network of nodes (IoT systems vendors, in this case), the even-faster-growing number of relationships, and the friction that naturally exists between each, the business environments in our cities and large institutions are becoming progressively more complex. All of this is accompanied by *rising uncertainty*. So, even though devising a strategy or policy around IoT systems deployment and IoT vendor management can be difficult to do, given the complexity and relative newness of the phenomenon, it is a vital task. But since we don't know what is going to happen next in IoT innovation, how do we establish strategy? Also, the strategy might cost something in terms of technical framework and staffing—and that can be particularly hard to realize internally. However, without some type of institutional strategy or policy for IoT system implementations, implementations will be driven by the motivations and priorities of the IoT Systems vendors. It is preferable that implementations are driven by citizens or city leadership.

This is natural in our market economy, but as business consumers, *we need to be aware of this tendency of vendor-driven-policy* and we need to manage for the greater good of our cities. Even though an IoT strategy or policy is almost guaranteed to be imperfect, incomplete, and ephemeral at this stage, the cost of not having one is much higher.

3.5 Raising expectations for providers of IoT systems

Cities and large city-like institutions need to raise expectations for providers of Internet of Things (IoT) systems. They can anticipate continued growth in the numbers and types of IoT systems in their environs. They should raise the bar regarding IoT system deliverables. This is not anti-vendor sentiment — cities need clever, reliable, and thoughtfully applied technology developed and delivered by trusted vendors. Further, vendors can sometimes assist by providing support staffing needs for short- or long-term arrangements dealing with IoT issues to address local staffing shortfalls. Naturally, however, vendors optimize engagements for themselves and their particular set of products or services. It is not the job of the vendor job to understand, support, and mitigate risks around the city's ecosystems. That's the job of city leadership, and to do it, cities must raise their expectations of IoT Systems vendors and contractors, articulate them, and communicate them clearly. Both institutions and their vendors benefit from strong, respectful, well-understood relationships.

3.6 An initial IoT Systems vendor checklist

Below is a possible starting point for a checklist or procedure for working with IoT systems vendors. While checklists deserve to be maligned when applied independently of a larger context, they are appropriate when applied thoughtfully within a larger system or process. When I am flying as a passenger on a plane, I want the pilot to be able to think out-of-the-box when the situation calls for it. Checklists applied in other phases of the flight can help free up the cognitive headroom for that out-of-the-box thinking by making common procedures methodical and rote. Similarly, a checklist can be very helpful in being expeditious and thorough with some standard things that occur in many IoT systems vendor engagements. But a checklist is only useful when it supports a comprehensive process that supports an overarching objective of thoughtful, diligent systems implementation.

An IoT systems vendor checklist can be used during Request for Information (RFI), Request for Proposal (RFP), contract negotiation, contract review, contract re-negotiation, and other planning activities. The following are some useful questions to ask when establishing a strategy for IoT vendor relationships:

3.7 IoT Systems strategy questions for the city/institution —

- Are there standard frameworks that the city can deploy to support requirements from multiple IoT vendors?

- For example, does every vendor need it's own dedicated, staffed, and managed database?

- Are there protocols that can be leveraged across multiple vendors for the city's IoT Systems portfolio?

- Does the vendor in consideration participate in open-source protocols?

- Does the vendor offer a VM (virtual machine) image or similar approach that will work in the city/institutional data center or with the city's cloud provider?

- Does the vendor offer a service that helps integrate its VM image into the data center or cloud environment?

- What city departments/organizations will be involved?
  o Who will oversee the whole system?
  o Do supporting organizations understand their roles and responsibilities in support of the system?

o Who will manage the vendor contract and vendor performance?

3.8 Questions for prospective vendors for selection, procurement, implementation, & management of a particular IoT system —

- If vendors demand a dedicated support infrastructure, are they willing to pay for it or otherwise subsidize it?
- Does the IoT vendor need data feeds/data sharing from your organization?
    - o Is the vendor consuming data? Sourcing/exporting data?
    - o Are the data feeds well defined?
    - o Reasonably defined? (Even written down?)
    - o Do the data feeds exist already?
    - o If not, who will create and support these data feeds?
    - o Are there privacy considerations or other considerations to the data feeds?
- How many endpoint devices will be installed?
- Is there a patch plan?
    - o Do internal city resources/support teams do the patching?
    - o Who manages the plan, the city or the vendor?
    - o What are the projected costs associated with patching (this might be large)
- Does this vendor's system have dependencies on other systems?
- How many IoT systems are you already managing?
- How many IoT endpoints do you already have?
- Are you anticipating or planning more endpoints on existing systems in the next 18 months?
- Are you anticipating or planning more IoT Systems in the next 18 months?
- Is there a commissioning plan the IoT System(s) in question?
    - o Or have IoT vendor deliverable expectations otherwise been stated (contract, memorandum of understanding, letter, other?)
    - o Is there a Design Guide or similar?
- What is the vendor's plan/approach to changing default logins and passwords?
    - o Has the password schema been shared with you?
    - o Are non-required ports and services closed on all your deployed IoT endpoints?
    - o How does the vendor demonstrate this?
    - o Has the vendor port scanned (or similar) all deployed IoT endpoints after installation?

- Is there a plan (for you or vendor) to periodically spot-check configuration of endpoint devices post-implementation?
    - Or a plan for accepting the risk of not doing this?
- Has the installed system been documented in a usable way?
    - Is there (at least) a simple architecture diagram?
    - Is the server(s) configuration documented?
    - Are endpoint IP addresses and ports indicated?
- Who pays for the vendor's system requirements (such as hardware, supporting software, networking?)
- Does local support (staffing/FTE) exist to support the installation?
    - Is local support capacity available?
    - If so, will it remain available?
    - If supporting IoT System servers are hosted in a data center, who pays those costs?
        - Startup and ongoing costs?
    - If supporting IoT System servers are hosted in the cloud, who pays those costs?
        - Startup and ongoing costs?
    - What is the total operational cost after installation?
        - Licensing costs
        - Support contract costs
        - Hosting requirements costs
        - Business resiliency requirements costs
        - Redundancy, recovery, etc. for operating systems, databases, apps
    - How can the vendor demonstrate contract performance?
        - Is the vendor willing to help establish a plan for this? (Willingness to do so can provide an indicator of vendor/contractor maturity in a rapidly growing field of technology providers)
    - Can the vendor maintenance contract offset local IT support shortages?
        - If not, then this might not be the deal you want.
        - For remote support, how does the vendor safeguard login and account information?
    - Does the vendor have a company policy or standard operating procedure that they can share with you that provides evidence of good information systems hygiene?
    - Is a risk-sharing agreement in place between you and the vendor?
        - When things go awry, who is liable for what?

In an address to the National Education Association in April 1957, Dwight Eisenhower made the statement, "Plans are worthless, but planning is everything." [20] No doubt his D-Day Omaha Beach experience — landing craft swamped or pushed off course, useless maps because soldiers landed in unplanned areas, artillery support unavailable because of radios lost on the swamped landing craft, and new beach obstacles from wreckage due to slipped timetables — contributed to that sentiment. The extensive D-Day planning created a breadth of knowledge that allowed for rapid adaptation to unforeseen events, a flexibility that otherwise would not have been possible.

4. SEAMS BETWEEN THE DEPARTMENTS WITHIN THE CITY

One of the unique characteristics of IoT Systems, and one that adds to the complexity of a system's deployment, is that they tend to span many departments and organizations within the city or institution. While traditional enterprise systems, such as e-mail or calendaring, are likely to be owned and operated by one or two institutional organizations, such the central IT organization, IoT Systems involve many organizations and are deployed in the working and living spaces of buildings and surrounding space. IoT Systems are deployed in a system of systems of systems.

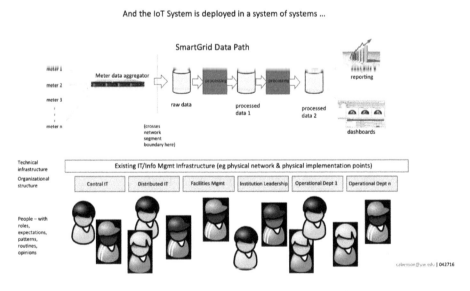

Problems of understanding in inter-organizational relationships:

[20] https://www.eisenhower.archives.gov/all_about_ike/quotes.html

- "emanate from the fact that participants in such relationships are accustomed to different structures, cultures, functional capabilities, cognitive frame and management styles" [21]
- they are aggravated "...because cooperating parties come from disparate backgrounds, and work in different industries, with dissimilar belief systems ... "
- "...in early stages of cooperation are frequently characterized by relatively high levels of ambiguity and uncertainty..."
- "...it confronts them with difficulties in understanding their partners, their relationships in which they are engaged and the contexts in which these are embedded."

These same phenomena are readily apparent in city departments and organizations. Some cities [22], even have departments to help mediate and resolve inter-departmental conflict. For example, a city's parks department will have different priorities than the city's transportation department and the transportation department has different objectives and priorities than the city's CIO/CTO office. And they all vie for parts of the same tax base. Collaborations often produce limited results, have difficult to manage and dissimilar goals and motivations, tend toward gridlock/fragmentation, and can even make things worse [23].

This rings true with what we know about governments and other bureaucracies – *the same ones comprised of those organizations and departments that must cooperate and collaborate to successfully implement IoT Systems.* City departments often compete for funds, have competing objectives, vie for attention with other departments, seek to leverage power and influence, and optimize for themselves while seeking to manage and mitigate their own risk. These issues of "resource allocation, policy change, ... power realignment" don't go away during IoT Systems implementations across these multiple organizations.

[21] Coping with Problems of Understanding in Inter-organizational Relationships: Using Formalization as a Means to Make Sense -- Paul W.L. Vlaar, Frans A.J. Van den Bosch and Henk W. Volberda -- Organization Studies 27(11): 1617–1638 ISSN 0170–8406 Copyright © 2006 SAGE Publications (London, Thousand Oaks, CA & New Delhi)

[22] http://www.seattle.gov/personnel/resources/specifications.asp?schematic=2153004

[23] Koschmann 2016

4.1 Similar challenges in city-like organizations

Facing similar challenges are large city-like specialized institutions such as Higher Education or large research corporations. For example, environmental control systems with multitudes of IoT Systems for large research spaces, whether corporate or Higher Education, are rapidly increasing in number. These systems often sense and regulate air temperature, humidity, particulate levels, light, motion, and many other factors. These measurements are used for safety, energy efficiency, regulatory compliance, and other research needs. Implementing an environmental control system will likely involve:

- the institution's central IT organization
- the facilities management group
- the end-user (e.g. researcher, principal investigator, staff scientist, etc.)
- distributed/local IT organizations
- many product/service vendors and subcontractors

In both the generalized case of smart cities and the more specialized case of city-like research institutions, gaps exist between these departments through which systems accountability and ownership can fall. For example, the city department that invested in or influenced the purchase of the system thinks that the central IT organization is monitoring and managing the system and keeping it secure. At the same time, the central IT organization doesn't know what is being plugged into the network backbone. Each department/organization hopes the other department/organization is managing the system well. Because of this spanning nature of IoT systems, there is often no organic overarching visibility, much less ownership and accountability, for the whole system.

4.2 Technology adoption in other aspects of the building industry

Research has been done in other areas of technology implementation in the building, space, and campus realms that might help provide a basis for understanding the multi-organizational challenge that IoT system implementations can bring to cities and city-like institutions.

Research in the Building Information Modeling (BIM) field suggests that buildings involve social and physical aspects that need a common framework. [24] Building Information Modeling seeks to codify or digitize the physical aspects of a space or place such that its attributes can be stored, transmitted, exchanged in a way that supports decision-making and analysis.

Competing obligations are identified within supporting/contributing organizations that limit technology adoption. BIM-enabled projects are "often tightly coupled technologically, but divided organizationally." I believe that their (Dossick/Neff) observations regarding BIM projects also share common aspects of deploying and managing IoT Systems.

The research suggests that mechanical, electrical, plumbing, and fire life safety systems can be as much as 40% of the commercial construction project scope. [25] It is likely that this number will only increase as our buildings and spaces become more alive, aware, and aggregating of information of what goes on in and around these spaces.

For the BIM implementations studied, the research suggests that there are at three different obligations of the people and organizations contributing to the effort (scope, project, and company) and that these can be in conflict with each other. This conflict, in turn, increases implementation uncertainty.

I believe that there can be similar conflicts and uncertainties when implementing IoT systems that also involve multiple, sometimes competing, parties in a city environment.

4.3 IoT System ownership for implementation & management

Like BIM and related technology adoption, successful IoT Systems implementations, and the smart cities that these systems support, have similar institutional organizational challenges. IoT Systems implementations are themselves a part of larger system of institution, organizations, and people. IoT System implementation and management success will also require learning to work with these multiple organizations that have inherent competing obligations. While there may be other approaches to evolve to solve these organizational challenges, a reasonable place to start might be to establish organizational-spanning system ownership and accountability. An example of where this is done well is Transport for

[24] Dossick, Carrie S., and Gina Neff. "Organizational Divisions in BIM-Enabled Commercial Construction." Journal of Construction Engineering & Management, April 2010, 459-67.doi: http://dx.doi.org/10.1061/(ASCE)CO.19437862.0000109#sthash.57vBt3I3.d puf.

[25] Dossick/Neff 2010

London[26] where a government body plans and coordinates the city's rail networks, primary roads, buses, taxis, river services and others.

5.　　SYSTEMS SOCIALIZATION FOR IOT SYSTEMS

Ultimately, smart cities and their underlying supporting technologies are a societal phenomenon and not simply a technical phenomenon. There are many non-technical and social aspects required for implementation success of an IoT System that in turn are required for success for a smart city or smart institution. Many more of these non-technology-based social aspects will be identified and articulated in the coming years. Here we'll discuss two:

- understanding expectations of data for all constituents (citizens, systems managers, users, etc.) will be an important and challenging problem
- socializing the concept of IoT Systems risk within cities so that that risk can be articulated, discussed, managed, and mitigated by the city leadership and citizenry responsible for the system

5.1 Understanding data expectations is essential to IoT Systems & smart city success

One of the subtle but powerful factors affecting IoT Systems implementation and management success in complex organizations such as a smart city is the change required in becoming a data-centric organization. In most cases, this is not a small transition. The evolutions of these cities and institutions has been from a place of relatively limited data available across multiple contexts. When an organization begins to shift, or seeks to shift, to an organization where data production, acquisition, consumption/analysis, and management are core to its operation and to its perception of self, subtle but powerful cultural and organizational change is required.

Data generation and/or acquisition is a major component in almost all IoT Systems that may be deployed in support of smart cities. It's where the money is, so to speak. The challenge is that the expectations of data from the many constituencies and consumers can vary in significant ways and these variances in expectation, in turn, influence perceptions of IoT Systems, and in turn smart city system, success. Further, early IoT System implementations that are viewed as failures in support of a smart city not only mean lost investment on those particular systems, but also that these

---

[26] https://en.wikipedia.org/wiki/Transport_for_London

failures will (understandably) make constituents wary of funding or deploying subsequent systems.

Reflecting on and planning for what expectations of data are in different constituencies and contexts can substantially help identify criteria for perceptions of successful IoT Systems implementations and smart city deployments.

6. A FRAMEWORK FOR AN ORGANIZATION'S EXPECTATIONS OF DATA

Fiore-Gartland/Neff have proposed a framework[27] for considering those data expectations in the context of health and wellness data from which we might borrow in considering IoT Systems data in smart cities and smart campuses in which the concept of data valences is introduced. In this context, the term valence is more closely aligned with Merriam-Webster's second definition of "relative capacity to unite, react, or interact."[28]

The authors identify six data valences:

- self-evidence
- actionability
- connection
- transparency
- 'truthiness'
- discovery

I'll briefly describe these valences within the healthcare context in which they were developed and then suggest how they might be applied to an IoT System/Smart City System such as an energy management or smart grid system.

6.1 Self-evidence valence

The idea of the self-evidence valence is that data is context-free or at least appears that way. The context-free-ness notion conflicts with the popular assumption of interpretation or mediation being required to make data meaningful as the researchers point out. I believe that data does indeed need mediation to be relevant. Data without mediation devolves to the 'just because' answer.

---

[27] Fiore-Gartland, Brittany, and Gina Neff. "Communication, Mediation, and the Expectations of Data: Data Valences Across Health and Wellness Communities." *International Journal of Communication* 9 (2015): 1466-484.
[28] https://www.merriam-webster.com/dictionary/valence

6.2 Actionability valence

Actionability refers to the expectation that the data does something or drives something. From the context of the data consumer, can that data be used to do something meaningful for that consumer within their context? The example is given of a physician being presented with self-collected patient data. This may well not be "clinically actionable" because the physician has no basis for comparison or reference.

6.3 Connection valence

This valence identifies data as a 'site for conversation.' This is a particularly powerful valence because the connection valence draws people to the same table to discuss data for one reason or another. An example given in the paper is that of a home patient contacting their case manager about data being collected as a part of the telemedicine system. The call was not particularly important regarding the telemedicine question, but rather because it provided an opportunity for the case manager and patient to connect and share other information which may have been recorded in an informal way.

Even if the data-discussion reasons are simple or seem unrelated to ostensible objectives, people are still showing up, meeting, and talking for whatever reason and in the course of that showing up, other things are shared and communicated. This is a powerful valence and yet not easily quantifiable.

6.4 Transparency valence

The transparency data valence is pretty much what it sounds like. It's the idea or expectation of real or perceived benefit of data being "accessible, open, sharable, or comparable across multiple contexts … Making data transparent across communities is one set of values or expectations." The transparency valence also introduces the idea that when there is data transparency, when it is indeed shared across contexts, then new questions around ownership, access, and confidentiality present themselves. Addressing these new questions/issues is important work and requires resources that have traditionally not been planned for.

6.5 Truthiness valence

Stephen Colbert introduced the word 'truthiness' [29] during one of his shows. He uses truthiness to describe something that feels right or just seems right, generally without regard to facts or evidence. Similarly, the truthiness data valence, in turn, has to do with the data quality of the data simply feeling right or seeming right and without reference or supportive logical argument. The concept of truthiness might also have more serious parallels to Ockham's razor where the simpler explanation is preferred to the more exhaustive and/or complex.

6.6 Discovery valence

The discovery valence "describes how people expect data to be the source or site of discovery of an otherwise obscured phenomenon, issue, relationship, or state." This is not inconsistent with the popular notion of Big Data where often broad assumptions are made that simply because there is an unprecedented amount of data, that there must be new patterns, knowledge, and possibly unsolved mysteries there.

7. DATA VALENCES IN AN IOT SYSTEM EXAMPLE – ENERGY MANAGEMENT

So how might the six data valences reveal themselves in an institutional energy management system such as a smart grid system or a part of a smart grid system — themselves IoT Systems? Here is one approach on how each of these valences might come into play in this context.

7.1 Self-evidence valence in energy management data

My initial reaction is that I don't see this valence playing out particularly well in the IoT Systems space. This energy management data sourced from thousands of energy sensors across a city or institution needs to have context and be interpreted to have relevance. Also, the data is too new, unfamiliar,

---

[29] Truthiness. (2017, February 6). In Wikipedia,
The Free Encyclopedia. Retrieved 01:31, February 15, 2017, from
https://en.wikipedia.org/w/index.php?title=Truthiness&oldid=763983368

sometimes abstract and often complex for there to be strong statements of self-evidence.

That said, the topic of climate change and all the misinterpretations and rhetoric therein comes to mind. So maybe the self-evidence valence has applicability here as well. Perhaps conclusions will indeed be drawn from energy data devoid of context.

7.2 Actionability valence in energy management data

Yes, this valence applies. Everyone — consumers, vendors, government, others — expect to do something useful here with energy management data collected via IoT Systems.

7.3 Connection valence in energy management data

Yes. This data provides the site, as the authors say, to come together to problem-solve. And in the course of that problem-solving, a parade of assumptions and expectations come quickly to the surface. Finance professionals, energy management professionals, IT and data professionals, vendors, and a variety of end-users bring their expectations, assumptions, and desires to these meetings.

This data valence is particularly important at this point in the evolutions of energy management systems, IoT Systems in general, and smart cities. Facilitating the opportunity for city leaders, citizenry, and systems providers to come together to problem solve is critical to success.

7.4 Transparency valence in energy management data

Yes. Everybody wants this. This distribution of data interpretation across contexts is exciting, challenging, and fraught with peril for misunderstanding. That said, addressing topics around this valence can bring important issues to the surface (and it's typically a lot of work).

7.5 Truthiness in energy management data

Not sure. I'm not sure about the utility of the truthiness valence in institutional energy management data. Similar to the self-evidence valence, I don't know that we have enough exposure to the data to have a truthiness feel about institutional energy management data. But again, there are plenty of examples of misinterpreting climate change data.

7.6 Discovery valence in energy management data

Yes. Almost everybody has this expectation of discovery. I do believe that capturing this data will yield useful, actionable (see above) data. However, I think it's going to be more work than is immediately apparent to create useful and actionable (see above) data.

7.7 Data valences in IoT Systems

How we, across our multiple constituencies within a city or institution, perceive various aspects of data has a strong influence on the perceived success of the system that produced the data. This is true for city energy management systems and I believe that that is broadly generalizable to IoT Systems of whatever governmental or city purpose.

Understanding data perceptions across an institution or population base is essential for successful IoT System implementations and hence Smart City or Smart Campus implementations. The capability and capacity of a city or institution to implement complex IoT Systems in a complex environment is essential to success. Understanding the varied data consumers and their perceptions and needs in a complex organization such as a city or campus is, in turn, a critical component to a successful IoT System implementation.

8.   SOCIALIZING IOT SYSTEMS RISK

IoT Systems hold much promise, yet concerns regarding security, privacy, safety, and other issues are valid. Addressing this new source of risk involves several challenges. It's easy for anyone to call out things that could happen with IoT growth and propagation: medical devices can be hacked, smart meters can be compromised to steal information, the utility grid has increasing exposure, drone videos are being intercepted and hacked. Misuse or malicious use examples that generate fear, uncertainty, and doubt are not difficult to come by. Highlighting these issues is important, but *the larger and more difficult task for a city or institution is to communicate risk around IoT in a way that allows that risk to be managed.*

Within an institution that already manages risk in some form, communicating and socializing the idea of IoT risk involves two broad components. First, IoT defies traditional classification/categorization and is still little understood. People have a hard time understanding the concept. To begin to manage IoT risk, institutional leaders must have some vocabulary and conceptual frameworks for it. IoT is still new, its effects are largely unknown and likely emergent, and its precedents and analogies are few. We need to surface some language and concepts so that it can be discussed.

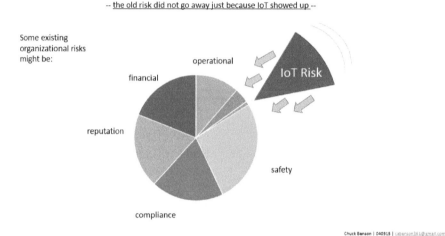

Risk from IoT is competing with existing organizational risk for attention
-- the old risk did not go away just because IoT showed up --

Second, the other risks that the institution faces are still there: safety, liability, financial loss, reputation damage, technology challenges, business competition, and more remain. They haven't gone away just because the IoT phenomena showed up. We are asking senior leaders to make room in their list of existing risks to add yet more risk to consider, manage, and mitigate, and perhaps substantially more. Nobody wants to hear this.

How we outline and explain these IoT security, privacy, and risk issues is, therefore, critical. Since we are competing for a small slice of available cognitive bandwidth of senior leadership amongst all of the other things that they are already concerning themselves with, we must use this opportunity to communicate as clearly as possible. Doing so could involve taking the following steps:

- Find out what other risks the institution is already dealing with. For example, is there a risk report for the city? What risks exist that already have leadership mindshare?

- Identify places where IoT and IoT systems are present currently in the institution or where they may be soon.

- Use the language of managing existing risk in the institution to begin to talk about managing IoT risk.

- Continuously iterate

A key to this communication is to get some IoT systems risk concepts out early. Give city leaders and constituents some language and conceptual framework to use in reflecting on IoT systems risk and discussing it with their peers. It's also important not to be heavy-handed in the approach. Yes, IoT systems risk is important, the dangers are potentially very high, and the opportunities for abuse are many, but the existing risks faced by a city must be managed too.

9.   THOUGHTFUL IMPLEMENTATION

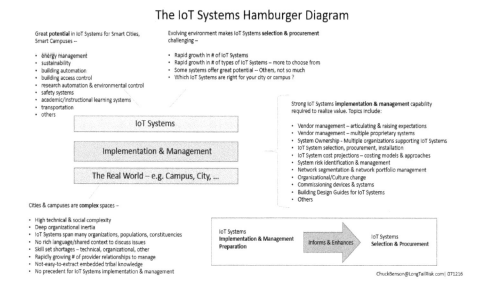

Smart cities and smart institutional campuses offer great promise to their users and constituents. However, the technology systems -- and the data that they produce and consume -- that underpin these smart cities must be implemented thoughtfully and with structure. Without self-reflection of institutional gaps on implementation and management capabilities of these IoT systems, return on investment will not be seen and, worse, poor implementation and management can actually make things worse for the population.

Implementing any new technology system incurs risk. Ideally, cities and institutions recognize this risk and can invest resources to actively manage and mitigate that risk. Of course, things are rarely ideal. Less ideal but still acceptable is that, cities and institutions recognize the risk and then make an informed decision about whether to accept the risk or not. It might be that the new system is perceived to bring such value as to be worth the risks incurred. Finally, the scenario that we want to avoid above all is where new technology systems bring risk into our environments and that risk is simply not recognized, acknowledged, or discussed. At this point in time, this unfortunate approach is likely more the rule than the exception.

CHAPTER 5

MANAGING CYBER RISKS IN SMART CITY SYSTEM OF SYSTEMS

Abhik Chaudhuri

Abstract: The smart city concept is a dynamic ecosystem created with integrated, live and interdependent cyber-enabled systems. Effective risk assessment and management of the interconnected systems is a prime necessity for ensuring security of the smart city services. The smart city council should take appropriate measure to identify and address risks of the interdependent systems on a round-the-clock basis to thwart cyber-attacks. This chapter discusses the dependent and interdependent components of a smart city system of systems and how the cyber risks of these systems can be managed to provide secure and trustworthy smart services to citizens.

1.   INTRODUCTION

There is a gradual demographic shift across the world to the cities, this means that providing basic services to the increasing number of citizens is becoming a challenging task for the City Councils. To meet the growing trend of human settlements shifting from rural to urban, cities are in expansion mode. In such a scenario, the concept of Smart Cities is promising to provide enhanced city experience with digitally enabled smart services to its citizens. New smart cities are also being developed to meet the needs of the growing population.

The smart cities are being designed on the premise of interoperability of Industrial Control Systems (ICS) and Information Technology Systems (ITS) for creating so-called 'smart' services spanning all spheres of life and economy.

However, like any other IT-enabled service, the smart city services should be risk managed and secured for use. To cope with the cyber security challenges in a smart city it is vital to manage the security risks of the interdependent systems. The interdependent systems in futuristic smart cities should interconnect devices and humans with confidentiality, integrity, availability and trustworthiness.

In this chapter we discuss the dependence and interdependence of systems in smart cities, the cyber risks of operation, and how we can manage these risks for a better living and working experience in smart cities.

2.   THE CONCEPT OF A SMART CITY

A smart city "*brings together technology, government and society to enable the following characteristics:*
- a smart economy
- smart mobility
- a smart environment
- smart people
- smart living
- smart governance"(IEEE, 2015).

One of the key features of a smart city is that it has a citizen-centric approach with a digitally enabled infrastructure. A smart city should "enable every citizen to engage with all the services on offer, public as well as private, in a way best suited to his or her needs. It brings together hard infrastructure, social capital including local skills and community institutions, and (digital) technologies to fuel sustainable economic development and provide an attractive environment for all" (Department for Business Innovation & Skills, UK Government, 2013).

Smart assisted living in smart cities includes features like smart infrastructure, smart energy management, smart transport and traffic management, smart water management, smart waste management, smart healthcare and other smart services, the term 'smart' mostly implying an ICT enabled and intelligence-based real time experience of the services.

3.   INTERDEPENDENT SYSTEMS IN SMART CITIES

If we look at the underlying systems design of a city, we will find that various services are being rendered to the citizens like the transport service, water distribution, power distribution, waste disposal, fire services, food distribution, healthcare services, education services, traffic management, street lighting and so on. The infrastructure facilitating these services is the underlying framework or hardware of the city. Based on the value rendered by the service and the impact of its loss, the infrastructure backbone of the service can be tagged as 'critical' and may be considered as an asset of national importance. The criticality of an infrastructure component can be decided based on a Criticality Scale (CPNI, 2008) having three impact dimensions of impact on delivery of the service, economic impact and impact on life, the last two factors arising from the loss of the service.

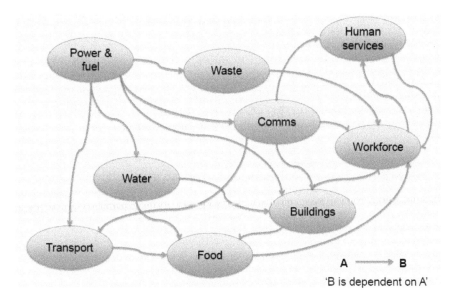

Figure 1: Dependent and Interdependent Systems in Cities
(Watson, J., 2014).

As shown in Figure 1, a city service 'B' can have a dependence on another service 'A'. Here 'service' is defined as: *"the output provisioned as a commodity through a system that "consumes resources, uses components, information assets and inputs, in the process"* (IRRIS, 2007). In a city that grows with the passage of time without proper design, most of these systems are randomly connected and grow in a scale-free topology as the infrastructure and service needs are implemented asynchronously in reactive mode. Hence, this unplanned growth results in uneven distribution of connectedness of the city's systems.

Direct dependence can be defined to exist *"between a pair of services if there exists a causal sequence of events, starting in one service, that results in a change of state in the other service and this change of state does not require events in any other identified entities in the service-model to occur"* (IRRIS, 2007). For example, transport service in a city has direct dependence on the availability of power and fuel.

Indirect dependence *"exists between a pair of services if there exists a causal sequence of events, starting in one service, that results in a change of state in the other service and this change of state requires events in other identified entities in the service-model to occur"* (IRRIS, 2007). For example, availability of food in a city has indirect dependence on power and fuel because food supply can get affected if distribution of water required for food production is affected for lack of power or when food cannot be transported to the city markets due to lack of fuel.

Interdependency exists between two services if there is a *"correlation between these services' changes of state"* (IRRIS, 2007). For example, electric power is required by transport system for powering locomotives and transport system and it is necessary to transport fuel to the power station for power generation. Based on the linkage between the city systems the level of interdependency varies from first-order up to the nth-order.

There can be six dimensions of infrastructure interdependencies as shown in Figure 2. These are – infrastructure characteristics, state of operation, types of interdependencies, environment, coupling and response behaviour and type of failure. The types of interdependencies have been classified as cyber, physical, geographic and logical.

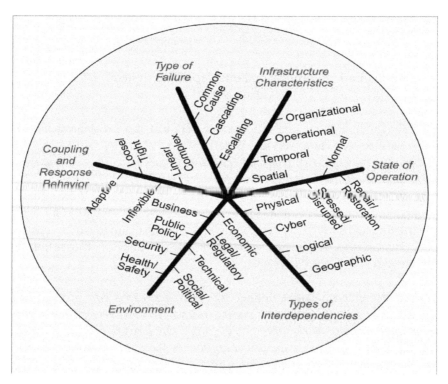

Figure 2: Infrastructure Interdependence Dimensions
(Rinaldi et al. 2001).

With the integration of the infrastructure systems and information communication technology, the interdependent systems in cities are becoming more tightly coupled due to information flow and functional dependency between these systems.

The dependent and interdependent systems in a smart city can handle all major services like smart water distribution, smart energy generation and transmission, smart mobility, smart garbage and waste disposal, smart street lighting systems, citizen connected smart healthcare, smart security and surveillance, smart traffic management and so on.

With effective utilization of ICS and ITS the live digital fabric of interdependent systems exchange data to create a smart city that is dynamic and synergistic in nature with features like instantaneous data gathering and analytics based decision making. The ICS have programmable logic controllers (PLC) to check inputs, execute programmed logic and regulate outputs of the infrastructure systems. The output from one ICS will provide input to the next ICS and thus help to create a series of actions for a programmed stimulus based action. There will be interfaces where ICS will communicate with the ITS. In a smart city all services will be digitised with ICS having supervisory control and data acquisition capability (SCADA). It will help to collect data from one or more remote technical units (RTU), perform data analysis and then send digitised working instructions to the PLC. For example, this will help, the power distribution system to sense a growing demand for electricity using smart meters as sensors in a certain region of the smart city and to then distribute power in the most efficient way.

4.   OPPORTUNITIES AND RISKS OF INTERDEPENDENT SYSTEMS IN A SMART CITY

The ICT-enabled synergistic interdependency of systems in a smart city has opportunities as well as risks, as shown in Figure 3. It can help Smart City Councils to identify necessary action based on continuous analytics of the huge volume of data collected from the subsystems. For example, the smart cities can analyze health data of its citizens to identify health scares like virus attacks at an early stage for necessary action. Data integration in smart cities can also be utilized for mapping energy efficiency of buildings, mapping social data for crime prevention, monitoring flood situations, citizen consultations, trend analysis and city development in areas like housing, education, transport, medical services, employment and so on. The other opportunities are to decrease the cost of operation with the help of digital automation and to improve the flexibility of the systems with predictive analytics and digitised response mechanisms.

However, this synergistic interdependency of the systems in a smart city also carries the risks of operation.

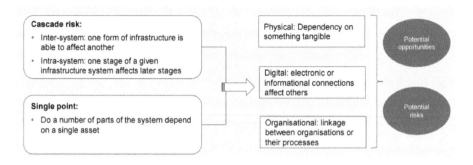

Figure 3: Opportunities and risks of interdependent systems in smart cities (Watson, J., 2014).

If one system fails to provide relevant information to the next connected system then it might create chaos in the smart city services. This is because the interoperability of the smart city systems creates a complex adaptive system of systems arising from the variation in interaction between these systems (Little, 2002). For example, a failure in the smart traffic management database server can cause hindrance to the seamless operation of smart transport management system as vehicles might continue to clog a particular highway junction instead of being diverted to a ring road due to non-availability of vital information from the traffic management system.

For smart healthcare services in a smart city, there can be new service opportunities like digitally monitoring the health of diabetic and heart patients through wireless data exchange on a 24x7 basis. Data captured by the sensors and smart glucose monitors implanted in the patients can be sent directly to the citizen health monitoring systems in the smart hospitals. In such a critical service if the internet connectivity to the glucose monitor or pacemaker is breached or authenticity of data cannot be verified then the patients' lives can be at risk.

5. NECESSITY OF RISK MITIGATION IN SMART CITIES

Due to the large number of devices that are expected to be connected in a smart city's digital infrastructure, enhanced security management for gateway devices is of prime importance to prevent data breach or leakage when one system feeds data to another system in the interdependent cyber systems. There can be no compromise of the security of digital infrastructure of a smart city because any security weak link in the digital architectural fabric of the smart city can be exploited as a single point of failure of the smart city information system. This type of failure can be cascading in nature (Rinaldi et al., 2001) when a software virus spreads from one smart system to another after injection, or it can be a common cause failure when multiple smart systems are infected at the same time by targeted cyber attacks.

A smart city will deal analytically with huge volume of data that will be generated from the communication between the smart city systems (Machine to Machine or M2M) and from the interaction of the smart systems with the citizens (Machines to People or M2P and People to Machines or P2M). Private and sensitive information directly obtained, intercepted or inferred from data flows in a smart city system of systems can be a cause of deep concern with regard to safety and security of smart city services and citizens. For example, smart healthcare system should be built with assurance of secured and effective transmission of data, including private health data, in the smart city network. Any incident of data breach or data loss will adversely impact the citizens' perception of security and trust of smart city services and living. Some information security concerns of citizens in a smart city can be the interception of wireless data in transit between sender and receiver, leakage of confidential information through man-in-the-middle attacks by motivated externals or malicious citizens (insiders), implantation of virus and Trojans at device level like sensors and so on. Cloud based information services and data storage in smart cities can be compromised through hacking and related subversive activities.

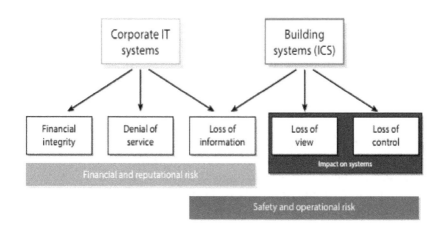

Figure 4: Risks arising from compromised interdependent systems in Smart Cities (Boyes, H, 2013).

As shown in Figure 4, the ICS and ITS can have safety and operational risks as well as financial and reputational risks. Any vulnerability in the security architecture of ICS or IT systems can open a floodgate of disaster like virus attacks, security breaches, compromise of sensitive data that can lock down critical services in a smart city. A key security concern about RTUs, PLCs and SCADA systems is that many of these use end-of-life technology and have cyber-vulnerabilities (for example hard-coded passwords, insecure operating systems like Windows 95) built into them.

The attacks targeting the SCADA ICS has risen by 100% in 2014 in comparison to the previous year, as per the data collected by Dell Global Response Intelligence Defence Network from millions of security sensors, firewalls, honeypots and shared intelligence network of research organizations and industry groups from more than 200 countries around the globe (Korolov, M., 2015). As per the Report, current hacking efforts on SCADA ICS are more of denial of service attacks aimed to shut down the devices. However, these trends can also lead to data theft and data tampering incidents in future that can affect smart city dwellers socially as well as financially. The Report also provides information that the malwares used to target the SCADA ICS are using memory scraping and encryption techniques that helps the malware to remain in hiding. A basic packet filtering firewall will not be able to detect these malwares and this is a growing cause of concern. The process control and SCADA systems are also becoming more reliant on information technology in order to create large scale smart system solutions with the growth in demand across the world. The increase in frequency and complexity of these cyber attacks is a cause of concern for smart cities because the prime necessity is safe, secured and trustworthy smart services.

6.   STEPS FOR RISK MITIGATION IN SMART CITIES

The standards and risk mitigation strategies currently being used to secure IT systems may not be enough to safeguard the interdependent systems in smart cities. As a system of systems grows in a smart city, the interdependencies increase manifold. This complexity can make the smart systems less resilient. We should therefore aim to design a risk tolerant digital architecture for the smart city that can proactively detect and respond to abnormalities like an immune system. The interdependent systems need an adaptive capability to arrest anomalies in the nascent stage and lock down the affected system or subsystem without disturbing other live system components.

New security and privacy standards are being developed for smart cities by ISO, ETSI and others. These will be available in the next three to five years. Until then various existing standards and frameworks for risk management can be utilized by the Smart City Councils. (Caralli, R.A. et al., 2007). A risk assessment framework like the NIST's Framework for Improving Critical Infrastructure Cybersecurity (NIST, 2014) can be utilized to identify the information assets of smart systems to qualitatively assess the risks and to secure these assets.

Business Continuity Planning (BCP) for Smart City is an effective risk management initiative that can help the Smart City Councils to understand the necessary measures they have to undertake to keep the smart services live and running. Periodic BCP drills should be conducted, audited and well documented for ready reference during criticalities. It will provide the smart cities a recovery oriented approach towards risk. The ISO 22301:2012, the "International Standard for Societal Security — Business Continuity Management Systems" (ISO, 2012) can be adopted by the Smart City Councils to prevent cyber disruptions with appropriate countermeasures.

Proper communication management is a prime necessity for smart cities to respond to emergencies and critical cyber threats. The communication channels with specific points of contact should be documented and regularly updated and these documents should be available to all stakeholders of a smart city, including its citizens.

Building resilient interdependent systems in smart cities will ensure that the citizens as well as businesses will be well prepared for cyber emergencies and to recover from it in a lesser span of time. An effective resilience strategy has to be designed, tested and implemented to pursue, prevent, protect and prepare for any eventuality. Resilience can be built in the infrastructure systems through four strategic components of Reliability, Resistance, Redundancy, and Response and Recovery as shown in Figure 5.

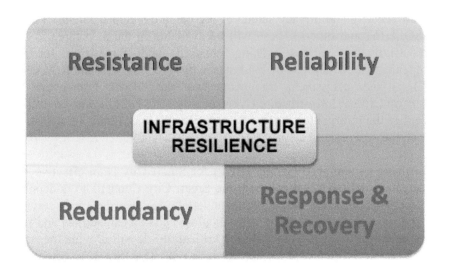

Figure 5: Components of Infrastructure Resilience (Cabinet Office, 2012).

Periodic system impact analysis should be performed for risk identification on critical interdependent systems and services in smart cities with appropriately defined recovery time and recovery point objectives. Smart cities should secure the data receivers and data storages to collect and store data generated from the ICS and ITS components for analysis, analytics, response and decision-making. The stored data should be periodically backed up as a precautionary measure to deal with any cyber emergency situation. Data flow from the ICS can be channelized using data diodes to prevent data contamination from ITS as a precautionary measure.

Component protection strategy can be developed by the Smart City Councils to identify the components of critical systems for agile risk analysis. Preliminary interdependency analysis can be performed to identify the order of dependency that can develop between the critical systems in a smart city like the smart grid and smart health monitoring systems. It also helps to understand the reliability requirements essential for continuity of the system functionalities and inter-system information flow in specific cyber attack scenarios (Netkachova, K. et al, 2015). This should be followed by probabilistic interdependency analysis of the systems to quantitatively assess the interdependency risks. The Good Practice Guide for Process Control and SCADA security (CPNI, 2015) can also be utilized to ensure security and trustworthiness of the smart systems.

Security of IoT installations should be ensured by the Smart City Council to prevent any physical attack or infiltration. Identity management mechanism should be employed for authentication, authorization and accounting of users and devices accessing the smart systems. Digital forensic capabilities should be integrated in the smart city cyber architecture right from the design phase to gather evidences of untoward incidents and to take appropriate action for making the cyber infrastructure more secure and robust.

7. GOVERNANCE AND POLICIES TO ADDRESS CYBER DEFENSE IN SMART CITIES

Effective Governance and policies are required for security, safety and data privacy of smart services. An architectural framework has to be put in place by the Smart City Council by taking into consideration the critical infrastructure and cyber components. The Smart City Council should create suitable policies for the implementation, maintenance and usage of the smart services.

Hasty designs and shortcuts to meet stringent deadlines for smart service implementation provides scope for errors and can create design weaknesses for hackers that can prove detrimental to the smart living concept. The Council should ensure that the notion of security and privacy is incorporated in smart services in the design phase.

Contingency measures have to be kept ready by the Smart City Council to counter any security incident that can jeopardize the seamless functioning of the smart services. The Smart City Council should continuously identify and assess the security risks of the smart city assets and take appropriate action for mitigation. The following queries, as shown in Table 1, have to be brought up repeatedly in the Council's service review meetings with due diligence of threat scenarios, history of the past attacks and future readiness plan.

1.	When and how the smart systems can fail? What will be the failover policy?
2.	Do we know the consequences of security breach on the critical interdependent systems?
3	Do the emerging cyber threats limit the extent to which we can make our city services smart?
4.	Are we appropriately addressing the security and data privacy requirements of the smart services?

5.	How can we ensure authenticity of the devices and users on the smart service network?
6.	What level of access privileges should we provide to the devices and users in the smart city cyber system?
7.	How can we enhance the cyber awareness of the citizens for appropriate usage of the smart services?

Table 1: Queries for Smart City Council on the security and privacy of interconnected smart systems

The citizens of smart cities will play a crucial role in ensuring security of the interdependent systems. This is because the citizens will feed and receive data from the interdependent systems for their day-to-day activities. So the citizens with smart devices accessing the smart services will become critical nodes in the cyber system that can be targeted by co-citizens and hackers for maliciously exploitation as weak links through various means like social engineering, spam emails, data streaming and so on. To prevent this, cyber awareness programs should be made mandatory for the citizens by the Smart City Councils with provision for penalties due to non-compliance.

8. CONCLUSION

The smart city concept is a multi-disciplinary and multi-stakeholder ownership approach to a dynamic ecosystem created with integrated, live and interdependent cyber-enabled systems. Effective cyber risk assessment and management of the interconnected systems is a prime necessity for ensuring security of the smart systems.

The system of systems in a smart city can generate huge volumes of data as a result of information creation, infusion and flow between the interdependent systems and for citizens' interaction with these live systems. The interdependency of the smart systems and the risk mitigation steps discussed in this chapter can be helpful for Smart City Councils to provide safe, secure, and reliable services to the citizens. The Smart City Council has to play a leadership role with an overarching governance authority to help the citizens realise the benefits of smart city living with a perception of trust and confidence.

REFERENCES

IEEE. (2015) Smart Cities. Retrieved from http://smartcities.ieee.org/about Department for Business Innovation & Skills, UK Government. (2013). Smart Cities: Background Paper. Retrieved from https://www.gov.uk/government/uploads/system/uploads/attachment_data/file/246019/bis-13-1209-smart-cities-background-paper-digital.pdf

CPNI. (n.d.) The National Infrastructure. Retrieved from http://www.cpni.gov.uk/about/cni/

Watson, J. (2014) The Resilience of City Systems. Retrieved from http://www.2014.csdm-asia.net/IMG/pdf/CSDM_Jeremy_Watson.pdf

Bloomfield, R. et al. (2007) Integrated Risk Reduction of Information-based Infrastructure Systems (IRRIS), Deliverable D2.2.4. Retrieved from http://www.irriis.org/File7864.pdf?lang=2&oiid=9247&pid=572

Rinaldi, S.M. et al. (2001) Identifying, Understanding, and Analyzing Critical Infrastructure Interdependencies. IEEE Control Systems Magazine, 11-25. Retrieved from http://www.ce.cmu.edu/~hsm/im2004/readings/CII-Rinaldi.pdf

Little, R. G. (2002) Controlling cascading failure: understanding the vulnerabilities of interconnected infrastructures. Journal of Urban Technology, 9 (1), 109-123. Retrieved from http://www.tandfonline.com/doi/abs/10.1080/106307302317379855

Boyes, H. (2013) Resilience and Cyber Security of Technology in the Built Environment. Retrieved from http://www.cpni.gov.uk/documents/publications/2013/2013063-resilience_cyber_security_technology_built_environment.pdf?epslanguage=en-gb

Korolov, M. (2015) Attacks against industrial control systems double. Retrieved from http://www.itworld.com/article/2911634/attacks-against-industrial-control-systems-double.html

Cabinet Office. (2010) Section A: Introduction, Definitions and Principles of Infrastructure Resilience. Retrieved from https://www.gov.uk/government/uploads/system/uploads/attachment_data/file/78902/section-a-natural-hazards-infrastructure.pdf

Caralli, R.A. et.al. (2007) Introducing OCTAVE Allegro: Improving the Information Security Risk Assessment Process. Retrieved from http://resources.sei.cmu.edu/asset_files/TechnicalReport/2007_005_001_14885.pdf

ISO/IEC 22301 (2012) Societal security - Business continuity management systems - Requirements, , International Standardization Organization/International Electrotechnical Commission. Retrieved from http://www.iso.org/iso/catalogue_detail?csnumber=50038

CPNI. (2008) Good Practice Guide – Process Control and SCADA Security. Retrieved from http://www.cpni.gov.uk/Documents/Publications/2008/2008031-GPG_SCADA_Security_Good_Practice.pdf

NIST. (2014) Framework for Improving Critical Infrastructure Cybersecurity. Retrieved from https://www.nist.gov/sites/default/files/documents/cyberframework/cybersecurity-framework-021214.pdf

Netkachova, K., Bloomfield, R. E., Popov, P. T. & Netkachov, O. (2015) Using Structured Assurance Case Approach to Analyse Security and Reliability of Critical Infrastructures. Retrieved from http://openaccess.city.ac.uk/12969/

CHAPTER 6

TIPPSS - TRUST, IDENTITY, PRIVACY, PROTECTION, SAFETY AND SECURITY FOR SMART CITIES

Florence D. Hudson
Mark Cather

Abstract: The deployment of Internet of Things (IoT) technologies to enable smart cities provides great opportunities to leverage information to improve city operations, enable process efficiencies, develop new services and enhance the citizen experience. A smart city is "smart" because it leverages information to make "smarter" decisions. This information may be acquired through various mechanisms including the Internet of Things, social media, systems and humans. The monumental increase in digital connections to physical devices, due to the wide deployment of IoT technologies in a smart city, also creates great risk. There is physical, statutory, financial and reputational risk. As evidenced by recent attacks through and on IoT devices, the key attributes of Trust, Identity, Privacy, Protection, Safety and Security (TIPPSS) need to be assessed and addressed for all IoT applications, devices, processes and services. Computer systems can be attacked by IoT devices, rendering them helpless (The Guardian, 2016). Similarly, IoT devices and the systems that manage them can be attacked and disabled, including transportation vehicles (Greenberg, 2015). This chapter is designed to give government officials, private companies, technical solution developers, and citizens an introduction to Trust, Identity, Privacy, Protection, Safety and Security (TIPPSS) considerations when designing and deploying Internet of Things enabled systems in a smart and connected city environment.

1.   INTRODUCTION

Many cities are already integrating Internet of Things (IoT) technologies into their municipal infrastructures (Smart Cities Council, 2015), a trend predicted to accelerate into the future (President's Council of Advisors on Science and Technology, 2016). These IoT technologies can be leveraged to enable cities to serve their populations in ways never possible, increasing efficiency and safety (Gudivada et al., 2016) and enhancing the citizen experience. Digitally monitored vehicles and roadways, working in conjunction with smart parking services, can improve the efficiency of work and life in a connected city, and potentially reduce traffic and carbon emissions. More energy efficient buildings and housing, leveraging microgrids of renewable energy, connected to more agile and reliable power grids, utilizing smart utility meters and infrastructure monitoring, can potentially reduce energy use, costs and carbon emissions. Collaborative emergency services leveraging communications from person to person and with transportation, utility and surveillance systems, can improve public safety. Autonomous vehicles and robots with assistive technologies can better serve citizens. Environmental monitoring services can inform healthcare services to anticipate needs and improve care. All these scenarios and implementations of Internet of Things technologies can improve the citizen experience.

1.1 The Internet of Things is Here

There are many examples of Internet of Things systems in smart cities and campuses already in service around the world. Examples such as the "Array of Things" in Chicago (Array of Things, 2016) is an urban sensing project. By leveraging sensors (Figure 1) on 500 nodes around the City of Chicago measuring environmental, air quality, light, and traffic data, this innovative partnership between the University of Chicago, Argonne National Laboratory, and the City of Chicago aims to better understand, serve and improve cities and the citizen experience (Computation Institute, 2016) Aspirations of this project include the idea of a light pole that can tell you to watch out for an icy patch of sidewalk ahead to improve your safety, or an app that told you the most populated route for a late-night walk to the train station by yourself to improve your safety and protect you from harm.

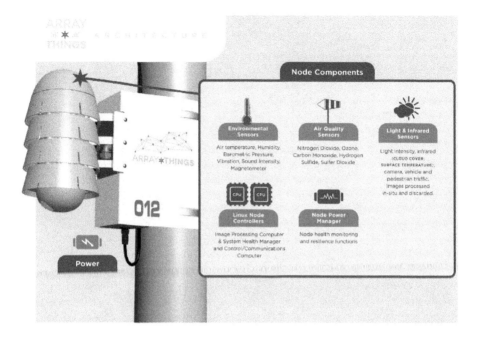

Figure 1: The Array of Things (https://arrayofthings.github.io/)

Smart water management systems such as in the Netherlands (IBM, 2013) will leverage sensors to harness the power of big data to improve Dutch flood control and water management systems and help keep the country safe. This innovation program called Digital Delta will integrate and analyze water data including precipitation measurements, water level and water quality monitors, levee sensors, radar data, model predictions, as well as current and historic maintenance data from pumping stations, locks and dams. By modeling weather events, the Netherlands will be able to determine the best course of action including storing water, diverting it from low-lying areas to avoid flooding, avoiding saltwater intrusion into drinking water, sewage overflows and water contamination. (Figure 2)

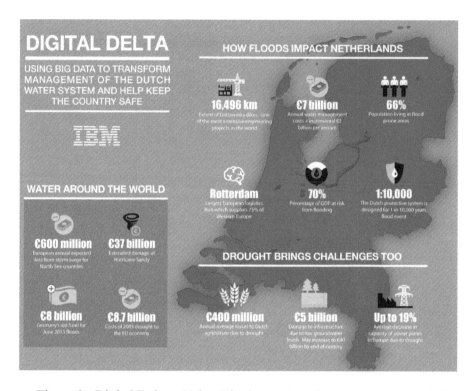

Figure 2: Digital Delta – Using Big data to transform management of the Dutch water system and help keep the country safe
(Link to hi-res infographic)

The value of smart city solutions will be realized only if we ensure the data is not altered. For instance, if sensor data on potential water levels is altered to suggest there is no water rising beyond an unsafe level when it is, thereby putting people and their possessions at risk of flooding damage, then emergency management systems and citizen safety can be compromised. As each new technology is being considered, the citizens, private industry participants, and cities will each need to consider their role in the safe and secure deployment of IoT systems.

1.2   TIPPSS for smart and safe cities

While advanced technologies deployed in cities can provide great benefits to a community, make city operations far more efficient, and improve the citizen experience, technology can also create increased risk to cities, private companies, and people if the technology or the data is compromised. When assessing the risks posed by the deployment of new technologies and interconnected solutions, everyone should consider Trust, Identity, Privacy, Protection, Safety and Security (TIPPSS) (Hudson, 2016).

- **Trust**: Allow only designated people/services device/data access
- **Identity**: Validate the identity of people, services, and "things"
- **Privacy**: Ensure device, personal & sensitive data is kept private
- **Protection**: Protect devices and users from harm
- **Safety**: Provide safety for devices, infrastructure and people
- **Security**: Maintain security of data, devices, people, etc.

Figure 3: TIPPSS Framework

These factors provide an essential framework (Figure 3) for measuring and mitigating the risks associated with the use of connected Internet of Things (IoT) devices (Sicari et al, 2015). TIPPSS needs to be integral in not only the deployment of IoT systems, but also in the design of IoT devices themselves. Internet of Things technologies will be successfully integrated into our cities and society if the concepts of Trust, Identity, Privacy, Protection, Safety, and Security are considered by all participants in the design and use of technical systems from the chips and low-level protocols through products, infrastructure systems, the user experience and usage instructions. It will be the responsibility of the citizens, private industry participants, cities, policy and regulatory bodies to ensure TIPPSS is fully integrated into all solutions.

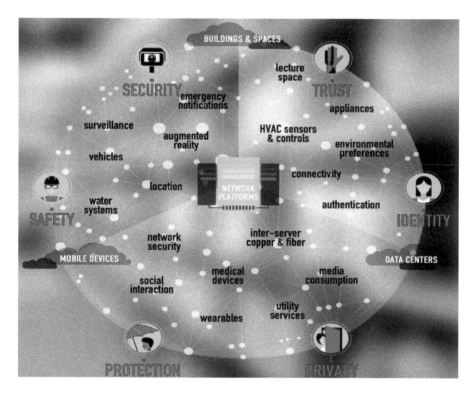

Figure 4: TIPPSS use cases for Smart and Connected Communities

TIPPSS is critical for many types of systems in smart and connected communities (Figure 4). We can consider each TIPPSS element in its own right.

The Trust aspect, ensuring only designated people have device or data access, is important for buildings, such as ensuring only designated family members or friends have access to your home. Ensuring that only trusted services providers have access to change the temperature or controls of the heating and air conditioning systems, not just for comfort of clients, employees or family members, but also to ensure they don't turn off the heat for the elderly during extreme cold weather.

Identity validation is important to ensure the person, device or service trying to access a network, home, secure building or datacenter holding all the data in a firm or hospital, is an authorized individual.

Privacy is a privilege we treasure, and it is regulated in some environments such as healthcare. Keeping data private has reputational considerations for instance for media consumption, as well as financial and

116

legal risk in regulated environments such as for healthcare data in a datacenter, in the cloud, or in a medical device.

Protection of devices and users from harm is critical for wearable medical devices. Patients could be given a potentially lethal overdose of medicine if medical devices are compromised to show a greater or lesser need for medicine from an infusion pump.

Safety of cars and other vehicles can be compromised, as well as safety of the people in the vehicles, if a vehicle is not protected from unauthorized digital access. Driverless or driven vehicles could have the engine turned off, or the brakes disabled. (Greenberg, 2015) Water systems with sensors could be compromised, having the sensors communicate no risk when indeed dangerous levels of chemicals or pollution could be in water, or flooding could go undetected until it is a severe physical hazard for people and infrastructure.

Security of data has been a focus for many years, especially for banks and commercial businesses. The Internet of Things increases security risks related to the physical and operational technology that connects people and infrastructure with digital technology, and can be used to cause physical harm. IoT devices can be compromised through the digital connections in connected devices, vehicles, networks and systems.

Just as the uses and availability of technology will continue to evolve over time, threats, attacks, and malicious motivations will also evolve. Imagine holographic doctors that that can make house calls to interact and treat patients leveraging Artificial Intelligence (AI). Perhaps holographic doctors could provide cost effective and highly skilled services to millions of people globally that do not have any source of medical care. Imagine the threat a hacker could pose if they impacted the operation or integrity of such a holographic doctor. If a hacker could impact factors such as the accuracy of data ingested or digested by a holographic doctor, or the output from the holographic doctor in the form of recommendations provided to a healthcare robot that then interacts with or provides medicine to a patient, the patient's life and health could be at serious risk. In this example, it will be essential for the patients, medical professionals, regulatory and government entities to agree with how a medical solution, like the one just described, will be designed and function.

New protocols and regulations will likely be needed to ensure that the concepts of TIPPSS are maintained. Without TIPPSS, patients may not trust the holographic doctors and refuse to adopt the technology; patients and system operators may not be able to identify users and control access to the system; patient data may become available to people who shouldn't have it and impact privacy; the patients and devices within the system may suffer physical harm; and the overall security and integrity of the system could be compromised. Through this example, we can see how all levels of society, from the citizen to the provider and the city, will need to be diligent and vigilant in assessing and ensuring Trust, Identity, Privacy, Protection, Safety and Security for the Internet of Things.

An end to end trust and security architecture enabled from a TIPPSS perspective will need to support new devices, protocols and use cases enabled by the Internet of Things for smart and connected cities into the future. Some say there needs to be agreement on one protocol, one standard, or set of standards, for the Internet of Things (IoT). The reality is that there will be more and more devices in the future, perhaps that have different needs than what we encounter and create today. The growing ecosystem of devices and evolution of society's opinions on technology will continue to prompt a need for new communications, security, and privacy protocols. Having a flexible and extensible framework for end-to-end TIPPSS will provide an opportunity for IoT systems and society's opinions to evolve while keeping a common set of principles and values in view.

2.   TRUST AND IDENTITY IN SMART CITIES

The Internet of Things (IoT) is creating a world where physical objects are integrated into information networks, to provide advanced and intelligent services for people, cities, campuses and enterprises; but for these intelligent services to be accepted and adopted, all the participants in the system must trust the system. Trust management plays an important role in IoT. It impacts everything from authenticating the identities of the devices and people in the system, to authorizing device and data access, and ensuring the context-aware integrity of the resultant analytics and services. Privacy and information security are also essential to creating a sense of trust in an IoT system. Overall, proper management of the authentication, authorization of access, privacy, and information security reduces uncertainty and risk, enabling user acceptance and consumption of IoT services and applications (Zheng et al., 2014).

Trust takes on many forms in a smart city context. There is the trust that vehicles will work as expected, and that only the people or services you trust can access your devices. There needs to be trust that the safeguards you have in place, such as locks on your front door or garage door, will keep out intruders. Now think about trust when those devices are connected to a network, in a world where just about everything is discoverable and everything is hackable (KPMG, 2015). Trust is critical to ensure security of people and things in an IoT-enabled world.

2.1 Genesis of the TIPPSS framework

IEEE, Internet2 (Internet2, 2016), and the United States National Science Foundation convened a conference focused on End-to-End Trust and Security for the Internet of Things in February 2016 (IEEE, 2015). Attendees at the conference brought forward their views of the risks associate with IoT, leading to a robust view including the need for Trust, Identity, Privacy, Protection, Safety and security. As a result of that conference including participants from around the world including academia, industry, government, and not-for-profits, the TIPPSS framework was envisioned. The goal of the TIPPSS framework is to envision an end-to-end trust and security architecture for the Internet of Things that is open, secure, and extensible to support devices and protocols in use today, plus those that we have not yet imagined, as we deploy today and plan for the future of the Internet of Things and smart cities.

A TIPPSS framework can be developed end-to-end from the intellectual property (IP) in the design of a chip, through hardware, system software, applications, data at rest and in motion, network and cloud services, servers and storage in the cloud, throughout a connected system of systems. These many layers and aspects of an end-to-end trust and security framework lead us to think about strategies across the system of systems, and device specific opportunities, across the Internet of Things in a smart and connected city.

2.2 TIPPSS Use Cases

To illustrate the need for TIPPSS, one of the attendees at the 2016 End to end trust and security workshop (IEEE, 2015) brought forward a simple scenario. The scenario is that Susie, a 6-year-old, gets a programmable IoT device for her birthday or perhaps at a maker space at her public library. Susie goes to the public library and learns how to make a garage door opener with her new IoT device, and it works. Everyone is excited for Susie and so proud of her. Her parents tell their neighbours and relatives, who all want one too. Soon, all these garage doors are being hacked and everyone is being robbed. Susie didn't intend to provide a way for people to be robbed; but by not considering TIPPSS, she enabled the risk and intrusion.

If Susie had considered the TIPPSS framework, the following thoughts could have been incorporated into her design process:
- Trust – To ensure only trusted individuals, devices and services can access and control the device.
- Identity - To support Trust, there needs to be a trusted identity provider to validate the person/device/service accessing the garage

door opener to ensure the person/device/service is who and what they think it is.

- Privacy - Privacy needs to be considered so only the owner of the house or an authorized person can access the data in the garage door opener, including when it was opened, who opened it, and the passcode.
- Protection - The data, the possessions within the home, people in the home, and the home itself need to be protected to ensure items aren't stolen and no harm is done, protecting the humans and things in a connected home.
- Safety - Safety needs to be ensured, not only physical safety with sensors so children and pets walking under the garage door are not harmed by a door hitting them, but also safety for the inhabitants of the home by ensuring intruders do not open the door.
- Security - Security needs to be maintained for the data, the home, the people and devices that access the garage door opener.

As another example, think of the trust you put in your car before you start the engine and begin to drive. You trust that the steering wheel will turn the car right when you turn it in a clockwise direction. You trust the brakes will stop the car when engaged, and if not that the emergency brake will stop the car and keep you from crashing into objects or people or off a bridge into water. You trust that the vehicle will speed up when you engage the accelerator as you merge onto a highway so you are not at risk from other vehicles moving at a faster velocity. You trust that the other drivers and vehicles will avoid crashing or disrupting traffic, and avoid harming vehicles, infrastructure and people. Now, consider how much you can trust the operation of devices when they are connected to a network and can be discovered and hacked from afar. There have been real demonstrations of hackers sitting in their homes while hacking into vehicles being driven by humans on the highway. The hacker exploits include turning off the vehicle engine so it cannot accelerate, disabling the brakes, taking over the steering, and distracting the drivers by remotely engaging the windshield wipers and blaring the radio (Greenberg, 2015). These digital attacks can be thwarted by ensuring trust and identity devices and services in an IoT enabled system.

2.3 Trust and Identity approaches for smart cities and IoT

As two components of the TIPPSS framework, Trust and Identity are foundational elements in any IoT solution. There are multiple technologies that can help establish trust in a device, including hardware roots-of-trust, software roots-of-trust, and encryption to ensure trust in accessing a device, access between devices, and between devices and people accessing systems.

These trust enabling elements can be deployed at various levels in a device and for end-to-end trust and security in a system such as a vehicle, or across a system of systems such as a vehicle communicating with transportation and public safety systems.

Let's consider a connected vehicle example. Suppose the connected vehicle has a wirelessly connected collision avoidance system and is told, "there is another vehicle coming from your right, turn left to avoid a crash." If there is indeed a vehicle approaching from the right, and turning to the left could avoid a collision, this technology could save lives, but what if a hacker sends the signal to turn left on a two-lane road with oncoming traffic. Turning left in this situation could cause the car to turn into traffic and cause an accident. Even worse, what if a hacker sent malicious commands to cars all over a city or country at the same time? Examples like this, while hypothetical, could become possible. Hackers could load malicious code on a vehicle's onboard computer to make the car crash. If the vehicles are capable of vehicle-to-vehicle communications, a malicious person could send a signal to your car from their car. Hackers could also hack potential servers connected to an emergency management system that sends alerts to vehicles and send false alerts.

These potential situations could cause people to neither trust nor invest in IoT technology. This is a key reason for TIPPSS to be included in the design of each IoT enabled system to avoid scenarios like these and create a sense of trust for the people using these systems. In this case, drivers, vehicle and systems manufacturers, and the city will need to develop ways to trust that the messages sent to avoid a collision are authentic and situationally appropriate. The ways that are developed to establish trust will likely be designed into new collision avoidance signaling protocols, and TIPPSS will be essential in the review and establishment of this protocol. The protocol will be a way to ensure that the systems will behave safely, predictably, and reliably. The safe, predictable, and reliable operation of systems and protocols will engender trust in people, the private sector, and the government, and help spur adoption and growth of smart cities to enable increased economic and societal value from IoT.

Identity also plays a critical role in a smart cities context. To provide customized services to the public and grant only the access and rights within the system that are appropriate, people and systems must be able to identify people, devices, incoming services and data.

Smart utilities provide a good example of identity considerations in a smart city. The proper identification of people, devices, and services can aid in maintaining the integrity of the smart utility system to provide utility services, while protecting citizens and the utility infrastructure. In this example, individual identifiers could be needed for the utility meters and infrastructure, the utility employees, the customers of the utility, and all the personal devices and tools that the utility employees and citizens could use with the system. These identities will need to be accurately determined so that access can be properly managed and the integrity of the system can be maintained.

Trust and identity considerations regarding emergency management services in a smart and connected community, including utilities and first responders, provides another interesting and pertinent use case. When there is a fire in a residence, multiple first responders could be involved, and must proceed in a safe, secure way. Fire fighters might need to disconnect power and natural gas sources to avoid explosions, reigniting of the fire, or risk to inhabitants, neighbors or first responders. Police departments may need the ability to terminate utility service to a building, or work with fire fighters and municipal employees to terminate public water service if a flood is reported. Giving first responders the ability to more safely and efficiently manage and manipulate utility services in an emergency could be possible if a city has a smart and connected utility infrastructure, providing trusted and secure access to the utility by authorized personnel both on-site and from afar. In such a smart and connected utility infrastructure, checking the identity of homeowners and first responders, as well as of the devices they use to turn utilities on or off, will be critical to ensure that someone does not maliciously manipulate the utilities of a house to do things like rob the house or harm the inhabitants, first responders, homes, and critical infrastructure in the community.

Trust and identity are established through various means for people and devices. First, the identity of a person accessing a device connected to a utility system may be validated by a trusted authority, perhaps a smart utility authentication system or smart home system, or both. Second, the device will need to be authenticated by a trusted authority, again perhaps a smart utility authentication system or smart home system. Third, people will need to authenticate to devices. This ensures that only the correct inhabitants, utility professionals or first responders, and not hackers, can connect to a device with the ability to monitor or alter the service. Finally, devices will need to be able to authenticate to each other if they are to work together. As an example, a handheld device used by a first responder or utility worker could authenticate locally to the device that locally turns a utility on or off. Device to device authentication can ensure that the correct customer device is being accessed and an authorized utility device is being used to turn service on or off.

To further ensure trusted access with a connected service or device, an extra layer of secure access management called multi-factor authentication

(MFA) may be used. Multi-factor authentication involves the validation of an identity through two or more factors. Factors can include things such as information that a person knows, a physical item that a person possesses, physical qualities of a person, or the physical location of a person. In basic terms, multi-factor authentication leverages something you know, something you have, something you are, or somewhere you are. Multi-factor authentication is already used for access to certain applications, such as online banking. When accessing these highly secure applications, a user first provides a password (something you know), then the application/service sends a text message to the user's device (something you have), requiring the user to validate he/she has that device through clicking on an authentication link, which provides a second factor of authentication beyond the password. Similar factors can be applied to devices. Devices can store digital certificates, similar to a person remembering a password. Unique physical characteristics, such as the electrical resistance through a given part of the device, could be used as factors to authenticate a device. A unique identifier could be embedded in every physical device. Finally, location information such as the GPS (Global Positioning System) location of a device may be useful for authentication.

2.4 Multi-Factor Authentication for Trust & Identity

Multi-factor authentication can be very useful for services deemed higher risk, meaning there could be more potential negative outcomes if the services are accessed by non-trusted people, devices or services. Turning back to our smart utility infrastructure example, a municipality could determine that reading the usage from a utility meter is a lower risk activity, but turning the utility service on or off is a higher risk activity. The municipality could decide that the lower risk activity of reading the utility meter only requires single-factor authentication, while the higher risk activity of turning the utility service on or off should require two-factor authentication. The one factor for reading the utility meter could be a password or the fingerprint of a utility employee, and the two-factor authentication for turning the utility service on or off could be a combination of a password or fingerprint plus the fact that the person is physically located within 50 feet of the utility meter. In this example, a first responder could meet the multi-factor requirements for turning off utility service by entering their password into an IoT device and physically being present at the scene, but a remote hacker could be blocked from turning off service since they would not be within 50 feet of the utility meter. This type of authentication example would also be a deterrent to large-scale remotely enabled cyber attacks. If the only way to terminate service is to be within 50 feet of the utility meter, it would be difficult for malicious actors to remotely impact utility service for a large area. The methods used to validate identities should be measured by the risk that an incorrect identification could pose.

Identities will also be essential to provide customized services for the public. This can include the use of public transportation, access to municipal athletic and social facilities, turning on and off appropriate assistive technologies for disabled members of the public, checking out resources from the digital library, or allowing or denying access to restricted areas. We will need to be able to reliably determine the unique identity of people and devices to manage the smart and connected communities of the future.

Ensuring trust and identity of devices and people in a connected smart city is a difficult challenge. There are technologies and processes that can help identify people and devices now, but there is much more research and development to be done. Developing and deploying ways to ensure the identities of various parts of an IoT system, both devices and people, based on the risk posed to the TIPPSS of the system will be essential.

3.   PRIVACY IN SMART CITIES

The volume of data flowing through the systems in a smart city will dramatically increase as more vehicles, building technologies, sensors, meters, cameras, and other devices connect to and utilize city systems. The data will also become increasingly personalized and detailed. Medical telemetry and data related to people's identities, locations, and actions could be transmitted across and processed through municipal systems. As people interact with transportation systems, their locations and schedules can be tracked. As they walk down the street, public safety systems may capture video footage of them. Commerce systems may track a person's spending and shopping activity. Doctors may monitor a patient's vital signs remotely. What a person looks at, where they go, and their conversations could flow across a city's systems. All of this data will be available to the operators and potentially other users of each system, therefore all providers and users of the systems will need to understand the privacy implications of the IoT data.

Location based data is a good example of data that could flow through a city system and create privacy concerns. Location data, as with all data, can be used for beneficial and harmful purposes. Examples of beneficial uses of data in a smart and connected city could include enhanced public safety and crowd control, quicker response to emergency situations, and the ability for parents to keep track of their children. On the other hand, allowing commercial companies to track the locations of people to improve marketing, stalking people, and using a person's location to know when to burglarize their home would be examples of harmful uses of location data.

As connected systems and services are being implemented, all designers and users of the system or service must be cognizant of these potential beneficial and harmful uses and consider ways that the beneficial goals can be achieved while limiting the harmful effects.

3.1 Approaches to address Privacy concerns in Smart Cities

De-identification is one tool that system operators can use to limit privacy issues and potential misuse of data to do harm. De-identification involves the removal of data elements from a system, to avoid the use of those data elements to determine the identity of a person. Identifying information can include elements such as names, government issued identification numbers, addresses, phone numbers, and other values that are unique to an individual. Sometimes combining elements can also lead to the identification of individuals. Researchers have determined that the combination of a person's date of birth, gender, and 5-digit zip code is unique for over 50% of the residents of the United States (HHS, 2017). Determining if the removal of identifying elements is useful for protecting privacy is something that must be reviewed on a case by case basis. For example, it could be very beneficial for an emergency medical responder to have access to fully identified data when assisting a person in a crisis. In this example, the privacy risks of giving the fully identified data to an emergency responder could be outweighed by the ability to provide timely and accurate emergency healthcare. In contrast, a city may decide that it wants to spend money on upgrading water distribution piping, and may want to use data to determine which pipes are carrying the most water. While the city's systems may be capable of polling individual water meters and providing fully identified data related to each building's water use, only de-identified data related to the number of gallons per minute that each pipe is carrying may be needed. This de-identified usage data could allow a city to maximize fiscal efficiency by addressing the pipes that see the most usage, while protecting the privacy of the users of their systems.

3.2 Privacy principles

The United States Federal Trade Commission Fair Information Practices Principles (FTC, 1998) and European Union Data Protection Directive (OECD, 2013) contain principles that users and operators of city systems should consider when integrating technology into the fabric of citizen services and city operations. In particular, privacy principles such as notice, choice, access, data minimization, and limited use will be critical to create a sense of trust among the users of the municipal systems in order to catalyze adoption and growth of the deployment of the Internet of Things in a smart city.

The first privacy principle, "notice", is one of the most fundamental and critical in establishing a privacy framework for a municipal technology system. "Notice" is the idea that the subject of the data must be informed about what data is being gathered, how the data will be used, how long the data will be held, why the data is being gathered, who will have access to the data, and how the data will be secured. Essentially, it is the way that the subject of the data can learn about how their data will be collected and used within the city. As an example of where "notice" around the use of data has been an issue, consider the issues that have arisen after the reported leaks of classified data by the United States National Security Agency (NSA). It appears that the classified programs of the NSA were gathering information about people without "notice"; and when the people found out, there was a backlash (Risen, 2013). The case of the U.S. National Security Agency highlights the fundamental tug of war that happens on a daily basis between privacy and security. In order to provide security, very often, some level of privacy needs to be given up. This is the argument that the United States National Security Agency and many other global intelligence agencies use to justify the data they gather, explaining that the gathering of data is essential to the safety of the groups that they serve. As cities consider technological solutions, each city will also need to consider the use of the data and how that data can be managed through the balance of security versus privacy. In whatever manner a city decides to manage the public's data, they should strive to have transparent processes and open discussions with the public. "Notice" regarding the use of data helps engender trust in the city and its technical solutions, essential elements in the adoption of municipal technology.

"Choice", sometimes referred to as consent, is the second privacy principle that city system operators will need to consider as they implement new technologies. "Choice" is the concept that a person should have the ability to opt-in, opt-out, or change their mind about allowing the use of data about them. "Choice" goes hand-in-hand with "notice". Notice provides a person with information about their data and how the municipality could use it, and "choice" allows the person to choose whether or not to permit the gathering or use of the data about them. "Choice" should not be thought of as an all-or-nothing concept. People could have "choice" on an element-by-element basis or tiers of "choice" could be created such as "No Gathering", "Anonymized Gathering Permitted", or "Fully Identified Gathering Permitted". City operators may find that as they weigh the privacy issues, there are times when the good of the community doesn't allow for people to have complete choice. This often arises in examples where the collection and use of a person's data provides benefit to people around them. For example, monitoring and recording the use of community resources can help to detect abuse of resources and help ensure that shared resources remain available to everyone. This could be especially important for utility monitoring. Cities will need to consider the situations in which they give people a choice in the data the municipality gathers as compared to the risks that "choice" could cause for the overall community. In coordination with the principle of "notice", the public should be informed of their "choice" options.

"Access" is the next privacy principle that municipalities should consider related to privacy. "Access" is the principle that a person should have access to see what data the municipality has collected about them and the ability to challenge information that the person feels is inaccurate. Some examples of where people currently have access to their data are driving records, credit reports, and educational records. In each of these examples, people have the right to request that the group holding the data provide them with a copy of any data about them. Upon receiving the data, the person has the right to challenge anything they feel is inaccurate. In some cases, the person can also request to have the data expunged. The monitoring of the use of city parks can be used to explain the concept of "access". The monitoring of the use of city parks can provide insights into which parks are best serving the communities and which park amenities are most attractive to the public based on their usage. If a city wanted to support the privacy principle of "access" in relation to park usage, they could give each person the ability to view the data recorded about them through a web portal. The portal would be able to show the person all the data that the municipality has saved, about the person, over time. It could take the form of a map that shows park visits according to date and time. Upon clicking on a particular park visit, the portal could show information such as the time the person arrived, the amenities the person used, and the time the person left the park. The portal could also give the person the ability to mark a particular visit, or the data within a visit, as incorrect. For example, if the system said that the person used the tennis court, but they actually used the basketball court, the person could challenge the incorrect data and request to have it corrected. The person could also request to have one, a subset, or all of their visits deleted from the system and possibly request that the system no longer records their visits in the future. Giving people access to see the data that a city has collected is another way in which a city can support privacy for the people who use the systems and enhance people's trust that the city is not abusing their data.

As cities review the large amounts of data that are available to be collected, data minimization and limited use are privacy concepts that may be considered. Data minimization is the concept that a group should only collect the minimum types and amounts of data necessary to achieve the goals of a particular project. Data that is no longer needed should be securely deleted. Limited use is the concept that collected data should only be used for the purpose for which it was gathered. For example, if a company providing a service to a city collected data in order to provide support to the public, limited use would restrict them from using the gathered information for marketing their products to the public.

In the end, the Fair Information Practices Principles complement each other to form a privacy framework that fits very well with TIPPSS. When a municipality has a goal that can be met through the collection of data from municipal technological systems, the concepts of notice, choice, access, data minimization and limited use can be combined into a deliberate process. The municipality should give notice to people about the data it plans to collect, allow people to have the choice about whether they would like to participate or not, plan to give people the ability to view and challenge data collected about them, only collect the minimum data required to meet the goal, only use the data for that specific purpose, and then securely dispose of the data as soon as possible.

As an example, we can model these principles against a municipal traffic system. Imagine that a municipality decides that it needs to determine which roadway to widen between two towns. The municipality could give notice to the citizens that they would like to gather data regarding traffic between the two towns. The town can allow drivers to opt-out, gather data from each vehicle that does not opt out, and give drivers a website to view and challenge their data. The vehicles may be able to provide all kinds of data such as the identities of the occupants, the starting and ending points of the trip, the vehicle make and model, vehicle speed, and many other values. Through the concept of data minimization, the municipality should only collect the essential data required for the goal of determining which roadway to widen between the two towns. In this example, only the count of the vehicles driving on the road and the journey start and end points would need to be gathered. None of the other data elements are truly essential to meet the goal of measuring traffic volume between two points. Limited use can also be applied to the same example. In this example, notice, choice, and access were given for the purpose of determining which roadway to widen between two towns. The concept of limited use requires that the data only be used for the agreed upon purpose. Once the municipality has the data, they could think of lots of other uses for the data. Examples could be estimating the amount of income tax generated by the people who commute to work between the two towns, evaluating the environmental impact of traffic congestion between the two towns, or determining where to locate toll booths to maximize revenue. The concept of limited use would require that the municipality only use the data for the purpose of determining which roadway to widen. If the municipality would like to use the data for another purpose, the municipality would need to give notice of the new use, give people the choice to participate or not, and give the people access to see and challenge the data under the new use. These concepts can be combined to help establish a firm foundation of trust between the municipality and the people.

3.3 Privacy policy and regulation

One last element of privacy that cities will need to keep in mind is the statutory and regulatory environment around data privacy. Data privacy laws and regulations are changing rapidly and vary greatly between jurisdictions and topic areas. Some laws protect citizens wherever they go, while other laws only apply to people within a particular jurisdiction. Some laws only apply in particular circumstances and some laws, between different jurisdictions, contradict each other. Cities will need to ensure that they have good legal resources available to interpret and keep up with the complicated legal landscape. Municipalities also must develop governance and compliance processes to translate laws and regulations into municipal policies, standards, and procedures. Once established, these policies, standards, and procedures need to be pushed down to all areas of the government and resources need to be allocated to ensure that all levels of the municipality remain in compliance. Without strong governance and compliance processes, municipalities may put themselves at legal risk within the rapidly changing legal and regulatory landscape. On a global basis, privacy regulations can vary widely and make data management even more complex.

As the number of municipal technologies increases, the volume of data available to a municipality will grow quickly. Municipalities may find that the data is a rich resource in supporting efficient and safe operations. As uses of the public's data are considered, applying principles like de-identification, notice, choice, access, data minimization, and limited use will help the public trust the municipal operators and the system. Public trust will help the systems grow, while strong governance and compliance programs will help the municipalities minimize legal risk.

4.   PROTECTIONS AND SAFETY IN SMART CITIES

Ensuring trust, identity, privacy and security of devices in a smart city are critical in ensuring protection and safety of the citizens and critical infrastructure. In a connected or self-driving vehicle, reducing the risk that a hacker can compromise the systems in the vehicle increases the protection and safety of the vehicle and its occupants. In 2015, it was shown that it is possible to remotely control and disable a moving Jeep Cherokee by connecting to it through the Internet and the vehicle's cellular connection (Greenberg, 2015). In this demonstration, the driver was distracted by the hackers who remotely accessed the vehicle systems to turn on windshield wipers, increase the radio volume, and turn off the engine while the vehicle was being driven on a busy highway. The hackers then told the driver to turn off the engine and turn it back on to enable acceleration, a non-intuitive action. Turning off an engine, disabling steering, disabling brakes can all be done through remote hacking of vehicles, which could obviously result in disaster for the vehicle along with the occupants of that vehicle and perhaps others. It is the responsibility of the designers, developers and manufacturers of the vehicle and all systems in it to ensure trust, identity, and security of the systems to provide protection and safety for the users, devices and city infrastructure.

5.   SECURITY IN SMART CITIES

Within the technical infrastructure of a smart city, the security controls that a municipality chooses to implement can have a dramatic impact on the trust, identity, privacy, protection, and safety of the public, and the efficient, reliable operation of municipal systems. Security, in a municipal technical infrastructure, can take many forms. For example, ensuring the physical security of municipal systems, devices, and the public can avoid physical harm and tampering. Information security is also essential to ensure the privacy and protection of personal and confidential information. Finally, the data and operational integrity of a system are directly related to the controls that are used to protect the security of the system.

5.1 Cybersecurity technologies and approaches for Smart Cities

Network segmentation is a security control that all municipalities will need to include in their infrastructure design. Network segmentation allows municipalities to separate, inspect, monitor, and filter network traffic. The granularity of the segmentation is something that each municipality will need to determine based on factors such as the functionality of the system and the risks posed by the devices and people in the system. At a very high level, segmentation could be as simple as having critical, non-public municipal devices on one network segment and devices related to access by the public on a second network segment, with an air gap between them to ensure one segment does not impact the other. A municipality could also decide to segregate network traffic between individual municipal systems and groups of the public. Segmentation could also be related to contractual access by commercial providers.

As an example, the public will likely not have a need to access the utility infrastructure of a library building, but will need to access public library services. In this scenario, the municipality may decide to have one city-wide network segment for all library building SCADA systems (Supervisory Control And Data Acquisition) for the building operational systems and infrastructure devices, and a separate city-wide network segment for all public library access systems across the city. As another example, a municipality may decide to segment the networks for devices within a water filtration plant from devices in other water filtration plants, devices within the water distribution system, and public devices such as water meters. In this scenario, the municipality may view the risk posed by access to the infrastructure at the filtration plants to be higher than the risk posed by having access to flow sensors in the distribution system, or access to water meters by the public so that members of the public can monitor their water usage and plan to pay their water bill. They may also have one contractor operating one filtration plant and a different contractor operating another filtration plant. The municipality may decide to separate the network segments for each contractor to ensure that the contractors are not able to interfere with each other's operations, or so a hacker infiltrating a system through one contractor cannot get into another contractor's infrastructure. Segmenting systems allows for improved controls and security.

In some cases, gateway devices will also be needed in order to facilitate the authorized passage of commands and information between network segments. These gateway devices provide a bridge between multiple network segments, and can filter, authenticate, and validate the flow of commands between the segments.

For example, in a traffic system, it may be beneficial for vehicles to know the state of traffic signals along a route; but to protect the traffic signals from tampering, a municipality may decide that the public should not have direct access to the traffic control devices. In this scenario, a municipality could decide to have a gateway act as an intermediary between the traffic control infrastructure and the public and their vehicles. When the public and their vehicles need to get information about the state of signals within the utility infrastructure, they could send their request for information to a traffic gateway device. The traffic gateway device can protect the traffic infrastructure systems by validating that the request is authorized and appropriate based on the identity of the person and vehicle, requesting the information from the appropriate traffic control devices, and passing the appropriate and authorized information back to the vehicle and public.

If properly engineered, the gateway can also act as a sacrificial part of the system when hit with a denial of service attack. A denial of service attack could cause the gateway to be overwhelmed with network traffic so it cannot respond or communicate, impacting the operation of a gateway device and public access to services. The gateway could also shield critical non-public infrastructure elements from an attack. To continue the example of our traffic infrastructure scenario, a denial of service attack may impact the operation of the traffic gateway and may impact the ability for information to flow between the public network segments and the traffic infrastructure network segments, but the gateway could block the attacks from reaching the traffic infrastructure segments and help ensure that traffic infrastructure devices like street lights and roadway sensors continue to function.

5.2 Managing security and updates across millions of devices

Municipalities will also need to make sure that devices within the municipal system are properly patched and maintained to ensure their security. This includes devices that the municipality owns and maintains, and devices the public owns that the municipality allows on the network. Municipalities may own and operate thousands or millions of devices that are manufactured by many different companies, and integrated by additional companies into solutions for the municipality. Furthermore, the devices may include electronic chips and components from even more companies, plus cloud services may be used as a part of the solution.

Using traffic systems as an example, the control electronics for a single traffic light may be made by one company, while the electronic chips, components, and firmware may come from other companies. The software control system to coordinate the status of the traffic light with vehicular traffic and other traffic lights in the area may run through software written by yet another company. Further, the software control system may be reached through network and security devices manufactured by certain entities with components from other entities, and the software control system may run on cloud servers operated by additional entities. Through this example, it is easy to see that from the component level up through the communications, control, and cloud computing infrastructure levels, many entities could be involved in the manufacture and operation of a single traffic light system, and all of them could have a part to play in the patching and maintenance of each of their components. Municipalities will need to have a way to coordinate the patching and maintenance of all the devices across these hundreds of vendors to keep the systems secure, efficient and effective. Now to put the full problem into view, we can extend this scenario to all of the traffic lights in an entire municipality. Given that not all the traffic lights, components or integration services may be from the same manufacturer, the number of manufacturers the municipality is dealing with to manage their traffic light system could become very large, perhaps in the hundreds across a municipality or region, and that is only for the end-to-end traffic light system.

If you extend the view to all IoT systems within an entire municipality, the effort to patch and maintain thousands or millions of components from thousands of vendors becomes difficult at best. For municipalities to keep up with their patching and maintenance responsibilities, municipalities will need to manage across an extensible and flexible TIPPSS for IoT in Smart Cities architecture which supports multi-vendor platforms for the monitoring, patching, and maintenance of the IoT infrastructure. Initially, municipalities may be able to use individual vendor solutions for patching and maintenance; but as described earlier, the size and complexity of the systems will grow so quickly that individual vendor management solutions will be unmanageable. The challenge of ensuring that device and system updates do not hinder interoperability across the system of systems in a smart city is yet another layer of complexity to be managed.

In order to protect the IoT devices and municipal system as a whole, the municipality may need to implement a network device admissions control solution to ensure that devices owned by the public have the security settings, patches and TIPPSS attributes necessary to protect the devices and the network before they are allowed to connect to the network. A network device admissions control solution could interrogate each device before it allows it to connect to the network. It can interrogate devices for anything from default usernames and passwords to antivirus software and patches that have been applied.

To illustrate the importance of interrogating devices before they connect to the network, consider the September 20, 2016 distributed denial of service (DDoS) attack against the security blog of Brian Krebs (Krebs, 2016). In this attack, hundreds of thousands of IoT devices were used to send 665 Gbps (gigabits of data per second) worth of Internet traffic to Akamai, the hosting provider for Brian Krebs's blog. At the time of the attack, this was the largest denial of service attack in the history of the internet, and it was done by commandeering improperly configured and unprotected IoT devices like Internet Protocol (IP) cameras, digital video recorders, routers, and other easily hackable devices. In the case of this attack, it has been reported that malware, dubbed "Mirai", scanned the Internet for devices with factory default or hard-coded usernames and passwords. Once the malware found these insecure devices, it was easy to log in to the devices and install malicious software. Imagine the many devices the public, businesses or municipalities own which might not be secure and could be used in a manner similar to the attack on Brian Krebs.

The denial of service attacks that could be launched from a municipal network could overwhelm the municipal network and any systems it targets; and when the municipal network and the targets are overwhelmed, the collateral damage to the municipality could threaten life, safety, and the overall functioning of the city. This issue becomes even more challenging when we consider that not being allowed onto the municipal network could itself cause safety and security concerns for the public. For example, a person who has a history of heart disease could be given a heart monitor to wear which will alert emergency responders in the event of a cardiac emergency. This cardiac monitor could be connected to the municipal network and could quickly signal emergency responders when the person needs emergency assistance, but what should a municipality do if a dangerous vulnerability is detected in the software of the cardiac monitor? The vulnerability could pose a significant technical risk to the municipal infrastructure, but not allowing the cardiac monitor to connect to the municipal system could keep the device from being able to call for help when the person needs it. To avoid this type of occurrence, it will be essential that municipalities use network device admission control solutions and ensure that devices which are allowed to connect to the municipal network have proper security settings, security software installed, and up to date patches, as the risk to personal safety will need to be considered.

Municipalities will need to develop procedures to ensure that IoT devices and systems are updated with security patches as needed to keep the systems secure. This will include the need to test and certify patches and maintenance activities before they are applied to active city systems. Many municipal systems will not be homogenous, and not all components of a complex municipal IoT system may react the same way to a patch or device security update. Municipalities that push maintenance patches and changes to production IoT devices may find that some of the devices stop functioning or begin to behave erratically. If the device is something like a wayfinding sign in a public park, the impact of a patch breaking the functionality of the sign may not be large; however, if a patch causes 10% of the traffic lights in a city to malfunction, that could cause impactful traffic and life safety challenges. As municipalities move toward incorporating IoT devices into their municipal infrastructure, the municipalities must develop testing and deployment procedures that ensure that software and maintenance changes to the system do not adversely affect the operation of the systems in the municipality. Depending on the devices impacted, the integrity of the system and thereby the trust, safety, protection, physical security, and data security of the system could be at risk.

5.3 Secure against "Hack In" and "Hack Out"

Municipalities will need to ensure that their IoT infrastructures are reliable and protected against attacks. Denial of service attacks are one critical type of attack and can include any activity that impacts the proper operation of a device or system. For example, if a criminal wanted to disable a video surveillance camera's ability to record their activity, they could block the network connectivity to the camera, send a signal to the camera that would cause it to turn off or malfunction, or send a power surge to the camera which could burn out the power supply and cut the power to the camera. The criminal could also cause the central monitoring and recording system in a building or the city to stop functioning. Denial of service attacks can be targeted at any part of a municipal IoT system at any level in the infrastructure. From attacks on a device at the chip level, through attacks on the device firmware, control software, communications links, and central management infrastructure, municipalities need to be prepared to protect a system against denial of service attacks. Unfortunately, not only could these attacks "hack in" to a system to turn off equipment or harm devices or people, but the system could also be commandeered to attack another device or "hack out" to other systems or devices. In order to mitigate these risks, designs for municipal systems should include redundancy for critical systems. As an example, if the vehicles on a roadway are going to rely on a gateway to obtain vehicle position information for autonomous operation, making sure that the gateways are always available will be essential for the safe and reliable operation of the traffic system. Redundant gateway and network connectivity designs would be needed to ensure that device failures and necessary maintenance activities do not interrupt the operation of an overall system.

Encryption will be an essential element of a safe, secure municipal IoT infrastructure. Data related to every facet of life, community, and city operations will be flowing over a multitude of networks. Information may flow through cellular networks, private corporate networks, city-owned networks, and home networks owned by members of the public, both wireless and wired. In order to ensure connectivity, information should be able to flow through whatever networks are available to the person or device at any given time. Since this may mean that data of a sensitive nature could flow over any number of untrusted transport networks, the security and privacy of the connections will need to be protected through encryption. In many ways, this is no different than how things work today. Today, if we need to send information related to banking or credit card transactions, encryption technologies like SSL (Secure Socket Layer) are used. Secure file transfer protocols and encryption of data at rest is also available with today's technology. The challenge in the future will be the scale of the IoT systems, and perhaps the protocols needed for new types of devices and data. Devices may need to be able to manage encryption keys for hundreds of relationships.

For example, a person's wearable devices may need to be able to communicate with family members' devices, devices installed in the person's home, municipal systems, IoT systems in stores, the systems managed by the person's doctor, and systems for every other relationship in the person's life, and every one of these systems could have a different set of encryption keys. Municipal and global key management infrastructures will be needed to handle the validation, issuance, revocation, and overall use of encryption keys on a global scale. Municipalities will need to be prepared to properly encrypt network communications within their infrastructures and support the public's use of encryption to protect their information while in transit over numerous untrusted transport networks.

Auditing and compliance policies, processes and procedures help a municipality ensure that the goals and principles that are initially built into the system are maintained throughout the lifetime of the system. Municipalities will need to implement continuous auditing and compliance systems related to trust, identity, privacy, protection, safety, and security (TIPPSS) to minimize the risk that a system poses to a municipality and help the municipality keep the system up to date.

6. TIPPSS EDUCATION FOR SMART CITIES AND CONNECTED CITIZENS

As smart cities technologies have a growing influence in urban environments, providing many potential economic and societal benefits, both citizens and government employees will need to be comfortable and fluent in their interactions with the technology. They will need to be educated in how to use and maintain new IoT technologies deployed throughout municipalities, to realize the potential benefits in a smart city while keeping the city and citizens safe. Cities are beginning their journey to a digital destiny such as the city of San Jose in California (Santosham, 2016), the county of Arlington in Virginia (Arlingtonva.us, 2016), and Chicago which is tackling the basic digital divide (Kim, 2014) as well as leveraging the

Argonne National Laboratory and University of Chicago to deploy an Array of Things test bed to enable a smart connected city (Mitchum, 2016).

While cities are engaging citizens and technologies together to build their futures, the awareness of the need for TIPPSS in managing and deploying new smart and connected city solutions is critical for safe smart cities. Privacy and security are a keen focus of a growing legion of government and industry leaders, including the U.S. Department of Homeland Security (DHS, 2016), Federal Trade Commission (FTC, 2017), National Institute of Standards and Technology (NIST, 2017), the Institute of Electrical and Electronics Engineers (IEEE, 2016), and the Industrial Internet Consortium (IIC, 2016). There will be an increased need for policy and regulations to address the safety, security and privacy aspects of smart cities technologies, and to protect the civil rights of citizens, while managing the safety of the city.

Municipalities will need to ensure that the citizens are aware of the risks posed by a technology. They will need to consider how best to monitor, regulate and manage municipal IoT services and technology deployments, to ensure safe services, address new risks that arise from new technologies or exploits, and advocate for the citizenry. Commercial IoT technology and service providers will need to ensure that their solutions take TIPPSS into account for all their solutions, at inception and throughout the life cycle of the solution.

The public will need to be informed about TIPPSS risks and actions they may take if there are concerns, so they can participate in maintaining TIPPSS within the municipal system and ensuring the safety of themselves and others. The public will need to maintain and troubleshoot their personally owned devices and report issues to the commercial providers and municipality when municipal IoT solutions do not operate as expected. Across all these groups, fluency with the technology will be required. Municipalities considering the addition of municipal IoT technologies will need to plan for how municipal employees, commercial providers, and the public will be trained on use and maintenance of each IoT solution.

TIPPSS awareness and education could be developed by a municipality, commercial solution and device providers, not for profit organizations, or an ecosystem of these groups. There could be general TIPPSS awareness training, such as through a public broadcasting system, an online channel, and in-person through local TIPPSS and smart cities advocates who could meet in community settings such as libraries, schools, senior centers, and town halls. Educating the public on the risks such as the potential hacking of an insulin pump (DHS, 2013) and what to do about it could be lifesaving.

7.   TIPPSS IN A SYSTEM OF SYSTEMS

Connected smart city infrastructures can be viewed as a system of systems, leveraging information and insights across a collection of individual devices and systems. An integrated view of smart city systems, including vehicle, transportation management systems, energy grids, water systems, buildings, healthcare systems, and public safety systems, can enable city efficiencies and improved citizen experience.

Figure 5: A system of systems in a Smart and Connected City

7.1   Smart city system of systems scenario starting with water systems

A system of systems view of a smart city could begin with a water main break. Sensors on the water pipes could transmit the location of the water main break to alert the water utility. This could result in the utility system shutting off the water in that area, and dispatching water utility experts to the area to fix the water main break, as compared to waiting for a citizen to call in the water main break. The "system of systems" could also alert the buildings in the area, and send text messages to alert building managers, companies, and employees in the buildings that the water will be off for a period of time, that a road is closed, and suggest they work from home or use an alternate entrance. The alert can also propagate the water main break information to emergency services such as fire and police to suggest they close the road with the water main break to traffic. The city transportation systems could be notified to divert buses or subways to other routes, and

138

provide toll incentives to increase tolls in the vicinity of the closed roads, while reducing the tolls for other roadways, in order to incent drivers and vehicles to proceed to alternate non-congested routes. The value of a system of systems view comes from the leverage of data and insight across systems to improve efficiencies and outcomes.

The opportunities are endless in leveraging city information for good, but the risks that the systems could be hacked and create mayhem in a city also exist. Cities will benefit from a TIPPSS for IoT in smart and connected cities framework, along with a management system across the technology and municipal departments to design and deploy a TIPPSS framework across the city's system of systems. The risk related to a lack of TIPPSS in a specific device or system is itself a challenge, but in a smart city of multiple connected devices and systems, individual challenges and weaknesses can be combined to create different and potentially greater risks.

7.2 Smart city system of systems scenario starting with transportation

In a connected smart city, there are many devices and connections that can be hacked or compromised. Transportation systems can be hacked to turn off the traffic management systems, or perhaps send vehicles to unsafe locations, coupled with water system sensor alerts that can be compromised or diverted. Imagine if many heavy trucks were diverted to a street with a water main break, which could cause the roadway to collapse, potentially harming people and infrastructure in or near the vehicles. For this reason, the "system of systems" in a city needs to have layers of TIPPSS. The trust and identity of services trying to access and inform transportation systems and vehicles need to be authenticated and secure, to certify that the alerts are genuine and authorized to ensure safety and to protect the vehicles, city infrastructure and citizens. The communications from the water main to the utility system to the transportation system to the vehicles need to be trusted and secure. The citizens and emergency workers receiving alerts will need to know that the communication is legitimate. TIPPSS attributes can be enabled in a "defense-in-depth" strategy to ensure safe, secure smart city communication and management. "Defense-in-depth" can be enabled by providing unique identifiers in the hardware in a device, and cyber security elements in the software and services.

Hacking of consumer devices could potentially harm not just the user of the device, but also city infrastructure, and many citizens. Consider a personal vehicle compromise such as the Jeep hack illustrated in 2015 (Greenberg, 2015) that allowed the remote control of the vehicle's transmission, braking, steering, and other systems. This attack was itself scary and dangerous for the driver and occupants, but consider the risk this type of attack could pose to the city infrastructure, citizens and vehicles in the surrounding area.

Automobile manufacturers often use the same parts on multiple models of vehicle; and in a city, there could be dozens if not hundreds or thousands of vehicles with similar components. These similar components could introduce similar vulnerabilities into other vehicles. This could provide a hacker with a large quantity of remotely controlled vehicles that they could use like weapons. For example, if a number of vehicles were hacked and directed to hit fire hydrants, the occupants may be injured, while the water pressure in an area of the city could also be lowered to a level where water for firefighting, fire sprinkler systems, and household use would not be available.

Vehicles could be strategically directed to create accidents and block roadways. By blocking roadways, traffic congestion could prohibit emergency responders from driving to emergency situations. If emergency responders can't get through the streets, people in need of emergency medical care would not be able to get assistance and could suffer grave consequences. Fires could rage unchecked due to the lack of water pressure and the inability of fire fighters to get through the streets. As this example demonstrates, one small security flaw in the wireless system of a vehicle could pose a far greater risk in an urban system of systems than the flaw poses alone. If every individual flaw in a city is considered in the light of how it could impact the ecosystem of the city, flaws take on a new dimension of risk that must be considered above the risk that the flaw poses in isolation.

8. IOT TIPPSS RECOMMENDATIONS

The Internet of Things and Smart Cities are being deployed today. There are steps cities can take to increase IOT systems risk awareness, and to mitigate risk from a TIPPSS perspective. For example:

- Leverage tools such as shodan.io and censys.io to become aware of the devices, in your environment, that are discoverable and searchable on the Internet. Devices that can be discovered with these tools can include facilities systems, power plants, cameras, smart TVs, refrigerators and more. The next step is to secure these devices from access by untrusted and unauthorized people and systems.

140

- Determine which connected devices still have a default password and change them. If these passwords are managed by vendors rather than the owner or user of the device, negotiate with the vendor to ensure the passwords are all changed, and are managed or known by the user and owner of the device.
- Develop an IoT device security upgrade plan for currently installed devices, including patching and updating practices. This could require contacting the device manufacturer or vendor.
- Map out the system of systems connected to your IoT connected devices. Then determine how to increase trust, identity, privacy, protection, safety and security. For instance, there could be a power plant system connected to a building management system connected to a camera that is discoverable and hackable. It might just take one open port to tunnel all the way through to the highest risk device.
- Develop a security-first approach, designed in from the start, with resilience to ensure security throughout the operating life of a device and system (Internet of Things Security Foundation, 2016)
- Leverage thought leadership for TIPPSS such as the Industrial Internet Consortium's Industrial Internet of Things Security Framework (Industrial Internet Consortium, 2016)
- Develop a comprehensive TIPPSS for IoT framework for the city's system of systems, leveraging security, safety, system, process and device experts. This will entail understanding the TIPPSS risks by use case and system, developing and leveraging known techniques to deploy TIPPSS, and evolving to a TIPPSS ecosystem of experts and technologies across a system of systems.

There are many more steps to take to ensure TIPPSS, and there will be more needed into the future as new IoT and smart city systems are developed and deployed. The need for TIPPSS vigilance will be endless as more and new devices and systems are developed; but the sooner you begin, the sooner you will reduce your risk and improve the sustainability of the devices and systems in a smart city.

9.   TIPPSS RESEARCH AND DEVELOPMENT INNOVATIONS AND OPPORTUNITIES

Research and development to infuse TIPPSS into the system of systems in a smart city will be an ongoing journey. There are approaches being developed which can provide additional elements of future TIPPSS implementations to reduce the risk in a smart city. A defense-in-depth strategy using various TIPPSS technologies and techniques depending on the use case and risk will allow multiple layers of trust and security. (Internet of Things Security Foundation, 2016)

Product and system developers need to design in TIPPSS at the inception of a device or system, including device, network and system level mechanisms. As systems and devices are more connected, blockchain and similar technologies that could add a layer of distributed and united trust and security, will provide additional opportunities to enable a TIPPSS environment (Ernst & Young, 2016). To improve security of IoT devices already in use, research is being done on IoT security gateways that can add a layer of security in front of devices with limited ability to be hardened against attacks (Yu, et al., 2015).

The end-to-end TIPPSS solution of the future will have multiple elements, which can be deployed in a defense-in-depth strategy. Defense-in-depth is the idea that there are multiple layers of defense in a system. Consider the castles of old. First, there might be humans and horses defending the perimeter of a castle. Then there was a moat. Then there was a large drawbridge over the moat that could be retracted. Then alligators in the moat. Then a wall. Then catapults and humans launching threats against attackers. This was defense-in-depth. The attacker gets past one layer of defense, and there is another waiting for them to reduce the risk of them infiltrating the castle.

A technology-enabled defense-in-depth strategy could be implemented at many layers of a device, from hardware to firmware, software and services (KPMG, 2015), and in multiple layers across an interconnected system. In a connected vehicle, there could be unique identifiers or a root-of-trust at the hardware level in the semiconductor chip that goes into a navigation device. Then there could be a root-of-trust or encryption layer in the firmware in the microcode of the chip. Then there can be defenses in the software, and at the application and service layer. The unique identifier in each chip would be different, so if one device is hacked then other similar devices cannot be easily hacked. Taking this further, there could be defense-in-depth for all the systems in a vehicle, and for the communications system which connects to the outside world, communicating with humans, other vehicles, devices, cloud-based manufacturer and application systems, and smart city systems.

While further research and development is needed, technologies and processes such as network segmentation (Kerravala, 2015), software defined perimeters (Cloud Security Alliance, 2013), blockchain for distributed trust (IBM, 2017), and named-data-networking (Shang, et al., 2016) are potential elements of the future of TIPPSS capabilities for the Internet of Things and smart cities.

A TIPPSS maturity model could be developed for a smart city, providing a framework to assess the maturity and potential effectiveness of the TIPPSS capabilities for a particular device or system in a city, and for specific use cases such as the internet of medical things, and connected vehicles. Ecosystems of experts will be needed with deep domain skills for each of these use cases to develop an end to end TIPPSS maturity model from device to network to application, including the technology, incentives and business models to support the development and deployment of TIPPSS elements in devices, cities, and systems.

10.   CONCLUSION

The safe and sustainable deployment of Internet of Things (IoT) technologies to enable smart cities requires robust trust, identity, privacy, protection, safety and security (TIPPSS) capabilities and expectations. Developers, governments, and citizens need to demand that technical solutions incorporate the concepts embodied within TIPPSS in every city system.   Systems that incorporate TIPPSS can improve city operations, citizen experiences, and enhance city services while ensuring safety and security. In a city environment, this responsibility falls not just on government officials, but also on the public and private industry. As smart cities are enabled as systems of systems, the TIPPSS attributes require coordination across the many systems to enhance the citizen and city experience, but also to ensure the citizens, physical devices and infrastructure in the city are safe for all IoT applications, devices, processes and services

REFERENCES

Array of Things (2016) Retrieved from https://arrayofthings.github.io

Arlingtonva.us (2016) Defining Arlington's Digital Destiny, Retrieved from
https://departments.arlingtonva.us/dts/digital-destiny/

Censys.io. Retrieved from https://censys.io

Cloud Security Alliance, Software Defined Perimeter (December 2013), Retrieved from
https://downloads.cloudsecurityalliance.org/initiatives/sdp/Software_Defined_Perimeter.pdf

Computation Institute (2016) Chicago Becomes First city to Launch Array of Things, Retrieved from
https://ci.uchicago.edu/tags/array-things

DHS, U.S. Department of Homeland Security, Strategic Principles for Securing the Internet of Things (2016), Retrieved
from
https://www.dhs.gov/sites/default/files/publications/Strategic_Principles_for_Securing_the_Internet_of_Things-
2016-1115-FINAL_v2-dg11.pdf

DHS, U.S. Department of Homeland Security, Industrial Control Systems Cyber Emergency Response Team (ICS-
CERT) (2013), retrieved from https://ics-cert.us-cert.gov/alerts/ICS-ALERT-13-164-01

Ernst & Young, EY (2016) Implementing blockchains and distributed infrastructure, Retrieved from
http://www.ey.com/Publication/vwLUAssets/EY-implementing-blockchains-and-distributed-
infrastructure/$FILE/EY-implementing-blockchains-and-distributed-infrastructure.pdf

FTC, United States of America Federal Trade Commission (2017) PrivacyCon. https://www.ftc.gov/news-events/events-
calendar/2017/01/privacycon

FTC, United States of America Federal Trade Commission (1998) Privacy Online: A Report to Congress, Retrieved
from https://www.ftc.gov/sites/default/files/documents/reports/privacy-online-report-congress/priv-23a.pdf

Greenberg, A. (2015) Hackers Remotely Kill a Jeep on the Highway—With Me in It, retrieved from
(https://www.youtube.com/watch?v=MK0SrxBC1xs)

Gudivada, V., Govindaraju, V., Raghavan, V., et al. (2016) Cognitive Computing: Theory and Applications, Vol 35.
Handbook of Statistics, Pages 350-370, Chapter "The Internet of Things and Cognitive Computing", Hudson, F.,
Nichols, E.

HHS, United States Department of Health and Human Services (HHS, 2017) Guidance Regarding Methods of
Deidentification of Protected Health Information in Accordance with the Health Insurance Portability and
Accountability Act (HIPAA) Privacy Rule, Retrieved from https://www.hhs.gov/hipaa/for-
professionals/privacy/special-topics/de-identification/index.html#_ednref10

Hudson, F.D. (2016) The Internet of Things Is Here. EDUCAUSE review, Retrieved from
http://er.educause.edu/articles/2016/6/the-internet-of-things-is-here

IBM, (June 2013) IBM harnesses power of Big Data to improve Dutch flood control and water management system,
Retrieved from https://www-03.ibm.com/press/us/en/pressrelease/41385.wss

IBM, (February 2017) What Blockchain means for you and the Internet of Things, Retrieved from
https://www.ibm.com/blogs/internet-of-things/watson-iot-blockchain/

IEEE Standards Association (2016) IEEE End to End Trust and Security Workshop for the Internet of Things in
Washington, D.C., cosponsored by IEEE, US National Science Foundation, Internet2, presentations and report,
Retrieved from http://standards.ieee.org/events/iot/index.html

IIC, Industrial Internet Consortium (2016), Industrial Internet of Things, Volume G4: Security Framework,
IIC:PUB:G4:V1.0:PB:20160926, Retrieved from http://www.iiconsortium.org/IISF.htm

Internet of Things Security Foundation (2016) Make it safe to connect, Establishing Principles for Internet of Things
Security. Retrieved from https://iotsecurityfoundation.org

Internet2 (2016) End to end trust and security for the Internet of Things wiki, Retrieved from
    https://spaces.internet2.edu/pages/viewpage.action?pageId=92471892

Kerravala, Z. (December 17, 2015), NetworkWorld, How network segmentation provides a path to IoT security,
    Retrieved from http://www.networkworld.com/article/3016565/security/how-network-segmentation-provides-a-
    path-to-iot-security.html

Kim, D. (2014) How Chicago is Narrowing the Digital Divide, Data-Smart City Solutions, An initiative by the Ash
    Center at Harvard Kennedy School and powered by Bloomberg Philanthropies, Retrieved from
    http://datasmart.ash.harvard.edu/news/article/how-chicago-is-narrowing-the-digital-divide-572

KPMG (2015) Security and the IoT ecosystem, Retrieved
    fromhttps://assets.kpmg.com/content/dam/kpmg/pdf/2015/12/security-and-the-iot-ecosystem.pdf

Krebs, B. (2016) Krebs on Security, Source Code for IoT Botnet Mirai Released, Retrieved from
    https://krebsonsecurity.com/2016/10/source-code-for-iot-botnet-mirairreleased/

Mitchum, R. (2016) Chicago becomes first city to launch Array of Things, Urban sensing project will measure air
    quality, traffic, climate and more. UChicago News, Retrieved from
    https://news.uchicago.edu/article/2016/08/29/chicago-becomes-first-city-launch-array-things

NIST, National Institute of Standards and Technology, U.S. Department of Commerce (2017) NIST Cybersecurity for
    IoT Program, retrieved from https://www.nist.gov/programs-projects/nist-cybersecurity-iot-program

OECD, Organisation for Economic Co-operation and Development (2013 Revision) OECD Guidelines on the Protection
    of Privacy and Transborder Flows of Personal Data, Retrieved from
    http://www.oecd.org/internet/ieconomy/oecdguidelinesontheprotectionofprivacyandtransborderflowsofpersonaldata
    .htm

President's Council of Advisors on Science and Technology (2016) Report to the President on Technology and the
    Future of Cities, Executive Office of the President of the United States, Retrieved from
    https://www.whitehouse.gov/sites/default/files/microsites/ostp/PCAST/pcast_cities_report___final_3_2016.pdf

Risen, J. (2013) Bipartisan Backlash Grows Against Domestic Surveillance, Retrieved from
    http://www.nytimes.com/2013/07/18/us/politics/bipartisan-backlash-grows-against-domestic-
    surveillance.html

Santosham, S. (2016) A Model for Closing the Digital Divide? In working to become a truly "smart city," San José is
    tackling issues that confront communities everywhere. Retrieved from http://www.governing.com/authors/Shireen-
    Santosham.html

Shang, W., Bannis, A., Liang, T., Wang, Z., Yu, Y., Atanasyev, A., Thompson, J., Burke, J., Zhang, B., Zhang, L.,
    Named Data Networking of Things, Proc. 1st IEEE Intl. Conf. on Internet-of-Things Design and Implementation,
    April 4-8, 2016, Berlin, Germany. retrieved from http://named-data.net/publications/ndn-iotdi-2016/

Shodan. Retrieved from https://www.shodan.io/

Sicari, S., Rizzardi, A., Grieco, L.A., Coen-Porisini, A. (2015) Security, privacy and trust in Internet of Things, Journal
    Computer Networks: The International Journal of Computer and Telecommunications Networking, Volume 76,
    Issue C, Pages 146-164

Smart Cities Council (2015) IBM investing $3 billion to tap IoT's full potential, Retrieved from
    http://smartcitiescouncil.com/article/ibm-investing-3-billion-tap-iots-full-potential

The Guardian (2016) DDoS attack that disrupted Internet was largest of its kind in history, experts say, Retrieved from
    https://www.theguardian.com/technology/2016/oct/26/ddos-attack-dyn-mirai-botnet

Yu, T., Sekar, V., Seshan, S., Agarwal, Y., Xu., C. (2015) Carnegie Mellon University, CECA Peking University.
    Handling a trillion (unfixable) flaws on a billion devices: Rethinking network security for the Internet-of-Things.
    Retrieved from https://users.ece.cmu.edu/~vsekar/papers/hotnets15_secureiot.pdf

Zheng, Y., Zhang, P., Vasilakos, A. (2014) A survey on trust management for Internet of Things, Journal of Network and Computer Applications 42, Pages 120

CHAPTER 7

IT STANDARDIZATION FOR SMART CITIES

François Coallier

Abstract: A Smart City is an IT intensive system of systems. The 'smartness' in a smart city is essentially driven by the proper and intensive use of various IT technologies and applications. This chapter will present an overview of how IT standards contribute to make a smart city possible, with an emphasis on de-jure and open standards. It will do so using an IT standard oriented smart city architecture model to position and illustrate the contributions of these standards organizations. The system of systems nature of a smart city will be visible through the interactions and complementary nature of the required standards. This means the need for a systems integration approach for smart city standardization: comprising the elaboration of frameworks and a more explicit governance of the standardization process.

1.   INTRODUCTION

A Smart City is an IT Intensive System of Systems (SoS) (JTC 1 2014), which is commonly defined as:

> *A large system that delivers unique capabilities formed by integrating independently useful systems* (ISO/IEC/IEEE 24765:2010)

While a 'normal' city is also a SoS, the 'smartness' in a smart city comes from the systematic and appropriate use of IT to realise desired outcomes.

SoS are complex by nature, and an IT intensive SoS is more so. Adding to the complexity are the social and economic components of a smart city. SoS are also different from systems in the sense that they have no life-cycle e.g. no 'beginning' nor 'end': SoS are continuously evolving with their constituents systems. And these constituents systems are themselves evolving along different timelines. One does not manage a SoS like a project: instead it has to be 'governed'. Typically, four types of SoS are recognized, and the differentiating factor is their governance, or lack of as illustrated in Table 1 from Annex G of ISO/IEC 15288:2015 'Systems Engineering Life- Cycle.

Table 1 System of Systems Types [ISO/IEC 2015]

Type of SoS	Characteristics
Virtual	• Lack a central management authority • Lack of a centrally agreed upon purpose • Emerging behaviors that rely upon relatively invisible mechanisms to maintain it
Collaborative	• Component systems interact voluntarily to fulfill agreed upon purposes • Collectively decide how to interoperate, enforcing and maintain standards
Acknowledged	• Recognized objectives, a designated manager, and resources for the SoS • Constituent systems retain their independent ownership, management and resources
Directed	• Integrated SoS built and managed to fulfill specific purposes • Centrally managed and evolved • Component systems maintain ability to operate independently • Normal op mode is subordinated to central purpose

As written in ISO/IEC 15528: 2015:

> 'SoS have been characterized into four types based on the governance relationships between the constituent systems and the SoS (figure G.1). The strongest governance relations apply to directed system of systems, where the SoS organization has authority over the constituent systems despite the fact that the constituent systems may not have originally been engineered to support the SoS. Somewhat less control is afforded for acknowledged SoS, where allocated authority between the constituent systems and the systems of systems has an impact on application of some of the systems engineering processes. In collaborative SoS, which lack system of systems authorities, application of systems engineering depends on cooperation among the constituent systems. Virtual systems of systems are largely self organizing and offer much more limited opportunity for systems engineering of the SoS.'

Another characteristic that appears in Table 1 is the emphasis on systems integration. Some of this integration may be accidental in a virtual SoS, but in the other types of SoS it reflects design intent.

It is very easy to make the parallel between the governance of a smart city and the governance view of SoS presented in Fig1. The 'virtual' level would be a city were 'smart city' projects are mostly ad hoc in nature and restricted to functional silos. While those 'smart' projects will add value to the city and its stakeholders, they will not be able to unlock the much higher value that are associated with the synergy brought by a more holistic approach.

This should sound very familiar to professional in corporate IT were it has been known for a long time that breaking organizational silos and sharing data can contribute to a more agile organization, and that one of the parameter for this is a strong IT governance enabled by what is called an Enterprise Architecture discipline. Enterprise Architecture being, for all practical purpose, a domain specific type of System of Systems Engineering. The governance associated with a 'Directed' SoS is very similar to the practices promoted by enterprise architecture frameworks such as the TOGAF (the Open Group enterprise Architecture Framework). Figure 1 The TOGAF Governance Model (TOGAF) illustrates this.

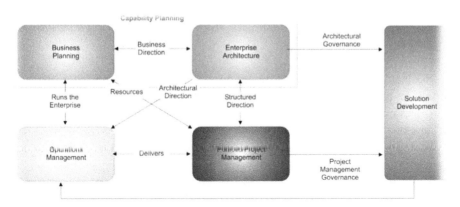

Figure 1 The TOGAF Governance Model (TOGAF)

Two standards have been quoted up to now in this introduction to smart cities: a joint one from the Internal Organization for Standardization and the Electrotechnical Commission (ISO/IEC 15288:2015) and one from the Open Group. These are two different types of what is commonly called Standards Development Organizations (SDO): the ISO and the IEC are both 'de Jure' organizations were the membership is country based while the Open Group is an industrial consortium.

This chapter will first start by an overview of the world of IT standardization. This will then be followed with an IT centric description of smart city architecture. We will then conclude by presenting an integrated model were de Jure standards activities are mapped to the smart city model.

2. AN OVERVIEW OF IT STANDARDIZATION

In this section, we will provide an overview of IT standardization with an emphasis on de Jure work.

2.1 A general standard taxonomy

Standards are an integral part of our socio-economical environment. They not only ensure that devices can be interconnected, but also help protect the operation of a wide diversity of city life e.g. the safety of the food we eat and our data privacy. But what is a standard? Lets consider the following definition[30]:

Standards are: *Guideline documentation that reflects agreements on products, practices, or operations by nationally or internationally recognized industrial, professional, trade associations or governmental bodies.*

Standards are thus first documentation. This documentation reflects a certain level on consensus by stakeholders on a given topic. This means that standards are not compulsory; it is the usage of standards that will define its influence.

We can classify standards based on who the stakeholders are and the degree of consensus required. In Table 2, we have the stakeholders view. This ranges from an organization (for instance company x) to countries (de Jure). When the degree of consensus is considered, the following classification is usually used:

- **'Technical Reports' or 'white papers'** in a semi-formal format. These are low consensus document issued in many cases to elicit comments. More formal standardization work may be initiated from these documents.
- **Guidance documents** (some time also called Technical Report). These are more formal that the previous type of document and written using a well defined structure and style. They are also

---

[30] http://www.atis.org/glossary/definition.aspx?id=1378

low consensus as they go through the design process. These guidance documents can, in some case, be standards that did not gather enough consensus to be published as such.

- **Standards:** These are formal document representing a high consensus and that can be used in a legal context. Standards are written using a very well defined and formal style and their degree of consensus is determined through a formal balloting process.

Table 2 Types of standards from a stakeholder perspective

Types of standards	Example	Experts/contributors from	Approval	Openness
Organization	CMMI	Organization	Organization	Usually private
Market (De facto)	Microsoft Windows	Organization	Organization, market share	Usually no
Professional	IEEE	Professional members	Professional members	Usually yes
Industry	OMG, The Open Group	Industrial members, academia, non-affiliated members	Industrial members	Varies
National (de Jure)	ANSI, BSI, BIS,...	National stakeholders	The country national organization, with national stakeholders inputs	Usually yes
International (de Jure)	ISO, IEC, ITU-T	Participating countries, liaison organizations	Participating countries' National Bodies	Yes

Standards are developed usually using the following process:
- A market or regular need acts as a trigger
- A group of experts elaborate a draft document
- The draft document is refined through a consensus building process
- The draft document is finalized through a formal balloting process
- A governing body approves the draft document once it has reached a defined level of consensus.
- Standards are formally published and adopted by organisations and regulators

Consensus is a key concept in the development of standards. ISO defines consensus as:

General agreement, characterized by the absence of sustained opposition to substantial issues by any important part of the concerned interests and by a process that involves seeking to take into account the views of all concerned parties and to reconcile any conflicting arguments.

In a nutshell, this means that standards need a development process where:
- All the involved parties are able to voice their views.
- The best effort is made to take into account all of the above views, and resolve all issues (meaning all comments tabled during a ballot).
- Ideally all, or close to all, the parties involved can live with the final result.

In IT, standards are elaborated on a wide range of topics. A possible classification is presented in Figure 2. The most fundamental IT standards, classified here as 'Base technology', are those that defined things like the encoding of characters. Ontologies are becoming more important with the spread of automated machine-to-machine transactions. At the 'Social and Cultural' level we have data privacy standards. Finally, in this age of complex IT systems, such as smart cities, frameworks and standards start to gain more importance to ensure reliability and flexibility.

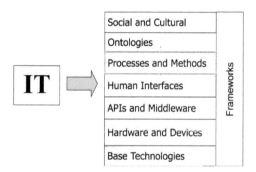

Figure 2 Range of IT standards

It is vital to realize that various stakeholders should not develop standards, in silos; especially in IT. One of the most significant sources of IT standards is not national organization, but rather Standards Developing Organisations (SDOs). The following section will elaborate more on this.

2.2 Standards Developing Organizations (SDOs)

SDOs, or Standards Setting Organizations (SSOs) are generic terms that designate all organizations that develop standards. In the de Jure standards world, it usually refers to all standards developing organizations that are not de Jure e.g. where consensus is not among countries.

The Web site Consortium Info.org, at the time writing this chapter was listing over 1000 SDOs, a significant proportion of these being in IT. Giving a complete description of all the SDOs involved in IT standardization would be too long for this chapter, therefore a summary of some of the main IT organizations that promote their documents to become de Jure is given in Table 3.

Table 3 Main IT SDOs

Name	Type	Mission
DTMF[31]	Industrial	*Creates open manageability standards spanning diverse emerging and traditional IT infrastructures including cloud, virtualization, network, servers and storage*
ECMA International[32]		*An industry association founded in 1961, dedicated to the standardization of information and communication systems.*
GS1[33]	Industrial	*A global, neutral, non-profit standards organisation that brings efficiency and transparency to the supply chain.*
Industrial Internet Consortium (IIT)[34]	Industrial	*The world's leading organization transforming business and society by accelerating the Industrial Internet of Things (IIoT).*
Institute of Electrical and Electronic Engineers (IEEE)[35]	Professional	*A leading consensus building organization that nurtures, develops and advances global technologies. Our standards drive the functionality, capabilities and interoperability of a wide range of products and services that transform the way people live, work and communicate.*
Internet Society[36]	Professional	*The world's trusted independent source of leadership for Internet policy, technology standards, and future development.*
OASIS[37]	Industrial	*A non-profit consortium that drives the development, convergence and adoption of open standards for the global information society.*
Open Geospatial Consortium (OGC)[38]	Professional & Industrial,	*An international not for profit organization committed to making quality open standards for the global geospatial community.*

---

[31] http://www.dmtf.org/about
[32] http://www.ecma-international.org
[33] https://www.gs1.org
[34] http://www.iiconsortium.org
[35] https://standards.ieee.org
[36] http://www.internetsociety.org
[37] https://www.oasis-open.org
[38] http://www.opengeospatial.org

Table 3 (continued) Main IT SDO

Open Grid Forum (OGC)[39]	Industrial & Professional	*An open global community committed to driving the rapid evolution and adoption of modern advanced applied distributed computing, including cloud, grid and associated storage, networking and workflow methods*
Object Management Group (OMG)[40]	Industrial	OMG Task Forces develop enterprise integration standards for a wide range of technologies and an even wider range of industries. OMG's modeling standards, including the Unified Modeling Language® (UML®) and Model Driven Architecture® (MDA®), enable powerful visual design, execution and maintenance of software and other processes.
The Open Group[41]	Industrial	*A global consortium that enables the achievement of business objectives through IT standards*
TM Forum[42]	Industrial	*The global industry association that drives collaboration and collective problem-solving to maximize the business success of communication and digital service providers and their ecosystem of suppliers.*
W3C[43]	Industrial	*An international community where Member organizations, a full-time staff, and the public work together to develop Web standards.*

2.3 International de Jure IT standardization organizations

De Jure standardization organizations have been with us since 1865, when the International Telecommunication Union (ITU) was founded. It is easy to understand that, in this area, standards were required for systems interconnection. The ITU nowadays is: *an international organization within the United Nations System where governments and the private sector coordinate global telecom networks and services.*

The other international de Jure standardization organizations are:
- **The International Electromechanical Commission (IEC),** founded in 1906 whose mission is being the leading global organization that prepares and publishes international standards for all electrical, electronic and related technologies[44].

---

[39] https://www.ogf.org/ogf/doku.php

[40] http://www.omg.org

[41] http://www.opengroup.org

[42] https://www.tmforum.org/about-tm-forum/

[43] https://www.w3.org

[44] http://www.iec.ch

154

- **The International Organization for Standardization (ISO),** founded in 1947 whose mission to promote the development of standardization and related activities in the world with a view to facilitating the international exchange of goods and services, and to developing cooperation in the spheres of intellectual, scientific, technological and economic activity[45].

We should also mention the UN/CEFAC, the United Nations Centre for Trade Facilitation and Electronic Business, that has published a series of standards in electronic commerce.

In 1988, ISO and IEC created a Joint Technical Committee, Joint Technical Committee 1 (JTC 1) with the mandate: *Standardization in the field of Information Technology*[46]. Information technology being defined as:

Information Technology includes the specification, design and development of systems and tools dealing with the capture, representation, processing, security, transfer, interchange, presentation, management, organization, storage and retrieval of information.

JTC 1 has thus a number of entities, sub-committees and working groups that elaborate standards on a wide range of topics. Theses are elaborated in Table 4

---

[45] https://www.iso.org
[46] https://www.iso.org

Table 4 JTC 1 Entities and technical areas at the end of 2016

Technical Areas	JTC1 Subcommittees and Working Groups
Application Technologies	SC 36 - Learning Technology
Cultural and Linguistic Adaptability and User Interfaces	SC 02 - Coded Character Sets SC 22/WG 20 – Internationalization SC 35 - User Interfaces
Data Capture land Identification Systems	SC 17 - Cards and Personal Identification SC 31 - Automatic Identification and Data Capture Techniques WG 09 - Big Data
Data Management Services	SC 32 - Data Management and Interchange
Document Description Languages	SC 34 - Document Description and Processing Languages
Information Interchange Media	SC 11 - Flexible Magnetic Media for Digital Data Interchange SC 23 - Optical Disk Cartridges for Information Interchange
Multimedia and Representation	SC 24 - Computer Graphics and Image Processing SC 29 - Coding of Audio, Picture, and Multimedia and Hypermedia Information
Networking and Middleware	SC 06 - Telecommunications and Information Exchange Between Systems SC 25 - Interconnection of Information Technology Equipment SC 38 - Cloud Computing and Distributed Platforms
Office Equipment	SC 28 - Office Equipment
Green IT	SC 39 – Sustainability for an by IT
Programming Languages and Software Interfaces	SC 22 - Programming Languages, their Environments and Systems Software Interfaces
Security	SC 27 - IT Security Techniques SC 37 - Biometrics
Software, Processes and Systems	SC 07 - Software and System Engineering SC40 – IT Governance and IT Management
Internet of Things	SC41 – Internet of Things and related technologies
Smart Cities	WG11 Smart City

The view in Table 4 is unidirectional and gives the impression that these IT areas are isolated silos. In reality, especially for newer areas like Smart Cities, covers many IT domains. This is illustrated in Table 5. In this table, the smart city committee and area have been enhanced.

Table 5 JTC 1 Entities and their interrelationships

JTC 1 Systems Integration Matrix
Version 1.3, 2017-06-08

	Application technologies	Cultural and Linguistic Adaptability and User Interfaces	Data Capture and Identification Systems	Data Management Services	Document Description Languages	Information Interchange Media	Multimedia and Representation	Networking and Middleware	Office Equipment	Green IT	Programming Languages and Software Interfaces	Security	Software Processes and Systems	Accessibility	Big Data	Internet Of Things	Cloud Computing	Smart Cities	3D Scanning & Printing	Smart Machines
SC 02 Coding	X																			
SC 06 Network							X								X	X	X	X		X
SC 07 Sw&Sys	X											X			X	X	X	X		X
SC 17 Cards ID			X												X	X	X	X	x	X
SC 22 Prog. Lang	x										X									X
SC 23 Disk					X															
SC 24 Graphic							X										X	x		
SC 25 Interc.						X												X		
SC 27 Security											X	X			X	X	X	X		X
SC 28 Office Eq.									X											
SC 29 Multimed.							X		x				x		X	X		x		
SC 31 Data Cap			X												X	X	X	X		X
SC 32 Data int.				X											X			x	x	
SC 34 Doc.					X															
SC 35 User Int		x																		
SC 36 Learn	X																			
SC 37 Bio											X							x		
SC 38 Middl							X						x		X	X	X	X		X
SC 39 IT Sust.										X					X			x		
SC 40 Gov & M													X				x	x		X
SC41 IoT		x					x						x		X	X	X	X		X
WG9 Big Data		x	x												X	X	X	X		X
WG11 Smart Cities		x	x		x	x	x		x			x	x		X	x	x	X		X

As we can see, the IT standardization world reflects the complexity and the dynamist of not only IT technologies, but also of its market. Smart cities standards appears clearly as drawing from many IT domains. In the next section, we will describe a smart city model that will be used to map the de Jure IT standards areas that are required to make a smart city 'smart'.

3. SMART CITY IT ARCHITECTURE

This section will describe succinctly, using a layered model, the architecture of a smart city from the perspective of IT standardization.

The approach used will be a layered model initially inspired initially from (Zygiaris 2013), but considerably modified. Each layer of the model will be described in this chapter, and the standardization components will be added after a review of the IT standard world.

Like any model of a complex systems, and in this case a systems of systems, this model will put in value some aspects while hiding a lot. This is normal given that any complex system needs many modeling 'views' to describe and communicate its structure.

The top and bottom layers of the models are respectively the desired 'outcomes' of a smart city, and the 'vanilla' city on which the IT layer is added. The IT technologies required to realize these outcomes will be added in layers in between.

3.1 What are the desired outcomes of more smartness

Making a city 'smart' has to be for a purpose. It has to bring value to the various city stakeholders, the most important ones being its citizen and the various economics actors of the city. Also, it is good practice to have a clear vision before undertaking the massive investments and reengineering that building a truly smart city requires.

The following outcomes are usually associated with a smart city projects:

- Citizen Well-Being
- Economic Development
- Sustainability
- Innovation
- Collaboration
- Transparency
- Efficiency
- Resilience

These outcomes are not interdependent: for instance, 'citizen well-being' is directly related to 'economic development' (job market, careers opportunities) and also to 'sustainability' (more healthy, agreeable city environment). 'Economic development' is directly related to 'innovation' (entrepreneurship, start-ups) and 'efficiency' (better city services at lower cost, efficient transportation network, etc..). 'Innovation' is related to 'collaboration' (active professional, trades, industrial associations, etc...).

Many other city enablers that are not *a priori* related to smartness are also contributors, or even prerequisites, to these outcomes. One of them is the city education infrastructure, including professional training.

It is noteworthy that an ISO Technical Committee (TC), TC 268 on Sustainable cities and communities, has published a standard, ISO 37120:2014 titled *Sustainable development of communities - Indicators for city services and quality of life,* that *defines and establishes methodologies for a set of indicators to steer and measure the performance of city services and quality of life*[47].

Another outcome oriented standards, or in this case technical report, that must be mentioned is the TMForum 'Smart City Maturity and Benchmark Model' who was initially released in May 2016 (TR259). This model '*allows a city to fairly quickly assess its strengths and weaknesses in five key dimension areas related to city smartness and to set clear goals as how it wishes to transform over the next two to five years. It enables the city to benchmark itself against similar cities and identify other cities with whom it*

---

[47] https://www.iso.org/standard/62436.html

can partner to tackle similar challenges'. Noteworthy are the rating criteria's used in this model that, at the more mature levels, are value based.

3.2 The base city

This brings us to what may be called the 'vanilla' or 'base' city. This is the basic fabric of the city excluding the "smart" IT component. Because the model is IT centric, it is normal that the base city is abstracted to a single layer with the following components:

- Citizens
- Socio-economics
- Governance and management
- Infrastructure

The Citizens are the most important components of a city. They live in a 'socio-economic' environment that includes all the economic stakeholders and entities as well as the cultural fabric. The city has a governance and management infrastructure. And finally, we have the city physical infrastructure that includes buildings and facilities, roads, energy, communication, water, finance, waste management, safety, security, disaster recovery, transportation and education.

3.3 The IT enabled services that will 'smarten' the city

The city 'smart' processes and services are enabled by an IT infrastructure of various technologies and applications that we will elaborate on later. These IT enabled services can be summarized as follows:

- E-Government
- Utility Management
- Public safety
- Transport and logistics
- Health services
- Environmental services
- Collaborative services
- Knowledge management

All those services existed before we started to talk about 'smart cities'. In an ideal smart city, many of these services should be:

- Integrated through shared data and processes: reducing silos
- Data enabled, using large amount of real-time and other diverse types of data
- Instrumented: relying on sensors for the real-time data
- Autonomous and semi-autonomous: being able to react in real-time to changes in the environment, using actuators to influence the physical world.

The collaborative and knowledge management services are usually associated with the internal working of an organization. In the context of a smart city, they are open to stakeholders that are external to the public administration to enable innovation.

3.4 The instrumentation (Sensing and control)

As we saw in the previous section, a smart city is instrumented and also enables IT applications to control the physical worlds. This is where what we call the Internet of Things (IoT) meet the smart city. Three types of devices contributes to a smart city instrumentation:

- Sensors
- Actuator
- Tags

In an IoT environment, sensors include cameras and GPS receivers. A camera can be used, with the proper software, to detect movement, assess traffic, visibility, etc.

Actuators are mechanisms by which a control system acts upon an environment[48]. They are included in remote controlled water for instance.

The tags are used, for instance, on vehicle transponders to give access to parking and transportation services. In a well-governed smart city, a single transponder should be sufficient to access all services.

The instrumentation can be embedded in devices that are semi or fully autonomous.

---

[48] https://en.wikipedia.org/wiki/Actuator

3.5 The IT infrastructure

All these smart things and services need an IT infrastructure to power them. This infrastructure, represented in the layer models by two layers, includes:

- An interconnection layer:
  - o Physical links
  - o Wireless links
  - o Networking (protocols, architectures)
- An integration, data and computing layer
  - o Data & Ontologies
  - o Geomatics
  - o Middleware
  - o The fog, or edge computing
  - o The cloud – abstracting the computing infrastructure

The computing infrastructure is abstracted in this model as either fog (edge) computing, for the real-time low latency computing that is close to the sensors and actuators, and cloud computing for the classical data center types of services.

While we casually talk a lot about data, ontologies are important to make this data (and human) machine understandable and amenable to coding.

3.6 The different types of software applications

The IT enabled services are powered by integrated software applications. These applications can be classified as:

- Control
- Transactional
- Analytics
- Collaborative

These are broads categories that do not preclude a given enterprise application architecture.

3.7 Engineering and Engineering Governance

As we saw in the introduction, the engineering of a smart city and its components is a complex endeavor where, to get the most of the potential outcomes, good engineering governance and practices are required. Thus the following domains are needed:

- Strategic and Policy Governance
- System of Systems Engineering
- Architecture
- Green IT

One could argue that these domains are not independents. They were chosen to communicate to the model readers some specific areas that the author believes significant, and also to match more closely IT standardization efforts.

3.8 Trustworthiness

Trustworthiness is a user oriented systems engineering concept that, in the author own terms, essentially translate in how much trust can a stakeholder have in the services provided by a systems. It encompass attributes such as security, privacy and availability. Trustworthiness is synonymous with the systems engineering concept of dependability, concept that is defined by a series of standards from IEC/TC56. The definition given in the IEC online dictionary[49] is:

> **dependability**, *<of an item>*
>
> *ability to perform as and when required*
>
> *Note 1 to entry: Dependability includes availability (192-01-23), reliability (192-01-24), recoverability (192-01-25), maintainability (192-01-27), and maintenance support performance (192-01-29), and, in some cases, other characteristics such as durability (192-01-21), safety and security.*
>
> *Note 2 to entry: Dependability is used as a collective term for the time-related quality characteristics of an item.*

Security and data privacy are design requirements that are very important to smart cities stakeholders, especially its citizens. It is a concern because a smart city is data driven, and significant part of this data is collected from sensors, including cameras. The data also includes sources related to e-government functions, data that may need to be anonymized for use in some applications.

Another security issue is the protection of the city infrastructure from malicious intents. The downside of an IoT enabled city infrastructure is that

---

[49] http://www.electropedia.org/iev/iev.nsf/display?openform&ievref=192-01-22

it becomes vulnerable to IT security risks. A good example of this vulnerability is the incident that happened at a German Foundry were industrial equipment was sabotaged by hackers who got access through an administrative PC using social engineering[50].

This protection is more than an issue of firewalls and network architecture. The software that is embedded in the 'things' that are part of the city' IoT infrastructure must be updated when vulnerability has been identified and corrected, like we do for PC operating system for instance. This is why an SDO named the Online Trust Alliance (OTA) integrate in its IoT trust model the management of the lifecycle of the 'things' that are part of IoT[51] (See Figure 2 OTA IoT Trust Model).

Figure 2 OTA IoT Trust Model

Real system risk means that trustworthiness need to be integral to the design of city infrastructure.

3.9 Smart city ICT frameworks

The last element of the model, cutting across all the horizontal layers, is the smart city ICT architectural frameworks. These architectural frameworks fall in the following categories:

- Generic Enterprise Architecture (EA)
- IoT
- Smart Cities specifics

Given the very close relationship between a smart city and a commercial or vanilla public organization, generic enterprise architecture frameworks do apply.

---

[50] http://www.itworld.com/article/2861675/cyberattack-on-german-steel-factory-causes-massive-damage.html

[51] https://otalliance.org/system/files/files/initiative/documents/iot_visionforthefuture_0.pdf

Since the Internet of Things is essential for making city infrastructure and facilities 'smart', IoT frameworks are pertinent.

Finally, there are smart city specific frameworks covering, for instance, data and business process architectures.

4.   IT STANDARDS AND SMART CITIES

Having defined a model tailored specifically to bring out the IT contributions to a smart city, we can now map standards development organizations to this model. This is done in Figure 3 ICT Smart City model with de Jure SDO's. The title of the JTC 1 Sub Committees (SC) that are in the figure can be found in Table 4 JTC 1 Entities and technical areas at the end of 2016.

The left column list the 'horizontal' generic categories that we described in the previous section while the three 'verticals' appear on the right. The domains of the three De Jure standards organizations have been mapped on the horizontals. A more detailed mapping has been done of the JTC 1 entities of Table 5 JTC 1 Entities and their interrelationships.

Traditionally, city experts and stakeholders have been involved in ISO Technical Committees: thus identification of ISO as the main source of standards related to the smart city outcomes. At the city infrastructure layer, we find ISO and the IEC as a main source of De Jure standards.

The ITU being focused on telecommunications is present at the Interconnection layer with JTC 1.

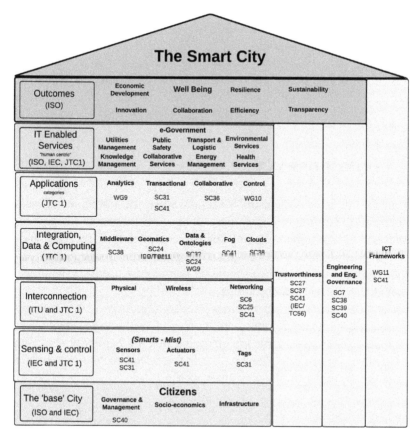

Figure 3 ICT Smart City model with de Jure SDO's

Of particular importance to smart cities are the IoT standards, especially the frameworks, and the smart cities specific standards.

IoT standardization is still relatively new, but very active. More than a dozen Software Development Organizations are involved directly in IoT standards. Of particular interest to smart cities are reference architectures, such as the ISO/IEC one that is currently (May 2017) at 'committee stage' and could be published at the end of the years (Project 30141 Internet of Things Reference Architecture (IoT RA). Standards related to what is commonly referred to as the 'Industrial Internet of Things' (IIoT) are also directly pertinent since they cover the application of IoT in settings that includes facility and infrastructure management and smart buildings.

ISO/IEC JTC 1, through its Working Group 11, is developing a smart city framework that covers standards for business processes, knowledge management and IT infrastructure (project 30145, Information technology - Smart city ICT reference framework). It is also developing a data ontology standards that will make smart city data machine interpretable (project

30182, Smart city concept model - Guidance for establishing a model for data interoperability). This last project will not only facilitate the creation of a global applications market, but it will also facilitate the global benchmarking of cities. This follows the publication in early 2017 of ISO/IEC 30182 titled Smart city concept model – Guidance for establishing a model for data interoperability.

5. CONCLUSIONS

As an IT intensive System of Systems (SoS), the implementation of a smart city requires many technologies, along with the standards associated with theses. To be able to build such a complex SoS the city and its contractors must follow good engineering practices. A large number of these practices are embedded in standards that can be used to advantage by all stakeholders in contractual settings.

Standards pertinent to smart cities are continuously being developed. Many are tracking the continuous evolution of IT technologies making them more valuable. Some standards are emerging that are explicitly about smart cities. However, in emerging areas, like IoT, general technology standards are beginning to transform the way cities work.

REFERENCES

ISO/IEC 2015, ISO/IEC 15528: 2015 Systems and software engineering - System life cycle processes, ISO and IEC, Geneva, Switzerland

JTC 1 (2014), JTC 1/SG 1 (Study Group on Smart Cities) Report on standardization needs for Smart Cities Submitted to JTC 1 2014 Plenary, ISO and IEC, documents N12211 and N12212.

Sotiris Zygiaris, Smart City Reference Model: Assisting Planners to Conceptualize the Building of Smart City Innovation Ecosystems, Journal of the Knowledge Economy, June 2013, Volume 4, Issue 2, pp 217-231

TOGAF, The Open Group Architecture Framework, TOGAF, version 9.1, The Open Group, December 2011, 692 pages

TR259, Smart City Maturity and Benchmark Model, TMFORUM, Release 16.0.0, May 2016.

CHAPTER 8

THE *INTELLIGENTER* ACTIONABLE FUTURE LIVING
AN UPDATE ON THE THEORY OF HUMAN MOTIVATION FROM A SMART CITY SYSTEM-OF-SYSTEMS PERSPECTIVE

Lluïsa Marsal

Abstract   You are right if you think this chapter is about revisiting Maslow's Theory of Human Motivation (1943) and his Pyramid of Needs in the context of today's digital transformation. Are digital technologies changing our human priorities? Indeed, they are changing our jobs, skills and interests. Is the Internet changing our lives? Certainly, it is changing our cities, industries and businesses. And there is a lot more but I do not intend to provide an exhaustive list of what digital technologies have changed, nor put Maslow's theories into question. No. This study has a much humbler and more practical interest. I want to think about the hypothesis that:

> **'Today we humans are facing different challenges compared to Maslow's times, and this has to have an effect on our hierarchy of needs'.**

I also want to reason the assumption that:

> **'Technology plays a big role in tackling our challenges and, therefore, in how we meet our needs'.**

To uncover the hypothesis and to unveil the assumption I will use the scientific method and to properly identify humankind's current challenges I will use internationally acknowledged precepts. It is globally accepted that the most challenging issue we are currently facing is the sustainability of our planet. And the international community recognises the three pillars of sustainability as environmental, sociocultural and economic. According to UN's Habitat New Urban Agenda, environmental sustainability has to fight climate change, sociocultural sustainability has to target a fully integrated society and, economic sustainability aims at responsible business ethics and fair labour conditions for everyone.

Countries do sign international policies and agreements such as the New Urban Agenda and, by doing so, they agree on the implementation and uptake of these global commitments. I will reimagine the implementation and uptake of these international instruments from an *intelligenter* perspective, which is a collaborative system-of-systems approach. The Intelligenter Method is based on the innovative idea of *collaborative discovery* in urban systems. The *intelligenter* methodology is data-based and uses technology to capture and process data that but escapes simplistic smart city approaches that have technology as an end in itself.

I will show how an *intelligenter* approach to the sustainability challenge better meets current human needs and how intimate is the relationship between humankind challenges and human needs. While doing so, I will have the necessity to measure the performance of the relationship between needs and challenges and I will have to create a new form of more technological metrics, what I will call Actionables, since traditional indicators and indices cannot do that. Finally, I'll show how today's human needs have a different hierarchy because our challenges are different and the way we tackle them in the digital era has an impact in our priorities

1. INTRODUCTION:
ON THE NEED FOR AN *INTELLIGENTER* APPROACH
TO SMART CITIES

The first ever bibliographical reference to the term smart appears in urban context, in the book The Technopolis Phenomenon: Smart Cities, Fast Systems and Global Networks (Gibson et al., eds.), published in 1992. In one of the chapters of this book, Tatsuno introduces the smart city concept. In his essay he defines smart cities as a "metaphor of intelligent cities". According to Tatsuno, smart cities "are global network cities of dispersed highly interactive economic nodes linked by massive networks of airports, highways, and communications; inhabited by 'knowledge processors' engaged in rapid information exchanges". Hence the metaphor of intelligent cities.

Interestingly, in this seminal book, published in 1992, we can see that smart cities and intelligent cities were presented as parallel concepts, but with the latter having stronger relationships with information, knowledge and science. Another author in a contemporaneous publication (Datty, 1990) referred to the intelligent city, as an informational city, along the lines of Castells' theories (1989), who first introduced the concept of informational city. A few years later, Mitchell (2002) anticipated something that we have not yet achieved, that telecommunications would offer not only the advantages of better communications and improved urban management but also "smart growth", consisting of "attractive combinations of economic and cultural vibrancy, social equity and long-term environmental responsibility".

These seminal publications call for revisiting the etymology of both terms intelligent and smart, in order to shed light upon the nuances of these adjectives. Etymologically, smart52 comes from both the old English form of smeart and the Proto-Germanic suffix -smartz. Both forms filled the current term smart, used as an adjective, with a variety of meanings, the most common of which are: 1. Causing sharp pain, stinging; 2. Sharp, keen, poignant; 3. Exhibiting social ability or cleverness; 4. Exhibiting intellectual knowledge, such as that found in books.

On the other hand, intelligence comes from the Latin form intellegēns, meaning discerning. Its present active participle form is intellegō, which means understand, comprehend. Intellegō is a compound term formed by the prefix intus- (transforming into inte-, after compounding), which means in between and the suffix –legere (turning into -legō, when compound), which means read inside, pick out, choose. Although the term intelligent has a more profound, complex, interactive, educational, collaborative and lasting meaning, the adjective smart has somehow been selected to characterise avant-garde features of cities, energy, transportation and any other highly evolving domains. After its first seminal appearance in 1990, the adjective smart applied to cities was not used again until the current "smart cities" initiative, which is considered to have begun as a global movement, circa 2010.

---

[52] http://en.wiktionary.org/wiki/smart#English

Etymology [as adjective]: From Middle English smart, smarte, smerte, from Old English smeart ("smarting, smart, painful"), from Proto-Germanic *smartaz ("hurting, aching"), from Proto-Indo-European *(s)merd- ("to bite, sting"). Cognate with Scots smert ("painful, smart"), Old Frisian smert ("sharp, painful").

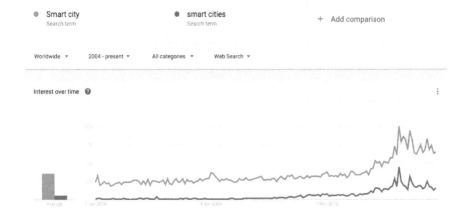

Fig. 1: The terms "Smart City" and "Smart Cities" have a peak of popularity between 2013-2014 (Source: Google trends)

Fig. 2: The term "Smart" has a more constant popularity since it has wide application to many fields (Google trends)

Some recent scientific literature on smart cities, interestingly, has indications of the etymological meaning of intelligent in the smart cities term, drawing from educational, discursive, holistic, and more human-interactive concepts. These are the qualities that the Intelligenter method brings into the process or practice being transformed. One of the first authors imbuing some intelligence in smart city theories was Shapiro (2006). In his article, Smart Cities: Quality of Life, Productivity, and the growth effects of human capital, he shows how a large percentage of employment growth for college graduates is due to the introduction of cognitive enhancement in productivity systems. This finding contrast with the common argument that only a critical mass of human capital along with adjustments in productivity scale is enough to generate employment growth in urban areas. Along the same lines, Winters (2011), in his article Why are Smart Cities Growing? Who moves and who stays, affirms that smart cities are "education pools". This strong statement comes from the belief that smart cities enrol more people in higher education programs, and grow in part because scholar immigrants often stay after completing their education.

To this, Caragliu et al (2011) add the importance of a creative class as a determining factor for urban smartness. Neirotti et al. (2014) sustain that evolution patterns of a smart city depend highly on its local context factors. In particular, economic development and structural urban variables such as population profiles and knowledge density are likely to influence a city's digital path. Campbell (2012, 2013) in his book, Beyond Smart Cities: How Cities Network, Learn and Innovate, goes one step further and sustains that for cities to achieve smartness, the conditions for continuous learning and innovation must be created; conditions that are created if cities connect together and learn from each other. Finally, in Greenfield's book (2013), Against the Smart City, a similar idea is presented in what is perhaps a too narrow dissertation about the effects of networked places and networked individuals. According to Greenfield, these interactions are only possible in cities built from scratch. The authors of this paper acknowledge the value of Greenfield's idea but disagree on the scope of this interaction, which is perfectly achievable in existing cities.

These examples show how the smart concept has already been touched by the intelligent etymological idearium, at least in the smart cities context. However, the *intelligenter* concept goes beyond that and brings intelligence in its truly etymological meaning by focusing on the intus- factor ("in between"), understanding that the right response and solution are something systemic and holistic, somewhere outside the traditional result and immediate answer. Moreover, the *intelligenter* concept also includes the -legere element ("choose", "read inside") and is therefore a more educated approach, highly collaborative, complex and sophisticated, and disruptive of the status quo. This two-tier *intelligenter* theory brought into practice unfolds as a cross-subsystem (intus- factor) and a multi-stakeholder (-legere element) collaboration. A possible materialisation of an *intelligenter* approach could be in the set-up of a *collaboratory* in which stakeholders, not only those relevant to the subsystem being studied but any others related to linked subsystems are brought into the collaboration, for an exercise of collective intelligence consisting of mutual learning, holistic discussion, in a more human-interactive environment. Similar to the use of the term *intelligenter,* we will coin the new term, *collaboratories* to distinguish these innovative and disruptive exercises of collective intelligence from other traditional forms of collaboration.

Whether is the collective intelligence of the proposed *intelligenter* approach or the smart intelligence derived from ICT sources, both intelligences rely on data. The main difference between the two is how data is processed. Whereas in the *intelligenter* approach data from ICT sources is analysed and humanised in the *collaboratories* to later take informed and consensued collaborative decisions, in traditional smart interventions data collection is the target being the technological devices an end in and on itself. In the *intelligenter* approach technology is only an enabler to take more collaboratively informed and consensued decisions. The *intelligenter* approach it therefore allows for the reimagining of any human process or practice to make it collectively informed and more consensued in its decision-making.

The *intelligenter* approach specifically targets processes and practices with global dimension so that these reengineering efforts can be replicated and reused locally. The *intelligenter* approach has been implemented and published as method in the reimagining of different processes, the design of Plans and Projects (Marsal & Segal 2016a), drafting of Policies and Regulations (Marsal & Segal 2016b), and in the development of Standards and Standardisation instruments (Marsal & Wood-Hill, 2016). I will now show how the delivery of international commitments and global agreements can be reimagined and vastly improved using the *intelligenter* methodology which leverages on data-enabled *collaboratories*, multi-stakeholder and cross-sector principles, and collective decision making.

Three big problems exist with international commitments and global agreements, and will be presented in detail in the following paragraphs.

1. Poor Implementation
2. High data requirements
3. Top-down process

We do need *intelligenter* global commitments and agreements like we do need *intelligenter* data-based practices and processes of any kind. Data is usually present in commitments and agreements as metrics -typically indices and indicators- allowing the user to monitor the performance of the implementation of these instruments. Agendas and programs are typically contained in international commitments and global agreements as executive/implementation tools. Therefore, agendas and programs are part of instruments such as treaties, conventions, charters, declarations, etc. promulgated by international bodies like the United Nations or the European Commission. Agendas and programs will be formulated if the former instrument allows for implementation mechanisms and/or requires a guided execution of its principles.

Typically, implementation and execution mechanisms are offered in the format of indicators and indices. It is at each country's discretion to adopt international commitments/agreements, and their corresponding agendas/ programs, and their current endorsement is far from global. Moreover, even in countries who do sign these agendas and programs, their uptake by the primary receivers -typically local administrations and regional governments- is low. Good examples of poor implementation of international commitments are the UN Rio Declaration of 1992 that included the Local Agenda 21 (LA21) as executive instrument; or the EU Strategic Energy Technological Plan (SET Plan) of 2000, which had associated the Covenant of Mayors (CoM) as implementing strategy. The LA21, although including several indicators to help measure sustainability, had poor uptake by cities around the world. The same occurred with the CoM, even though it included several indicators to deliver the European 20/20/20 energy goals, it failed to be implemented.

In author's opinion, the main reason for this poor uptake and implementation of both agendas and programs is the high data requirements to feed indicators and indices, putting off poorly resourced potential receivers. And this, inevitably, results in poor implementation and uptake. Moreover, if this costly and titanic task is actually completed, the benefit-realisation in society is very low. This is particularly important because typically the receiver of agendas and programs are public administrations and data resourcing efforts are to be paid with public money, hence the importance of improving the benefit-realisation towards the tax-payer, which is actually the final end user of these.

Finally, the last major problem with international agendas and commitments is the commonly too much top-down delivery process, with poor societal engagement which ends in poor uptake by the final end user. This top-down approach also contributes to a misrepresentation of actual human needs that will result in a failed implementation, as citizens' requirements will not be properly identified. We can thus affirm that the current delivery of both agendas and programs is not successful.

Using the *intelligenter* approach we will now reimagine the current process and practice of delivering both agendas and programs and suggest a reengineered version to deliver these built on the idea of *collaboratories,* which will allow for a collectively informed and consensued data-based delivery. Specifically, under the *intelligenter* approach we will tackle the three main shortcomings of the current delivery of agendas and programs described in the previous paragraphs. This will be illustrated by proposing a novel delivery strategy for the new UN's Habitat 'New Urban Agenda' (NUA).

To that end, we will use an inverse engineering approach to reinvent the current top-down delivery of agendas and programs, proposing a bottom-up implementation mechanism for the NUA in which citizens will be responsible for the implementation and, not in isolation, but in collaboration with the society as a whole. Secondly, this innovative bottom-up delivery and its novel citizen-owned implementation will have an immediate benefit-realisation in society, solving the three big issues described earlier. Implementation can be now made by society at large through a revolutionary role-based mechanism that will pay special attention to the non-motivated and non-engaged segments of society by giving them an essential role. This will very much improve uptake rates. Third and last, a pioneering format of metrics will be created to better visualise the newly achieved benefit-realisation, the so-called Actionables and Aggregators:

Actionables *will measure actions and therefore will require less* data efforts than indices and indicators while providing higher benefit-realisation since they will be easily understood by the common citizen. Aggregators will measure collective Actions, thus being a sum of equivalent Actionables; or measuring an Action collectively initiated.

Moreover, this benefit-realisation will be emphasised through an 'actionable' and 'aggregated' dashboard, which is an *intelligenter* version of typical mayor's dashboard. This is all explained in the coming sections.

2.   PROBLEM DESCRIPTION: LACK OF COLLABORATIVE AND SYSTEMIC DESIGN OF AGENDAS AND PROGRAMMES RESULTS IN POOR IMPLEMENTATION AND UPTAKE OF INTERNATIONAL POLICIES

The main problem faced by agendas and programmes delivering international commitments are their poor implementation and uptake. In the author's opinion, this is due to three reasons outlined in the previous section (too much top-down delivery, low benefit-realisation, and too costly data resourcing). In this section, these three reasons will be analysed along with the alternatives proposed by the *intelligenter* approach. We will start with the study of the measurement of performance in the implementation and uptake of agendas and programmes through indicators and indices, and suggest a new system of metrics, that are less costly and better serves benefit realisation. Moreover, this new system of metrics, the so-called Actionables and Aggregators is a bottom up resource, thus achieving the purpose of reengineering the current top-down delivery. Therefore, Actionables and Aggregators go beyond metrics, not only providing performance measurement but also achieving policy purposes.

Currently, indices and indicators used for performance purposes are the so-called KPIs (Key Performance Indicators/Indices). It is commonly accepted that there are three types of performance appraisal, namely: Individual, Operational and Strategic. The first to appear was Individual performance and it is believed its first expression was in the third century, when the emperors of the Wei Dynasty rated the performance of official family members (Banner & Cooke, 1984; Coens & Jenkins, 2000) by measuring individual achievements within the group (family). As an evolution of Individual performance, line management performance emerged in the early 1800s in the industrial context when Robert Owen monitored employees' outputs in his cotton mills with cubes of different sizes and measures installed at the workstation of each employee (Banner & Cooke, 1984; Wiese & Buckley 1998).

The origin of Operational performance appears before line management performance and it is linked to the evolution of accounting and management disciplines as it measures business outputs of organisations. The earliest example of Operational performance can be found in the 13th century in the measurement of the performance of a Venetian sailing expedition, as the difference between the amount of money invested by ship owners and the sum obtained from the sale of goods shipped (Lebas, 1995). Until the 19th century there was no distinction between operations and processes (Dainty & Anderson, 2008) and the first differentiation is attributed to Frederick Taylor. Processes performance has been since then the analysis of the effectiveness of methods and taylorist work practices and therefore linked to the study of time and motion (a new discipline previously developed by Lillian and Frank Gilberth). Whereas operations are still understood as transactions, concepts such as "Return on Investment (RoI)" and "tableau de bord" ('balanced scorecard' in Anglo-Saxon countries) are evolutions of the operational performance of processes (Bessire & Backer, 2005).

Strategic performance is the third type of performance appraisal. It is a discipline dating back to the sixties. It was triggered by Peter Drucker's concept of 'corporation' (1946) and the revolutionary inclusion of intangible assets as elements that will affect the performance of an organisation or even of an individual. Strategic planning (also known as long-range planning) has its origins in Drucker's theories as well. Since then various 'performance measurement tools' have been developed for organisations to capture, besides the operational performance, the value of more impalpable and strategic activities. These performance measurement tools had their heyday in the early nineties, coinciding with the creation of Key Performance Indicators/Indices (KPIs) as essential metrics to measure performance. And, since performance measurement tools can assess Operational (including processes) and Strategic performances, and even Individual performance; KPIs are the instrument used to inform all performance types.

Whatever KPIs are used, there is an important a distinction between Indices and Indicators: While **Indices** are a summarised representation of a set of indicators, and are used to provide a single description of related elements that can be individually measured with indicators (Marsal et al. 2014), **Indicators** are individualised measures informing a single element.

Whereas background instruments in which agendas and programmes are built on (charters, treaties, agreements, etc.) do not include indicators or indices, agendas and programmes typically do as they are meant to be the executable tools of such background instruments. In agendas and programmes, indicators are a more common metric than indices thus indices require additional elaboration to aggregate indicators, and the purpose of agendas and programmes is to offer detailed and individualised guidance (Marsal at al. 2014). Since the objective of agendas and programmes is to help achieve performance in the implementation of the key elements of the topic being addressed by the background instrument, indicators included in these instruments are Key Performance Indicators.

In order to monitor performance, KPIs require both a measurable baseline and a measurable benchmark. Some high-level agendas and conceptual programmes do not include KPIs (like the NUA) but provide a set of practical recommendations and guidelines that the user will have to implement and asses its performance using its own criteria. Experts and advanced users of these conceptual agendas and programmes are capable of elaborating the so-called 'proxies' to substitute the lack of indicators. **Proxies** are measurable equivalences created when a concept cannot be measured with its native units (Wilson, 2014). In other words, a proxy is something that can be counted or measured and that reasonably represents or is related to what it is desired to quantify; but it remains something different.

Although proxies can be created for agendas and programmes -if these do not already include KPIs, they still lack implementation and uptake. As mentioned earlier, the main reason for this is the costly data resourcing efforts that administrations (responsible for the delivery of agendas and programmes) must undertake to feed KPIs or proxies. Moreover, if this effort is eventually done, the demonstrable benefit-realisation of compiling these measurements is poor and it is difficult to justify its public expenditure to the taxpayer. Finally, since agendas and programmes currently have a strong top-down delivery, the process of filling indicators and proxies is a sort of self-indulgent exercise for administrations who already know they are in good compliance with agendas and programmes and something to avoid for those administrations that know they will not be conformant with the terms of agendas and programmes.

What is important in agendas and programmes is the guidance and recommendations they offer to help succeed in implementing international polices and global agreements. Both guidelines and recommendations will benefit from the bottom-up delivery proposed by the *intelligenter* approach as it implicitly brings the currently lacking benefit-realisation towards the final or end-user, the citizen. However, this proposed change of direction in the delivery of agendas and programmes will imply the reimagining of current performance metrics so that they can properly reflect the end-user benefits of this bottom-up implementation of agendas and programmes. Actionable metrics are, the main innovation of this reimagining exercise. This new measurement system using Actionables addresses the shortcomings of existing performance metrics – they are easy to understand and efficient to report. I will explain the use of Actionables in the next section with the use-case of the NUA and the proposed *intelligenter* Actionable Future Living.

It has been already described where KPIs come from and their origins in the early nineties. We will now add to these the most recent developments in performance measurement and show how Actionables link with the latest thinking. In the nineties, KPIs still used statistics as data sources (Marsal & Boada, 2013). Back then, baseline indicators were elaborated from the latest statistical data available and benchmarks were aspirational thresholds based on statistical projections. Since then much has changed regarding data availability and the timely readiness of data sources. Nowadays KPIs (and proxies) will use Internet of Things (IoT) as main data source, providing timely if not real-time data. IoT is essentially a data capture mechanism from one Machine (device) that sends to another Machine (computer) for processing and display. This process is the also called M2M (Machine to Machine) communication.

Once data from the IoT about a given system has been processed and displayed it still has to be siloed (as with statistics) to populate each KPI. A more holistic report on the performance of the system will be only possible if KPIs are combined to create indices. In terms of feeding KPIs, if we compare IoT as a data resource with data from statistical sources, we will notice that there are no advancements made regarding the same siloed reporting about a system. Moreover, in the move to using IoT data, we lost something very valuable, the human communication, which was still present during the statistical phase, as statistics need human processing. The Actionables do address both of these issues as they allow automated holistic reporting of the system in combination with human interpretation and interaction. To do so, Actionables capitalise on IoT precedents -mainly the science of Cybernetics-, which is much more humanised. Let's see how.

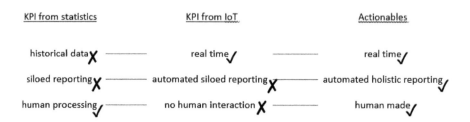

Fig. 3 Diagram showing the advantages (✓) and disadvantages (✗) of IoT for the creation of Actionables and how Actionables address these

IoT has its origins in Mark Weiser's (1991) modern Ubiquitous Computing, whose works in turn build on Robert Pask's (1968) early Ubiquitous Computing who, essentially, evolved late Cybernetic theories by including the 'feedback principle' seeking a more 'conversational' Cybernetics. Robert Wiener is considered the father of Cybernetics (Wiener, 1961) since he elaborated the first cyber theories on how communication is established between the animal (Humans) and the Machine (Wiener, 1948), what we could call today 'H2M (Human to Machine) communication'. Since our goal is to reengineer performance metrics so that benefit-realisation of implementing international commitments can be better communicated to and visualised by people, we will leverage on Pask's 'conversational cybernetics' and Wiener's 'H2M communication'. Pask, in his work Cybernetic Serendipity, proposes a conversational model between the human and the machine (Reichardt, 1968), the so-called Colloquium of Mobiles. In his model, pendulum mobiles and elastic structures react to human actions thus being responsive machines. This is a more interactive feedback than today's IoT machines reporting to another machine first for later display to humans. In Pask's system machine response is live and it is a reaction to human input (eg., in Figure 4, the "interactive flower": when the human gets close the flower it is programmed to turn to the human so that it can be smelled).

Fig. 4 Pask's Interactive Flower: screen shots from a video of the Cybernetic Serendipity Exhibition showing how the electric flower follows the movement of the human (source: http://cyberneticserendipity.net/page/2)

Pask's Cybernetic Serendipity interaction is the kind of synergy that the *intelligenter* approach seeks for the proposed bottom-up delivery of agendas and programmes in which, not only the bottom/final users (citizens) interact with the system but they actually have the prominent role, triggering the machine response that will improve the overall performance of the system.

In other words, the *intelligenter* delivery of agendas and programmes is a bottom-up process initiated by citizens that occurs and it is implemented through citizens' Actions, hence its unit of measure are the Actionables. *Intelligenter* delivery enables citizen to report their implementation Actions into a digital dashboard, a reengineered mayor's dashboard that will be described later in the chapter. These pioneering metrics, the Actionables, together with their compounded form, the Aggregators, will measure the performance of citizens' Actions in their delivery of agendas and programmes. Individual Actions will be measured with Actionables (which substitute KPIndicators) and community Actions will be measured with Aggregators (which substitute KPIndices).

On the other hand, and for our measurement purposes, from Wiener's Cybernetical principles, the *intelligenter* approach will capitalise on his findings about the correlation between entropy and information and how this results in what he calls 'integrated entropy'. Wiener asserted that accurate measurements of complex systems will only be possible if the whole system is measured and this is due to the indissociably nature of systems' entropy (which is the informational order in a complex system or non-isolated system). In other words, complex systems cannot be measured in parts or silos and therefore the whole system must be considered if an accurate reading is to be made.

The Intelligenter Method takes Wiener's 'integrated entropy' principle as the basis to build both Actionables and Aggregators, thus acknowledging that Actions -either individual or collective- must be measured holistically, considering all subsystems involved and not just the main subsystem.

Main subsystem's accountability would provide a siloed and dominance-biased measurement. An exemplified comparative between holistic and siloed measurements is given in the next section along with a practical demonstration of how Actionables and Aggregators are created and used in the reimagining of the delivery and implementation of a specific agenda, namely the NUA, in the so called *intelligenter* Actionable Future Living

3. INNOVATION: CREATION OF ACTIONABLES AND AGGREGATORS TO IMPROVE UPTAKE AND IMPLEMENTATION OF AGENDAS AND PROGRAMMES. THE REENGINEERED DELIVERY OF THE UN-HABITAT NEW URBAN AGENDA (NUA) AS USE CASE

This new system of metrics, the Actionables and Aggregators, emerged from the need to find a way to measure the performance of the proposed and pioneer bottom-up delivery of agendas and programmes which, in turn, will help their uptake and implementation through the active involvement of the end-user the citizen. Moreover, as shown, these novel metrics carry additional innovations and benefits to systems measurement. The first innovation brought by the Actionables has been already discussed in the previous section but it will be briefly recalled to go beyond what has been already said:

- **Actionables** will measure individual Actions improving the performance of the system
- **Aggregators** are to measure collective Actions.

Taking the delivery of the NUA as an example, Actionables measure individual efforts improving the sustainability of the urban system and Aggregators measure collective executions with the same goal.

The Action-based nature of the Actionables makes them novel overarching metrics uniquely able to measure overall systems' performance. Indeed, an Action, either individual or collective, involves multiple subsystems operating seamlessly (e.g.: an individual who reports regular recycling Actions; in this example, the Action of recycling involves many subsystems, primarily waste, but also energy, might include mobility as well, built domain, etc. The overall Action of recycling has an impact in these secondary subsystems and therefore its measurement cannot occur at primary subsystems level only).

One advantage of the uniquely holistic nature of Actionables is that identical individual Actionables can be combined and produce an Aggregator for a given Action, as if a collective -and not the sum of individuals- would have been doing the Action (e.g.: the sum of individuals reporting equal recycling actions can be grouped in an Aggregator and therefore generate a collective Action). With this, the uniqueness of Actionables has been now defined and its novelty described. We are now ready to show their *genesis et modus operandi* using the NUA as a use case and how Actionables and Aggregators will transform it into an *intelligenter* Actionable Future Living.

The New Urban Agenda (NUA) is UN's Habitat roadmap towards global urban sustainability. To create Actionables for the NUA, we first need to <identify the system> for which we want to improve performance. In the NUA, this will be the <urban system>. Next, we will establish what <needs to be improved> that for the NUA will be <sustainability>. Last in this identification round, we have to determine what <defines performance> in the system being studied, which will be what we will be measuring. The NUA defines urban sustainability performance as achievements in 'sustaining' the social, economic and environmental pillars of sustainability, thus the performance will be this <three-folded sustainability>, which is what we will be measuring and for what we have to create Actionables.

The overall goal of improving urban sustainability could be thus summarised as *not leaving anyone (Social), anything (Environmental) and in anyway (Economic) 'unsustained'*. Starting with Social Sustainability, it aims at *not leaving anyone 'unsustained'*. This will be possible through inclusive and integrative Actions across all segments of society to help close today's phenomena of Social Divide. Indeed, 'closing the Social Divide' is much of a challenge and its tackling should begin by having 'everyone connected'. Certainly, good connectivity, from transportation to telecommunications, is essential to achieve inclusive and integrative societies.

Regarding Environmental Sustainability, its performance lies on *not leaving anything 'unsustained'*. And this includes built and not built domains in both rural and urban areas since all these conform the global environment. Improvements in Environmental Sustainability will occur through Actions minimising the use of natural resources and emissions. Urbanisation excesses, especially low-density settlements causing sprawl, carry an intense use of natural resources and emissions. However, a compact city does not necessarily mean positive environmental performance. In recent years, we have seen massive high-density urbanisation across the globe due to rural and economic migration. These metropolises -or even megalopolises-, generate huge environmental imbalances as the loss of rural population and the abandoning of the fields collapses the agricultural sector and landscape. Thus, to address 'urbanisation excesses' it is important to prioritise urban renewal Actions instead of new development areas using brown fields.

Moreover, and now linking with Economic Sustainability, urban renewal actions should aim for more and include the green element by means of urban agricultural production within to promote local self-sufficiency, thus becoming what we call 'ruralised urban renewal' interventions. Lastly, Economic Sustainability, which has strong connections with the previous two sustainabilities. Actually, all three sustainabilities are intertwined and indissociable, as shown in Figure 5, since they all conform the urban system. Economic Sustainability will aim at *not leaving any way 'unsustained'*. Today's economy has gone digital and this has created an unprecedented 'middleman crises' due to job losses caused by the automation of many middle and handling positions in the service sector. The 'middleman crises' adds to the already existing chronic unemployment derived from the disappearance of obsolete professions. Economic Sustainability can only be achieved with no-unemployment and, to achieve this, the tackling of Social and Environmental sustainabilties offers great economic opportunities.

Fig. 5. Conceptual model of the intelligenter Actionable Future Living

We have just defined the problems and possible solutions in the three areas of sustainability. However, in the *intelligenter* approach we prefer to use the word 'challenge' instead of 'problem', since it is more inspiring; and 'target' instead of 'solution', as it is more realistic. Thus, after defining challenges and targets, performance measurement can be created since we now know what needs to be measured.

Starting with the Social Sustainability challenge, 'closing the Social Divide'; and its target, 'having everyone connected'; the assessment of its performance results in the measurement of **'connectivity'**, both physical and virtual. Complex systems (or non-isolated systems, like the urban system) tend to maximise entropy as they always seek equilibrium. To achieve that, different parts of the system need to enter into contact and therefore be connected. And this is for both kinds of entropy, Thermodynamics (physical systems) and Informational (virtual or digital systems). Therefore, Connectivity applies to both physical and virtual systems but it has a different manifestation. Whereas in physical systems Connectivity will be achieved through mobility Actions, in digital systems it will be through telecommunication Actions.

The earliest distinction between tangible and intangible elements in physical mobility is made in the early nineteenth century when Henry Drury Harness, a surveyor of the British Army in Ireland, compared his 1837 mapping of the traffic between Dublin and the countryside with John Carey's 1792 survey of high roads. As a result of this comparison, Drury established the first distinction between physical "flows" and "networks". We can say then that John Carey draw the earliest known map of a network, properly distinguishing between different types of connections (intersections and links) and Henry Drury Harness draw the first ever representation of flows.

The early nineteenth century is also when virtual mobility was born, with the naissance of the telegraphy, the first telecommunication system. Sir Charles Wheatstone and Sir William Fothergill Cooke invented the electric telegraph in 1837 and since then virtual networks and flows have been represented like in physical mobility.

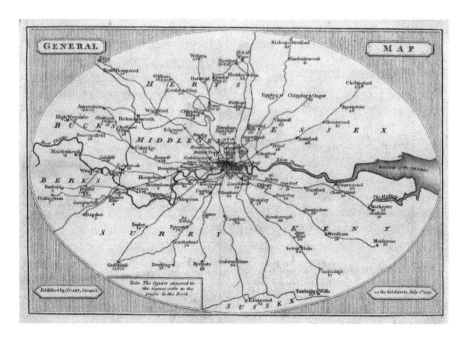

Fig. 6.1. The network map of Cary's Survey of the High Roads (London) 1792. (Source: http://mapco.net/london.htm)

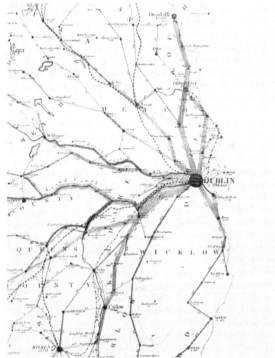

Fig. 6. 2. Ireland's flow map in 1873 from Henry Drury Harness, a surveyor of the British army (Source: http://urbandemographics.blogspot.com.es/2012/07/flow-maps.html)

In the early sixties Constantinos Doxiadis, together with a group of architects and telecommunication engineers including Buckminster Fuller (1963) and Marshall McLuhan (1962), created the Ekistics movement (Doxiadis, 1968) to study and anticipate the effects of what they foresaw as the excessive growth of urban settlements, facilitated by what they called "connectivity fever". Thus, the Ekistics were the first to merge physical and virtual Connectivity and its representation in networks and flows. The Ekistics movement was continued by the Metabolists (Renzo Tange, Arata Isozaki, Kisho Kurokawa are the well-known ones), the Cybernetics (Cedric Prize, Iona Friedman, the Archigram group, among others), and the Webbists (mainly Khan and Tyng, Jackson Pollock, and Andre Waterkeyn) (Friedman, 1971, 1978). The architectural expressions of these groups were physical representations of virtual networks and flows. The Ekistics legacy has been carried forward and even reached us. The current combined expression of virtual and physical Connectivity is the so-called Internet of Spaces (IoS) where architecture automatically adapts to connectivity results (i.e. moving walls able to automatically adjust room dimension to adapt to people connected to a given event who said will be attending). In all cases,

from Ekistics to IoS, the representation of this combined physical and virtual Connectivity responds to flow connections per network capacity:

$$\text{Connectivity} = \frac{\textbf{Flow Connections}}{\textbf{Network Capacity}}$$

We will use this equation to measure citizens' Social Sustainability Actions performance. Social Sustainability pursuits having 'everyone connected', it thus promotes Connectivity Actions. According to the above formulae, we will measure these Connectivity Actions as the 'number or social flow connections established within the capacity of the network'. An example of Connectivity Action would be a retired person who signs up to an online social platform, but also an unemployed person who walks every day to the employment office to take back-to-market classes. In these two examples 'flow connections' will be '1' as there is just one person in the flow whereas network capacity will vary: in the example of the on-line social platform, let's assume it has a capacity of 1000 users, then Connectivity=1/1000=0.001. In the example of employment courses, we will fix a capacity of 20 students, being Connectivity=1/20=0.05.

The results obtained are both Actionables. Aggregators will be obtained when individual actions can be added or a collective action is actioned (e.g: from the overall sing ups in the online platform, an Aggregator could be extracted aggregating retired people within sign-ups. In the second example, an Aggregator could be obtained from the Action of closing a company and signing up the whole group of employees made redundant to employment classes as unemployment benefit. The Aggregator would represent this group within the overall capacity of the course). Accountability of flows can help control the number of necessary networks. Excessive flow can collapse the network. Therefore, flows and networks should be designed in parallel, not only for optimisation and efficiency purposes, but also for the safety and resilience of the system.

In Environmental Sustainability, we want to tackle 'urbanisation excesses' through 'ruralised urban renewal' Actions. Complex systems (non-isolated systems) spontaneously maximise their thermodynamic entropy by combining parts of the system in opposed condition. The system enters in energetic equilibrium when the dynamics of its masses can be balanced. Therefore, a complex system cannot have its masses in the extremes (i.e. absolute compact or only empty) Informational entropy does not intervene in balancing of the dynamics of masses thus, energetic equilibrium is a pure thermodynamic process. Accordingly, the key factor to control in the Environmental Sustainability will be the amount of urbanisation which cannot be zero or totally compact since urbanisation is happening in a complex system. Hence, what we want to measure is **'compactness'**.

Ildefons Cerdà is considered the father of the compact city. In his Theory of City Construction (1859) he presents a method on how to build a compact city and himself executes an implementation in Barcelona (the so called "Eixample"). He also creates the first indicators and standards for urban planning. To highlight, his "density allowance" indicator, today renamed as "constructability", which is the total surface (m2) per unit of surface (m2). Constructability (C) informs about the number of storeys per m2. For instance, C=1 means one level allowed, C=2 means two levels allowed and so on. But C=0,5 means that only half of the construction site can be built at one level high or equivalents (e.g. building one quarter of the construction site built at two levels). Low density settlements usually have a C range between 0,5 and 0,25. C values between 1 and 2 are considered optimal for compact city fabrics since they allow for moderate building heights in good proportion with public unbuilt spaces.

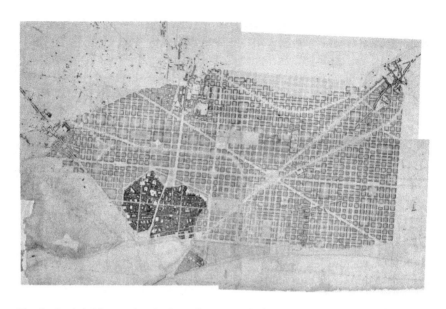

Fig. 7: Cerda's Master plan for Barcelona, note the huge extension (L'Eixample) outside the old city, quite similar to what the city size is today. Also to highlight Cerda's solution for intersections: an example of his good control of the proportions between empty and built space (Source: http://www.anycerda.org/web/)

The debate on the right balance between built and open spaces was initiated by Le Corbusier in the context of the International Congresses of Modern Architecture (Congrès Internationaux d'Architecture Moderne, CIAM), a series of conferences between 1928 and 1959 with the objective of spreading Modern Movement ideas around the world (Le Corbusier, 1973). CIAMs dealt with all topics relevant to the modern city, basically: city expansion, functionalism, minimal habitation unit and its proportion regarding unbuilt space. CIAM II (1929) and CIAM III (1930) dealt with these proportion issues in the context of new development areas and the precursors of these debates were Le Corbusier and Walter Gropius. Was only in later CIAMs, namely CIAM IV (1937) and CIAM VIII (1951) when the debate on the balance between the built and the unbuilt opened up in the context of city renewal, mainly due to the need for reconstructing cities affected by World Wars.

The debate on city renewal continues today and it is still the preferred formula before city expansion using new development sites as it is more environmentally friendly (no brownfield land consumption, possibility to reuse existing buildings and materials, preservation and expansion of existing green spaces, etc.) However, in too many occasions -specially for low-density settlements- we see how brown fields are preferred and used in first instance. This heavily contributes to the urbanisation excesses we suffer today. Although CIAM efforts between 1937 and 1951 to promote the

190

compact city formula, yet we will have to wait until the seventies for the concept of "compactness" to appear.

As we will see next, Compactness 'humanises' Constructability. Moreover, Compactness informs about the proportion between occupied and free spaces. Ramon Margalef is considered the father of Urban Ecology as he established a series of unifying principles in ecology (Margalef, 1963) by developing mathematical models to study populations of species in different environments. In general terms, urban ecology (ecology applied to urban systems), is a discipline that encourages an intensive, efficient and collaborative use of the urban domain, emulating the use species make of their natural environments. Therefore, the basic principles of urban ecology are the promotion of density and diversity. In other words, urban ecology advocates for the right balance between occupied and empty spaces as well as good mixture of activities and population. However, as we will see next, density has a stronger influence in Compactness whereas diversity has higher effect in Complexity.

Margalef established the definition of (ecological) Compactness as the number of species in a given habitat:

$$\text{Compactness} = \frac{\text{population of species}}{\text{unit of habitat}}$$

Compactness, in the urban domain, should not be confused with Constructability. Compactness applied to the urban context should be defined as inhabitants per city unit -such as district or neighbourhood-, whereas Constructability is an indicator of built surface, hence the statement earlier of Compactness as the metrics 'humanising' Constructability. Moreover, Compactness implicitly informs about the balance between built and non-built spaces while, in Constructability, this is unknown and therefore uncontrolled. Hence, Compactness is a more systemic and holistic metric.

As mentioned earlier, the purpose of Environmental Sustainability is to tackle urbanisation excesses through ruralisation of urban renewal. In this sense, Compactness Actions will be individual (Actionables) or collective (Aggregators) urban interventions promoting green-friendly urban regeneration. Moreover, and linking with Economic Sustainability, green-friendly-productive Actions (such as kitchen gardens, orchards, urban farming, etc.) should be encouraged. An example of a Compactness Actionable could be individual Actions of organic recycling to create on-site compost. An example of a Compactness Aggregator could be the collective transformation of a sideway used as an informal parking plot into a kitchen garden.

Lastly, Economic Sustainability, the purpose of which is to 'cut unemployment down to zero' by tackling the 'middleman crisis'. The digital transformation of our society has also transformed economy and thus, jobs. Many processes and workflows have been automated, what caused the disappearance of intermediate posts, hence the so-called 'middleman crises' which adds to traditional and more chronic unemployment rates. Economic Sustainability requires the reimagining of obsolete skills and professions so that societies can enjoy full employment. As mentioned earlier, tackling the previous two sustainabilities offers a great deal of economic opportunities. Let's analyse how Economic Sustainability leverages on the other two sustainabilities to create economic opportunities.

Complex systems are non-isolated systems tending to equilibrium (maximum entropy) although these are continuously disrupted by external factors due to their open nature and continued evolution. Johann Heinrich Von Thünen is considered the father of the understanding of the city as a system. In his treatise, The Isolated State (1875), he developed the first theory of urban spatial economics. Its relevance is because of his comprehensive consideration of the different land uses that would conform a self-sufficient and economically feasible urban system.

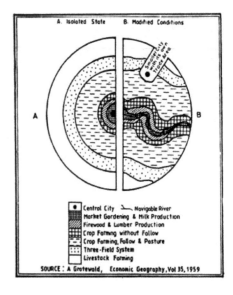

One century later, Walter Christaller developed the theory of Central Places (1933) that evolved Von Thünen's works by adding the concepts of "hierarchy" and "size" into the different subsystems classes (former "land uses" in Thünen's theories). He also proved the presence of "subcentres" in urban subsystems and the existence of a major "centre" for the overall urban system. Shannon's Information Theory (1949), to which we have referred earlier when discussing informational entropy, will be the definitive contribution to arrive to a complete definition of urban complex systems as they are understood today. In Shannon's Information entropy formula:

$$H = \sum_{i=1}^{n} p_i \log_2 p_i$$

H (Informational entropy) is a direct measure of diversity and an indirect measure of the organization of the system, where Pi is the probability of occurrence that members of a community with a certain profile interact with members of the same community with a different profile. It is therefore a measure that needs to know the number of portrayers of information with capacity for contact, in quantity and variety, in a given space. Its unit is "information bits".

A decade later, the architect Christopher Alexander in his book A Pattern Language (1977) combined Christaller's and Shannon's previous findings and created a planning-architectural system based on mathematics to unfold urban **'complexity'**. He also considered Berry's and Garrison's (1972) latest developments on central places theories. According to Alexander's theories, cities are sets of overlapping subsystems whose diversity can be modelled in lattices (a sort of mathematical decision tree). Thus, Alexander's efforts to model Complexity lie on the premise that it is possible to create a pattern in which all features and possible land uses mixings and combinations can be allocated. More recently, he made some advances to his seminal book in The Nature of Order: An Essay on the Art of Building and the Nature of the Universe (2003), which is a more dynamic interpretation of the older A Pattern Language. According to his predecessor, Shannon, Complexity would lie on the probability that portrayers of diverse information encounter and exchange. What Alexander adds to this is the modelling of the urban support where those encounters occur and, for that he uses Christaller's centrality principles.

In the compact city, there is a higher probability of information exchange since there is more variety of profiles and backgrounds; plus higher centrality, which brings mixture of uses. Indeed, the compact city is naturally multifunctional, offering a mixture of uses such as residential, retail, services, manufacturing, etc. On the other hand, in the low-density or sprawled city, the probability of exchange of information is much lower, and this is for various reasons. First, there is less population density; second, profiles are highly stereotyped which means similar backgrounds; and third, it is clearly monofunctional, with the sole use of residential. The reimagining of obsolete professions and skills will find a better environment In the compact city than in the sprawled city since it can leverage on the diversity that higher densities and mixed societies can offer. Thus,

Complexity Actions improving Economical Sustainability have to be calculated accounting   the number of jobs created out of the opportunities identified:

$$\text{Complexity} = \frac{\text{Jobs created}}{\text{Opportunities identified}}$$

For instance, if an opportunity has been identified in the Environmental pillar of sustainability (e.g.: the farming of the newly created kitchen garden mentioned earlier) and, let's say, it reintroduces into the jobs market three unemployed, then the Complexity of this Action will be equal to "3" (three jobs created/one opportunity).

4.   METHOD AND RESULTS: OUTCOMES OF THE *INTELLIGENTER* DELIVERY OF THE UN-HABITAT NEW URBAN AGENDA (NUA) AS ACTIONABLE FUTURE LIVING

The new metrics proposed, Actionables and Aggregators, are a big step forward for the *intelligenter* approach itself as the original four steps of the Intelligenter Method (Marsal & Segal 2016a, 2016b; Marsal & Wood-Hill 2016) are embedded in the new metrics. In previous implementations of the Intelligenter Method, the four steps were used to formulate the so-called *collaboratories,* an inter-system and multi-stakeholder collaboration environment (which included the monitoring of the performance of the cross-sector pluri-stakeholders' collaboration through indicators and indices), and were the following steps:

1. Identification of relationships between subsystems involved

2. Discovery of multi-system and multi-stakeholder collaboration
3. Definition of static and dynamic monitoring
4. Integrated monitoring and control

Steps 3 and 4 of the Method required the creation of qualitative and quantitative indicators and indices for monitoring purposes. The new metrics developed are a step forward since they are able to measure both quantitative outcomes and qualitative outputs in a combined manner, being thus a more complete form of measurement. Moreover, besides this innovation in measurement, the bottom-up nature of Actionables and Aggregators implicitly has both inter-subsystem and multi-stakeholder collaboration, absorbing Steps 1 and 2 too. Hence, the non-application of the former Intelligenter four-Step Method in this particular implementation for the reimagining of the delivery of agendas and programmes. It is yet to be seen if future implementations of the Intelligenter Method can be executed through Actionables and Aggregators or they will still need the four original steps. Further research is needed to answer that questions and this will be author's future work.

The *intelligenter* approach executed as Actionables and Aggregators for the reimagining of the delivery of agendas and programmes has indeed succeeded in improving the implementation and uptake of the use case proposed, the New Urban Agenda (NUA), reborn as *intelligenter* Actionable Future Living. The Actionable Future Living allows for bottom-up uptake through Actions and discovers a novel role-based implementation the performance of which is measured with a new form of metrics, the Actionables. The bottom-up approach brought by Actionable Future Living's new metrics is actually a new form of governance since the policies proposed by the NUA are now owned and governed by citizens. This has an empowering effect in society as the challenges tacked by policy instruments -such as the NUA-, are now passed to the society by giving them an active role. This specifically contributes to Actionable Future Living's Social challenge of closing the Social Divide. Segments of the population that were chronically out of the society are now brought back in thanks to Actionable Future Living's motivational and inspirational citizenship roles that they will be assigned with. This will result in a more inclusive and participated society globally secured through societal consensus, with antagonist societal forces clearly reduced.

Fig. 9. UN Habitat schemas summarising the main principles of the New Urban Agenda

This role-based nature of *intelligenter's* Actionables and Aggregators is technology-based, what will help the creation of new e-jobs and the development of ICT skills in segments of the population not yet participating in the digital transformation of cities. Of course, analogic participation will still be possible in the Actionable Future Living but we expect new digital users joining, seeking access to employment opportunities brought by these achievements in Economic Sustainability. In the Actionable Future Living, citizens will be reporting their sustainability Actions into a Dashboard (similar to a Mayor's Dashboard but bottom up, and imputed solely by citizens) that will be showing in real time the delivery of the NUA. In author's opinion, these 'bottom-up dashboards' can become the next social media revolution as they will allow for pairing up and teaming up participants like virtual agents acting as advisory peers in the delivery of their citizenship roles. We can therefore summarise what we could call the Actionable Future Living Dashboard as the informational representation of the performance of a new form of governance emerged from the bottom-up implementation of public policies actioned by citizenship roles.

Lastly, achievements in both Economic and Social sustainabilites will introduce a new form of urban ethics since these economic and social developments will result from a more responsible attitude towards the environment and a return to the basics. Indeed, employment and social inclusion will inspire self-sufficiency spirits to individuals, something that will wake up the desire and need for being more connected to the essentials and more physiological elements of liveability, namely, food, nature and rest: a sort of inverted or top-down implementation of Maslow's pyramid of needs in which self-actualisation will be achieved first and will unfold down to the biological covering of bodily needs. Perhaps, thus, the intelligent response to a more sustainable Future Living starts by Actioning an inverse hierarchy of needs.

REFERENCES

Alexander, C., Ishikawa, S., Sliverstein, M., et al. (1977) A Pattern Language: Towns, Buildings, Construction. Oxford University Press. New York.

Alexander, C. (2003). The Nature of Order: An Essay of the Art of Building and the Nature of the Universe. Book 1: Phenomenon of Life. Center for Environmental Structure, United States

Banner, DK., Cooke, RA. (1984) Ethical dilemmas in performance appraisal. Journal of Business Ethics, 3, 327-333

Batty, M. (1990). Intelligent Cities-Using Information Networks to gain competitive advantage. Environment and Planning B-Planning&Design, 17(3), 247-256

Bessire, D., Baker, CR. (2005) The French Tableu de Bord and the American Balanced Scorecard: a critical analysis. Critical Perspectives on Accounting 16, 645-664

Berry, BJL., Garrison, WL (1972) Recent developments of Central Place Theory, in Zentralitätsforschung. Wissenchaftliche Buchgesellschaft. Dramsstadt

Campbell, T. (2013). Beyond Smart Cities - How Cities Network, Learn and Innovate. International Journal of Sustainability in Higher Education, 14(1), 105

Campbell, T. (2012). Beyond Smart Cities - How Cities Network, Learn and Innovate. Earthscan, Taylor and Francis, London-New York

Caragliu, A., C. Del Bo and P. Nijkamp (2011). Smart Cities in Europe. Urban Studies, 14(2), 65-82

Castells, M. (1989). The Informational city: Information Technology, Economic, Restructuring and the Urban-Regional Process, Basil Blackwell, Oxford

Cerdà, I. (1859) Teoria General de la Urbanización. On-line resource in: http://www.anycerda.org/web/es/arxiu-cerda/fitxa/teoria-general-de-la-urbanizacion/115 (last accessed 20/01/2017)

Christaller, W. (1933) Die Zentalen Orte in Suddestduschland, G. Fischer Jenna. Berlin (translated into English in 1966 Central Places in Southern Germany. Englewood Clifs, New Jersey)

Coens, T., Jenkins, M. (2000). Abolishing Performance Appraisals: Why they backfire and what to do instead. Berrett-Koehler Publishers, San Francisco, California.

Dainty, P., Anderson, M. (2008). The MDA companion. Melbourne Business School, Palgrave Macmillan, New York

Doxiadis, CA. (1968) Ekistics: an introduction to the Science of Urban Settlements. Oxford University Press. New York

Drucker, P. (1946). Concept of Corporation. John Day Company, Transaction Publishers, New Jersey

Gibson, DV., G. Kozmetsky and RW. Smilor (1992). The Technopolis Phenomenon: Smart Cities, Fast Systems, Global Networks, Rowman & Littlefield, Boston

Greenfield, A. (2013). Against the Smart City. A pamphlet by Adam Greenfield. Part I of the city is here for you to use, E-book, Do projects, New York

Friedman, I. (1971) Pour une Arquitecture Scientifique. Pierre Belfont. Paris.

Frideman, I. (1978) La arquitectura movil. Poseidón. Barcelona

Fuller, RB. (1963) Nine chains to the moon. Southern Illinois University Press. Carbondale and Edwardsville-Feffer and Simons, Inc. London and Amsterdam.

Lebas, MJ. (1995). Performance measurement and performance management. International Journal of Production Economics, 41 (1-3), 23-25

Le Corbusier (1973). The Athens Charter. Grossman Publishers. New York.

Margalef, R. (1963). On Certain Unifying Principles in Ecology. The American Naturalist, 97 (897), 357-374

Marsal-Llacuna, ML., Boada-Oliveras, I. (2013), 3D-VUPID. 3D-Visual Urban Planning Integrated Data, Lecture Notes in Computer Science 7974, 17-32

Marsal-Llacuna, ML., Colomer-Llinàs, J., Melendez-Frigola, J. (2014), Lessons in Urban Monitoring taken from Sustainable and Liveable Cities to better address the Smart Cities Initiative: the Need for Intelligent Indexes. Technological Forecasting and Social Change, 90, 611-622

Marsal-Llacuna, ML., Segal E, M. (2016a). The Intelligenter Method (I) for making "smarter" city projects and plans, Cities, 55, 127-138

Marsal-Llacuna, ML., Segal E, M. (2016b). The Intelligenter Method (II) for "smarter" urban policy-making and regulation drafting, Cities 61, 83-95

Marsal-Llacuna, ML., Wood-Hill, M. (2016) The Intelligenter method (III) for "smarter" standards development and standardisation instruments. In press in: Computer, Standards and Interfaces (on-line first)

Maslow, A. H. (1943) A Theory of Human Motivation. Psychological Review, 50, 370-396

McLuhan, M. (1962). The Gutenberg Galaxy. University of Toronto Press.

Mitchell, W. (2002). Electronic Cottages, Wired Neighborhoods and Smart Cities, in Szold, T.,   Carbonell, A. (Ed.) Smart Growth: Form and Consequences. Lincoln Institute of Land Policy, Cambridge, 69-83

Neirotti, P., A. De Marco and AC. Cagliano (2014). Current trends in Smart City initiatives: Some stylised facts. Cities 38, 25-36

Pask, R. (1968) Cybernetic Serendipity: the computer and the arts. Studio International- Journal of Modern Art (special issue), 3-107

Reichardt, J. (1968) Cybernetic Serendipity. Studio International-Journal of Modern Art, 176 (905), 176-177

Shannon, CE., Weaver, W. (1949) The Mathematical Theory of Communication. The University of Illinois Press-Urbana

Shapiro, JM. (2006) Smart cities: Quality of life, productivity, and the growth effects of human capital. Review of Economics and Statistics, 88(2), 324-335

Von Thürnen, JH (1875) Der Isolirte Stadt. Berlag Von Biegaudt. Berlin (reprinted by BiblioLife)

Wiese, DS., Buckley, MR. (1998). The evolution of the performance appraisal process. Journal of Management History, 4(3), 233-249

Weiner, N. (1948) Cybernetics or Control and Communication in the Animal and the Machine. The Technology Press. John Wiley & Sons, Inc., New York-Hermann et Cie, Paris

Weiner, N. (1961) An Approach to Cybernetics. Hutchinson of London. London.

Winters, JV. (2011). Why are smart cities growing? Who moves and who stays. Journal of Regional Science, 51(2), 253-270

Weiser, M. (1991). The Computer for the Twenty-First Century. Scientific American, September 1991, 94-100

Wilson, A. (2014). Quantifying Roman economic performance by means of proxies: pitfalls and potentials. Pragmateai 27, 147-167

199

CHAPTER 9

SORG ALGORITHM
(SUSTAINABLE ORGANISATION ALGORITHM)
HOW DOES IT GIVE US INSIGHT INTO BECOMING
A SMART CITY?

Miguel Reynolds

Abstract   The Sustainable Organisation algorithm, SORG, offers an easy and simple way for anyone to check the sustainability of any endeavour, even at the genesis stage.

The sustainable organization is based on four pillars of: cooperation, recognition, meritocracy and fair rewards, and the SORG Index.

Imagine that every structure and space idealised in the city, is analysed using a SORG perspective to study its real contribution to the whole sustainability of the city as a community. Although ROI is already considered in most investment decisions, SORG will offer a deeper understanding of the whole and total outcome of any project. The city will be envisioned as a facilitator of human collaboration and interaction towards sustainability, social peace and happiness.

By integrating the SORG analysis in the core architecture of smart cities and its organizational components, we might expect a significant aggregate result by having cities designed with happiness and sustainability as their main criteria.

1. INTRODUCTION

Organisations are the realisation of human collaboration efforts. It might be just a two or a two million person organisation. It can be a family, a football club, a government or a church. Either way, it's just a set of rules bringing the power of collaboration to reach what one human being can't reach alone. The way people organise themselves is highly conditioned and empowered by the way cities are organised. This is not news, but the reality is that in the last two centuries much of the effort that has been dedicated to urban development has cantered on efficiency or aesthetics as the main criteria for organising cities, frequently forgetting the human essence in collaboration. Consequently, we create cities that instill isolation, competition and loneliness instead of an environment that integrates people, nature and facilities promoting social and intellectual development as a whole for families. One of the many reasons that might be at the heart of this evolution, is the fact the sustainability is seldom considered as a central and holistic criteria to empower happiness and healthy collaboration between current and future generations...this regressive mind-set must change!

For this change to occur, we first need to demystify sustainability, and turn it into a central belief understood by anyone. We can then start to identify cities as just another instrument to allow us to live in harmony, enjoy this life on earth as much as we possibly can and always ensure that the next generations have the same opportunities.

SORG - the sustainable organisation algorithm is a first attempt in that direction offering an easy and simple way for anyone to check the sustainability of any endeavour, even at the genesis stage.

SORG offers a new perspective over, the common and widely accepted financial instrument, of Profit and Loss (P&L). SORG analyses the economic flows between the three main groups of people found in any type of organization: the TEAM that works in the organisation, the OWNERS and the COMMUNITY that benefit from the work of the organisation. It focuses on real assets and non-speculative information. Hence it offers a reliable unambiguous and transparent perspective of the organisation's real impact over time. It bases its analysis on a balanced distribution of the economic flows among the team, owners and the community, while considering that any sustainable relationship is always structured on a balance of the rewards perceived by all members.

Imagine designing cities to place emphasis on structures that celebrate the human experience, over structures that are solely dedicated to corporations and companies. These cities would integrate the human experience of daily life into the fabric of the city. Such designs would incorporate sustainable materials while minimising the use of unsustainable ones. Such cities would keep the experience of daily life by the members of society, at foremost importance. Imagine cities wherein the welfare of the person is taken into consideration during the design stage, placing it at a higher priority than the welfare of companies. If we are able to keep in mind that an organisation — a sustainable organisation — is a term not only handed to corporations, but also to families, classrooms and neighborhoods, then we would be elevating the importance of these, which can have a positive impact upon the steps that we consider when designing our modern day cities.

Now, imagine that every structure, every space in the design of the city, is analysed using a SORG perspective to study its real contribution to the whole sustainability of the city as a community to engage and empower people in collaboration, towards development. Although ROI (Return on Investment) is already considered in most investment decisions, SORG will offer a deeper understanding of the whole and total outcome of any project. The city will be envisioned as a facilitator of human collaboration and interaction thereby enabling sustainability, social peace and happiness

In nature, sustainability is achieved by balance and equilibrium of complex and interconnected systems, the same happens in organizations. Our hope is that by this simple and transparent approach, we can engage the general public in understanding the relevance of sustainability. This understanding is both at an individual and societal level, thus creating a sensibility to the need for a fairer model for our development where trust and transparency become the pillars to share intelligence critical to our future as a species.

By integrating the SORG analysis at the core architecture of smart cities and its organizational components, we might expect an aggregate result by having cities designed with happiness and sustainability as their main criteria.

2.   THE SORG INDEX

2.1 Measuring Sustainability

Over the last century, despite all changes, the measurement system and the focus of organisations have remained highly concentrated on profits and shareholder value. This has highly influenced people's perspective of value, since the way that any organisation performs using these measurements defines the very results that may be expected. The same happens in a city's architecture where the focus was not the empowerment of sustainable organisations.

We need to change this paradigm to use a new measurement that we can all understand and compare the real impact any organisation has in our lives and in the lives of generations to come - a simple, transparent and speculation free index that will rank organisations according to their real impact on our society.

That is the meaning of the SORG index where using data publicly available from organisations anyone can simply analyse and evaluate how sustainable an organisation is. Sustainability is the most important criteria to evaluate an organisation's performance since it measures impact over time. It is a trans-generational criteria that considers all costs and benefits of the organisation's activity. Taking into account SORG as criteria, when designing smart cities, will provide a dynamic system relating urbanism with its impact in instilling sustainable organisations.

Considering that in a sustainable organisation there is a balance among the economic benefits of the organisation's owners, its employees (the Team) and the community it serves the SORG index measures the internal harmony of the organisation and its impact in society. It allows a transparent comparison of any organisation, regardless of its size, location or purpose.

This vision can be described by the following formula to assess how balanced the organisation is, both at an internal and an external level:

$$SORG = \frac{C^2 \times M^2}{O^2 \times A \times E}$$

Where:
C = is the economic benefit of the community as a result of the organisation activity
O = is the economic benefit of the owners of the organisation
M = is median salary of the employees of the organisation
A = is the average salary of the employees of the organisation
E = the highest salary in the organisation

Through the use of the SORG, we believe that anyone – inside or outside an organisation – can easily and freely understand the real outcome and usefulness of any given organisation, regardless of its size, location and purpose, anywhere at any point in time. This is still unique today! In fact, in a Sustainable Organisation, the SORG offers a much wider and comprehensive perspective of organisational value when compared to market capitalisation, as it focuses solely on sustainability.

2.2 Explaining THE SORG INDEX

Our aim is to create a new sustainability indicator – the Sustainable Organisation Index (SORG). Like any index, "it is something that helps you understand where you are, which way you are going and how far you are from where you want to be", Sustainable Measures explains.[xxxiv] Furthermore, it becomes increasingly important as it helps any organisation receive an alert to a problem before it gets too bad and obviously, it helps the organisation progress through a better-positioned indicator.

In the case of a sustainable economy, an indicator would focus on areas where there are weak links between the economy, the environment and the society. In the case of organisations, we will focus on the link between the owners of the company, the people working for the company (employees, or the team) and the people affected by the company (the community).

In our hypothesis, an organisation is just a group of people, gathered around a common purpose, to serve the community. It is sustainable if there is a balanced distribution of economic flow among the owners, the team (employees) and the community. The direct value of the organisation's activity is measured by its revenue and the positive or negative impact it may generate over time - after all, it represents the value the community assigns to the organisation's product(s) or service(s).

Our main challenge is to compare organisations transparently regardless of their size, industry and purpose, using only data available to the public. This is the purpose of the SORG. In the cases presented, what we want to show is not a definite solution, but rather a possible approach using the limited information available. Our challenge has been to make sense of this limited information and our hope is that this will show how further transparency could bring significant results by making this information fully available to everyone.

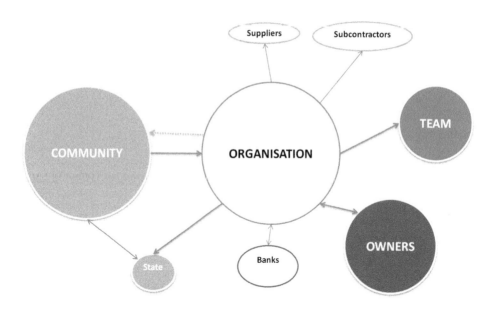

Fig.3 – The Organisation relationship model

The diagram above illustrates the economic flows between the organisation and the internal and external groups that affect it: revenues, salaries, interests, costs, taxes and dividends (blue lines). In the case of non-profit organisations with no revenues, the flow comes from the organisation to the community in the form of donations or voluntary work (green line).

In our hypothesis, we assume that organisations can only be sustainable if there is a balance between COMMUNITY, TEAM and OWNERS.

So in a sustainable organisation C+T≥ O and C≥T. Additionally, as we mentioned in the previous chapter, in a sustainable organisation, the distribution of all salaries should follow a bell-shaped normal curve and the highest-to-median salary ratio should be lower[xxxv] than 12 to guarantee harmony among all members.

COMMUNITY, TEAM and OWNERS are defined   in the following way:

(NB: all the data is taken from financial reports available online):

COMMUNITY = revenues - cogs - interest + taxes + impact

Revenues (r) represent the value recognised by the community impacted by the organisation's activity. COGS is the cost of goods sold (suppliers and subcontractors). We deduct the cogs and interest (banks) because that flow goes to external organisations to the one under analysis. Taxes are added since taxes are flows that theoretically return to the community.

Impact (I) is the positive or negative consequence of the organisation's activity over time. It's an important indicator associated with each industry, activity. Impact should be a factor determined as a function of revenues. In a form:

$$I(r) = \sum_{i=1}^{n} Fi \times r$$

Where **"I"** is the Impact, **"r"** are the revenues; **"F"** are the factors for each of the **"n"** criteria affected by the organisation activity. This concept is further developed in the book "The Sustainable Organisation – a paradigm for a fairer society"

As a wrap-up to this chapter, we propose an example of a model considering the environmental, health, security and development criteria to determine the impact of any activity/industry.

TEAM = Team Salary + All Benefits

TEAM represents the sum of employee salaries. It should include any type of equity compensation (benefits).

Owners = Net Income - TEQUITY

TEQUITY is the proportion of net income owned by the team. This is because we consider team ownership in TEAM, so it must be deducted here. Some members of the organisation may have two roles, as TEAM and OWNERS. When this happens we include all the flow in TEAM. However, TEQUITY is not always publicly available.

Now to analyse the distribution of the flow between these three entities, for one fiscal year, we use the following ratios.

$$SORG\ I = \frac{C}{O}$$

The SORGI (Sustainable Organisation Index I) measures the balance between the owners of the organisation in the community. The higher the value, the higher the benefits the community gets. It only applies when net income is positive. In a sustainable organisation SORGI $\geq$ 1

$$SORG\ II = \frac{T \times H}{O}$$

The SORGII (Sustainable Organisation Index II) measures the internal balance of the organisation. The higher the number, the better and it only applies when net income is positive. Harmony measures fairness. It is given by:

$$H = \frac{M^2}{A \times E}$$

M = is median salary of the employees of the organisation
A = is the average salary of the employees of the organisation
E = the highest salary in the organisation

The TEAM MEDIAN and TEAM AVERAGE are the average and median of the salaries and benefits from all people that work in the organisation. The CEO represents the total salary and benefits of the highest salary in the organisation, normally the CEO. The HARMONY index measures internal cohesion. In a sustainable organisation, harmony is always greater than 1. The higher the index, the better.

$$SORG\ III = \frac{C}{T}$$

The SORGIII (Sustainable Organisation Index III) measures the balance between the TEAM of the organisation in the COMMUNITY. The higher the value, the higher the benefits the community gets. In a sustainable organisation, SORGIII$\geq$ 1

To assess how balanced the organisation is, both at an internal and external level, we use the following formula:

$$SORG = \frac{C^2 \times M^2}{O^2 \times A \times E} =$$

$$= \frac{(revenues - cogs - interest + taxes + impact)^2 \times M^2}{(net\ income - TEQUITY)^2 \times A \times E}$$

The SORG (Sustainable Organisation Index) is a product of SORGI, SORGII and the SORGIII Index and indicates a cumulative effect. In a sustainable organisation SORG is $\geq$ 1. In a multi-year analysis, which offers a more precise evaluation of the organisation's activities, each variable should be calculated by the sum of its values for all the fiscal years under analysis.

It is important to note that this can be calculated using only public data but more accurate results could be assured if organisations made salaries publicly available and the IMPACT factor known. Still, even within the limits of current information, it is useful to assess any organisation regardless of its size, industry or purpose.

Overall, the SORG is a valuable tool to acquire a clear image of how the organisation behaves in the society and whether or not it is free from speculation. It is based on factual information publicly available: it is very simple to calculate and it offers a transparent assessment of the sustainability of any organisation.

3. APPLYING THE SORG INDEX

To illustrate the application of SORG I have chosen in 4 completely different types of organisations. By considering the data in the table below, we calculated the SORGI, SORGII, Harmony and SORG indexes for MacDonald's, Boeing, Google and Wikipedia.

Company	Market Cap	Revenue	Employees	Net Income	COst of Goods Sold	Taxes	Interest	Average Salary (USD per year)	Median Salary (USD per year)	CEO x MEDIAN
MacDonald's	89,04	28,11	440.000	5,59	11,19	2,6200	0,52150	20.000	22.000	434,53
Boeing	87,05	86,62	168.400	4,58	73,190	1,6500	0,4610	75.000	79.300	198,00
Wikipedia		44.667	208	12930	19.721			76.846	76.846	1,00
Google	346,3	59,73	55.030	12,21	25,820	2,2800	0,08300	70.000	115.900	1,00

Note: Market Capitalization, Revenue, Net Income, COGS, Tazes and Interest are in Billions, excepting Wikipedia data that is in Thousands

Fig. 4. Company data

All financial data was collected from Wolfram Alpha (2013 filing data), median salaries from PayScale.com Dec 2014, average salaries from Careerbliss.com and Wikipedia data from Wikipedia's financial report 2013. Wikipedia revenue, cogs and net income are in thousands. TEAM was calculated using average salaries x employees. For these examples, we did not find information about TEQUITY, so TEQUITY was considered zero. In these analyses, we did not consider the IMPACT factor, since it is not yet available.

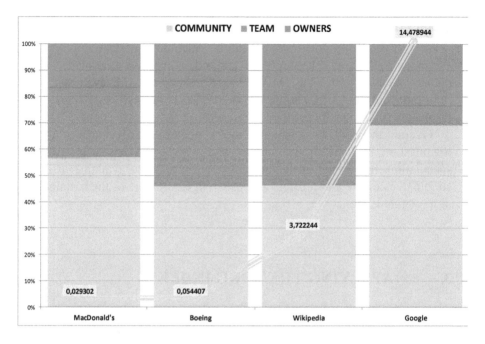

Fig. 5– Applying the SORG

This graph synthesises sustainability of any type of organisation. We overlap graphs of different scales just to offer a simplified analysis.

At first glance — using a colour graph where green represents community, blue represents team and red represents owners – we get the impact of the colours in the background graph. In this case the difference in colours is evident. The colours represent the proportion between COMMUNITY, TEAM and OWNERS. The bigger the green area, the better and the opposite goes for the red area. In a sustainable organisation, considering our hypotheses, BLUE+GREEN ≥ RED. As we can see from this example, MacDonald's clearly does not benefit the community. Boeing and Wikipedia look balanced and Google clearly benefits the community.

Looking at the SORG Index line, we can see that Google's sustainability index is 494 times higher than MacDonald's ... and only 5 times higher than Wikipedia's. The difference in this example is so big that the line had to be skewed to fit both extreme points in the graph.

Now, why are Google and Wikipedia's SORG so high? Because those organisations, besides providing clear benefits to the community and a high leverage owners' effect, they have outstanding internal cohesion. This probably explains our first observation and the results presented by those organisations.

3.1 Going deeper in the analysis: breaking up SORG

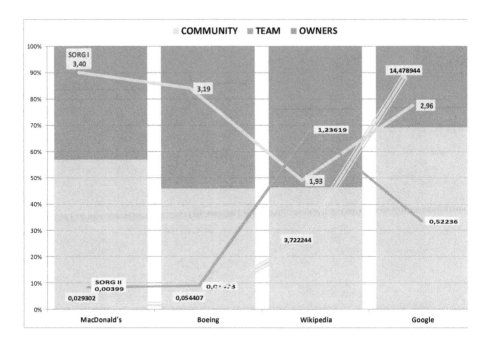

Fig. 6. Breaking up the SORG between the team, the community and the owners

Looking in more detail, we can further explain our first analysis by separating the external and internal impact of the owners' leverage – SORGI and SORGII. Again, each line uses a different scale but we overlap it just to offer a simplified analysis.

We observe the consistency of Wikipedia and Google and even MacDonald's. Boeing's inconsistency is due essentially to the HARMONY factor. That can be explained looking at the CEO-to-median salary ratio (see Company Table on "Applying the SORG"). The harmony and cohesion champion is clearly Wikipedia.

This analysis is thus useful to explain the behaviour of the SORG Index further.

*It is important to note that this data did not consider the impact factor. Empirically, we know that if we had considered the impact factor, the results would be even more emphasised but with the same trend.

3.2 Going deeper in the analysis: looking inside the organisation

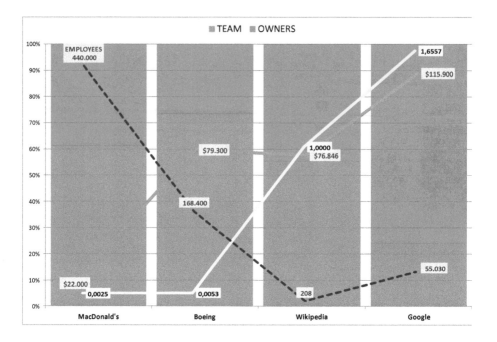

Fig.7. Internal assessment

Here, we can see the Harmony Index that so strongly influenced SORGII. It is easily explained by the distribution of the salaries and the CEO-to-median salary ratio. Besides, we clearly see that, despite having a USD 22,000 median, the TEAM factor in MacDonald's is high because of the organisation's 440,000 employees. This means that the TEAM factor is obviously influenced by the size of the organisation, even if the salaries are low. This makes sense because even when distributing low salaries, the organisation has a big impact in the society.

The "blue" factor in Google, associated with its harmony factor, means that the organisation generates a high income per employee. It is known that an organisation like Google has a strong Employee Ownership and this may be one of the reasons behind such a high proportion directed towards owners.

3.3 Concluding the SORG Analysis

Observing these three graphs, it is easy to understand how the value generated by the organisation is distributed among the COMMUNITY, the TEAM and the OWNERS. In this example, it becomes clear how much the HARMONY factors affects both Boeing and MacDonald's and how unbalanced MacDonald's seems to be. On the other hand, it also becomes evident that Google and Wikipedia are balanced in the way they benefit the COMMUNITY. If the IMPACT factor was known, the trend would be accentuated: more unbalance to MacDonald's and Boeing and more balance to Google and Wikipedia.

This analysis becomes especially interesting if these results are compared with the market capitalisation of these organisations, with the advantage of being immune to speculation. A wider analysis considering 5 or more years of the organisation's activities will provide a more accurate perspective of the organisation's sustainability.

3.4 The IMPACT factor

As noted in the definition of Community, the IMPACT factor is considered strongly relevant. Unfortunately, we did not find a universal and normalised analysis of impact by industry or activity. In our perspective, to truly and transparently analyse the real outcome of an organisation, it is extremely important to measure the result of the organisation's activity over time. Empirically, it is very easy to realise that some activities have a strongly negative impact, as is the case of oil & and gas, armament and fast food, while others can have a very positive leverage, like education, health and environment. So, the purpose of the Impact factor is to determine the net benefit of any activity over time.

As we defined previously, the IMPACT factor can be calculated by:

$$I(r) = \sum_{i=1}^{n} Fi \times r$$

Where I is the Impact, r are the revenues, F are the factors for each of n the criteria affected by the organisation's activity.

Taking the oil & gas industry as an example, the social cost of carbon is widely known and publicly available. According to data by the US government from May 2013 (Interagency Working Group on Social Cost of Carbon), the cost of cleaning 1 ton of CO_2 is USD $221. Therefore, turning these calculations into something easy for everyone to understand, the cost of cleaning one barrel of oil is $95.03. We do not know what price oil is while you are reading this sentence. However, this will probably come as a surprise to you.

As an example to demonstrate the influence of IMPACT, running the SORG index on oil & gas major ExxonMobil and just taking into account the environmental criteria, we can show that the SORG goes from 2.12397 to -16.8853[xxxvi], which shows how deeply the impact factor can affect the sustainability of an organisation, which is obvious because someone will have to pay for the mess…

Company	Cap (bn USD)	Revenue (bn USD)	Employees	Income (bn USD)	Cost of goods sold	Taxes	Interest	Average Salary	Median Salary
ExxonMobil	421,7	436,5	75.000	5,82	284	22,03	0,066	$44.000	$96.900

Company	Impact	SORG
ExxonMobil	-667,90	-16,885

Fig.8. Impact table: Calculation with the impact and without the impact

Unfortunately, the environmental impact is never considered when analysing organisations and so we tend to be misguided by the real value of some organisations. Apparently, they generate a positive outcome when looking at the revenues, but when we go deeper, we see that their activity will negatively impact the environment for generations to come.

It is not fair that our taxes will be, at least partiality, wasted on cleaning or recovering from the mess some industries generate. That has a price but unfortunately, most people ignore it and the transgressors benefit from it.

As you can see, one of the critical points when calculating the impact is to use units that are directly comparable. Revenue is a factor common to any organisation (with the exception of non-profit organisations with no revenue).

The idea is very simple. Imagine that we could calculate the average profit someone would get from a USD $1,000 investment in education. It's not difficult to realise that, empirically, this profit will be several times those $1,000.

Taking another example, we can calculate the impact of an organisation like Médecins Sans Frontières (MSF) considering two main criteria: health – we could look at how much it would cost to treat someone with MSF, a positive impact measured in terms of the number of people treated – and development, because every healthy person will at least have the capability of generating a minimum amount of US dollars per year.

Looking at Walmart, we can analyse a different kind of impact on the community. According to a study undertaken by Americans for Tax Fairness, a coalition of 400 national and state-level progressive groups[xxxvii], published on April 15, 2014, the multinational retail corporation's workers are costing US taxpayers an estimated $6.2 billion in public assistance including food stamps, Medicaid and subsidised housing. The report found that "a single Walmart Supercenter cost taxpayers between $904,542 and $1.75 million per year, or between $3,015 and $5,815 on average for each of 300 workers".

A similar study showed that the American fast food industry outsourced a combined $7 billion in annual labour costs to taxpayers, accounting $1.2 billion of that total to MacDonald's alone.

Impact analysis can also be useful to value non-profit organisations. In the case of Wikipedia, for instance, it is estimated that it could be worth tens of billions of dollars, according to an article on Smithsonian Mag[xxxviii]. The blog and cooperative resource site hosted by the American University InfoJustice (www.infojustice.org), researchers Jonathan Band and Jonathan Gerafi identified a few factors that could help value an organisation like Wikipedia, namely market value, replacement cost and consumer value.

They reached this conclusion by looking at what other sites that get similar traffic are worth, how much people would be willing to pay for Wikipedia and how much would it cost to replace the site[xxxix]. In the end, they concluded it is worth "tens of billions of dollars" with a replacement cost of $6.6 billion dollars. "The millions of hours contributed by volunteer writers and editors leverage this modest budget, funded by donations, into an asset worth tens of billions of dollars that produces hundreds of billions of dollars of consumer benefit", they wrote.

We could use the same rationale to calculate any impact from an activity through four criteria that are essential to human life: environment, health, security and development. Those are all the needs humans can aspire.

INDUSTRY	TYPE OF IMPACT			
	ECOLOGICAL	HEALTH	SECURITY	DEVELOPMENT
OIL ITS EASY TO RELATE BARREL WITH REVENUES	- $96x Barrel THIS IS AN OFFICIAL VALUE	-0,2x Revenues		
JUNK FOOD		- 2x Revenues		
COMPUTERS	-0,5 Revenues			+2 x Revenues
LEARNING				+3 x Revenues
HUMANITARIAN NGO		+500xPeopleHelped		+100xPeopleHelped
ARMAMENT			- FxRevenues	

Fig. 9. Types of impact

These are merely simple ideas. What we aspire to achieve with this concept is to inspire people, especially academics, to go deeper in this analysis and generate a full impact table that shows the real economic impact of any activity humans may develop. Such an impact table would be useful, not only for the purpose of supplementing this SORG analysis, but also as an additional framework to guide investment decisions.

3.5 Conclusion

The SORG is a corollary of the Sustainable Organisation model proposed in our book "The Sustainable Organisation – a paradigm for a fairer society" and originates from our curiosity to understand the world we live in as well as an attempt to improve this world. We simply want people to understand, think, compare and make wise decisions, based on the premise that wisdom is the foundation of security and development. Founded on new values, relationships, metrics and purposes, this Sustainable Organisation model is our attempt to change the way that organisations are built and perceived by society.

As a transparent society is our major guarantee to security and development, we hope this will represent a decisive contribution to a fair and sustainable society built on sustainable organisations. We see Google as a great example of how an organisation can prove to be useful and become profitable in a sustainable manner that shows balance at all the levels of the organisation.

The way a city is designed conditions or empowers decisively the kind of relationships and organisations that are created. It might inspire ingenuity, creativity, collaboration, harmony, peace and happiness, or, in contrast, transmit fear, oppression, competition, depression and conflict. SORG might be a tool to help any citizen, or decision maker, clearly understand what direction to expect at the genesis of any building, structure or organisation when aiming sustainability.

REFERENCES

1 http://www.sustainablemeasures.com/node/891 As suggested by Peter Drucker

1 For this example we considered that all the revenues come from barrels of oil

1 http://www.americansfortaxfairness.org/files/Walmart-on-Tax-Day-Americans-for-Tax-Fairness-1.pdf

1 http://www.smithsonianmag.com/smart-news/how-much-is-wikipedia-worth-704865/?no-ist

1 http://gondwanaland.com/mlog/2013/10/08/wikipedias-economic-values/

CHAPTER 10

THE MEASUREMENT LADDER:
EXPLORING A 4-STEP LADDER ON METRICS FOR SMART CITIES

By Hisakazu Okamura

Abstract: What are the goals is the Smart City? This is the fundamental question that needs to drive the measurement and evaluation system. From my experience of Smart City projects across several continents, the goals of a Smart City can vary widely. Therefore I am proposing a '4-Step Ladder' for cities to use to align their Smart City projects and increase the chances that the project will deliver appropriate value to citizens, business and city governors.

The 4 steps are:

Step 1: Discovering the purpose of Smart Cities
Step 2: Exploring the focus of Smart City measurement
Step 3: How we measure the Smart City
Step 4: Judging the Smart City

1.   INTRODUCTION

We need start by briefly looking back to the history of the city industry over the last 30 years to begin to understand the business model for Smart Cities.

I started my career with IBM Japan in 1982. In that era, the structure of the technology business was much simpler than it is now. Because we were at the beginning of a so-called "Growth economy" it meant that companies did not need to consider the collaborative social structure in their business. Most companies just had to think deeper about how they could generate revenue through their own products or services and within their own business domain. The hyper-connected world of business had not yet emerged.

Companies were only thinking of selling products and service from one company to another. We now call this simple model B2B. For the city the business model was the same thing, there was just a seller and a buyer involved, and most of the technologies were rather simple.

B2B

Figure 1 Buisness to Business

Some companies specialized in delivering products and services to the customer. This was a very stable process in large part because there was no Internet. Developed countries had well-established infrastructures and consumer income was good enough to support the consumer society.

B2C

Figure 2 Business to Consumer

In the 80s and also 90s the consumer was 'king'. Few people were worrying about the impact on 'place' that is where they lived and work, the natural environment or the planet as a whole. They didn't worry about the systems of the land and the Earth.

The first big opportunity that people in the world started to working together and considering the 'place' was COP3 (The UN Conferences of Parties), famously known as the Kyoto protocol. However, people and companies did not change much, they kept on looking inwardly at only their own business, while paying lip service to the remediation of the degrading global natural environment.

After the COP3 discussion to reduce CO2 emission had occurred globally, people in society started to consider the ground on which they were standing. At this time the new, internet-enabled, business model B2C had just started and businesses started to consider 'place' as markets became more global.

Figure 3 Business to Consumer Internet Enabled

Before this discussion, most of business had 'location or geographical position', the global warming correspondence projects all need to define 'place' as an important entity such as seller, buyer, budget and other business important factors. However, discussion of CO_2 reduction was far from the minds of many in business since people at that stage did not know how they could effectively slow down and stop the progress of global warming.

Of course, at this time in the 1990's, there were a number of smart city projects beginning to develop with a rather narrow focus like just re-development of the station and surrounded short distance areas or some new transportation ways. In many cases, it was about stimulating more business and growth in cities. These early projects considered the city as an asset for business; a place to be worked systemically. The business model to this point was focused on B2B. B2C business for the city was just to provide what people personally want to buy. There is no sophisticated products or services to people from the view point of the city development as Business..

In addition, the emergence of a new business model B2S (Business to Society) had started to emerge. This B2S model understood the complexity of cities; it employed new tools like the Internet and started to build the importance of 'place' into the success of the business.

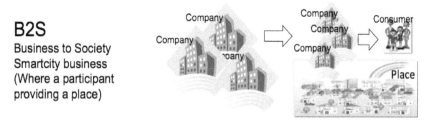

Figure 4 Business to Society

The 'City' that was becoming a focus for new business ideas and the title Smart City began to be used more frequently. B2S simply means 'Business model dealing with a society that includes consumers, companies and place provided by local Government, as buyers.'

2.   STEP 1: DISCOVERING THE PURPOSE OF A SMART CITY

Early stage Smart Cities had 'dumb' foundations

In early Smart City Projects, their purpose was unclear. The word Smart City had more of a buzzword for something new, however, there was little deep consideration and projects were more marketing than substance. This was very similar to the hype around many other new technologies. Recently, business projects using the words 'big data' are becoming popular in Japan. However the Japanese word 'Ookii' means just 'Large sized', there is no separate word distinguishing big from large. Therefore most of the software, technology and services for aggregating data in Japan is focused only on large volume of data. The new era of big data in Japan is understood more in terms of: e-Business, IOT, and other emerging trend in technology.

The issue was that with these early projects people did not feel the need to have a real purpose for the Smart City because it was not considered as a real business for those involved. In addition when new technology was being proposed it would have little regard to the 'place' and the culture where the technology was to be implemented. It was technology for technologies sake.

In this early stage municipalities and cities had one of two strategies for a smart city:

- **Simple City Investment.** They thought simplistically that if a city invests in infrastructure like buildings, shops, transport and housing, then industries in the city would get orders. These initial smart city projects did not change the old business model for the city. It was just more of the same, limited to seeing the city as an asset, not as a 'place'.
- **Reduce CO2.** In this case, consultants were simply asked to bring new ideas to the city that would reduce CO2. There was a little about differentiating the city, however, in most cases, it was about 'Green Washing' the existing way the city worked.

As you can imagine, most of those projects did not motivate the society to undertake effective Smart City projects. Real outcomes were poor; cities did not appear to be getting any smarter. The benefit is not given directly to the city or people.

In the early 80s and 90s even 00s, companies did begin to sell products and services for preventing global warming, however, at this point, there was no philosophy in business for creating the smarter city. City projects operated in isolation and rarely took a systems perspective. Budgets, governance and performance measures were all fragmented and managed separately.

The difference between the strategy of the cities at this early time and now is the recognition that cities need an integrated goal and a coherent design. Smart city projects require a systems perspective to have any chance engaging business and society in making significant change that could be described as 'Smart'. The goals of the projects can vary but having a defined clear goal and a way in which people can make a profit are the most important aspects in any project.

Tokyo, Singapore, Shanghai and Hong Kong, are examples of cities that were rapidly built with a lot of skyscrapers after the Second World War. In that era, development was just about growth. Plots of land were built on in isolation with no place for ideas like city collaboration and linking of functions across the city. The purpose was just 'build'.

The vital foundations of a Smart City, its purpose and its ability to create 'place' were missing.

2.1 Smart Cities require a business purpose

At their outset Smart City projects were naïve. The business model was as simple as asking businesses to join them, as a combined team, in the design of new projects. The city wanted access to expertise at little or no cost and the businesses were keen to explore new markets for their products and services. It was a useful start to collaboration but had little real world outcomes to make cities better places. Some Smart City projects have a goal like 'Relaxing city or city where people love to live'. When viewing Smart City as a business, there should be something that payers want to pay for, and some practical measures of success.

However, as the hype and the marketing developed it generated new interactions with citizens and organizations that were interested in the benefits that a Smart City could bring to them. Citizens were interested to learn how the city could respond to the threats of global warming and then redesign the city to create a better quality of life and a more vibrant economy. Citizens could see the opportunity to make life better: more convenient with Smart Transport, more economical way to consume electricity by looking at the usage and making best use of various prices with Smart Grids, more environmentally friendly with Smart infrastructure for services live waste, housing and water. A Smart City could deliver huge improvements by taking a systems perspective to the challenges of healthcare, shifting trends in employment and good governance.

In these early days the leaders of Smart City projects were the city Mayors who wanted to 'Make the city great again' and construction companies who wanted to build new infrastructure. But this rarely translated into real change that benefited the citizen. Mayors would get re-elected and 'white elephant' pilot projects would get built, but systemic change where IT companies can show hard use cases with real benefit for citizens were hard to find.

Gradually the aspirations for citizens and society were beginning to be heard by the business community. And wherever there are aspiration and demand there is money to be made providing products and services. This is when the 'business purpose' for Smart City project began to emerge. Business could help cities operate better, at lower cost, more reliably and with less environmental impact. If the city could design Smart City projects with a clear business purpose it had the foundations to deliver real change for the citizens. The projects could be viable socially, environmentally and (the important business system perspective) economically.

This shift towards a new 'business purpose' meant that the business model for Smart City projects changed from a philosophy of One-to-One (Client-Supplier) to One-to-Group (a network of different clients which included citizens, city organizations and the businesses as partners able to make a return on investment)

For example, when a city wanted to re-develop the run down park area in front of the train station making use of the latest ideas from urban design, infrastructure and technology it would turn to business for help to design a network of benefits that a new system could deliver. In past 50 years, the bullet train network called Shinkan-sen has been developed all over Japan. As width of the rails is wider than existing railways, so there are many train stations that could not get any benefit of this development. So a strategy of those cities with existing rails was to re-development their train stations and added park facilities by moving residences away. So many new train stations were developed in cities where no Shinkan-sen service runs. The big question is whether these developments were required and whether they gave benefit to the cities.

Often a city would provide the property and the vital local knowledge and context. While the business would re-imagine how the natural spaces and the railway infrastructure could operate as a system delivering value to the citizens, attracting investment and reducing costs for the city administration. This systems perspective allowed both economic benefits and improved environmental performance to be designed at the same time. The 'place' could become an attractive location for people; a profitable place for business and it could be more efficient for the planet by reducing its CO_2 footprint.

2.2 Smart City Business shifting from narrow interests to connected groups

Initially, projects were hyper-local, targeting a specific issue in the city. The earlier example of the park and the train station is hyper-local. It seems to be providing benefit to the local society but in reality it was often not the case.

Today Smart City projects are going beyond this narrow systems perspective to engage larger groups of stakeholders: the park, road, buses, trains, retail, education, healthcare, energy providers and residential areas. The projects also add to this the difficult questions of climate change as a common issue across all sub-systems.

The most significant change in emphasis is that the industries can now propose sustainable business projects and earn money as part of a group proposal. This made the Smart city a new model for business. There was somebody to sell and somebody to buy.

In most of Asian developing countries they have problems such as poverty, crime, parking, water, sanitation but from experience I know many Smart City projects where projects were more about delivering products that developed countries or companies from developed country could provided. The real things happening there is 'Developed country are bringing money to help raise living standards but this often results in developing country sacrifice their 'place'. This miss-match is getting very common. Most of their issue and problems of the developing city are still not solved.

So we need to clarify two pre-conditions for a smart city:

- Somebody interested in selling a solution and somebody willing to buy
- The city need and the proposed solution needs to completely match.

This creates the conditions where the 'B2S', Business to Society, business model could emerge. Each of the players can invest and deliver a return.

These city investments create a 'place' where companies can do business and where citizens are happy to pay for products and services. In essence, cities become smart when they create the conditions where business, culture, environment and society can thrive.

2.3 What makes a city into a 'place'?

In the old context of city development, the idea of "place" used to mean just a position or administrative boundary of cities. This is because the leaders of the city development were nations, municipalities or other public organizations and they started the planning based on the administrative boundaries and the existing properties. It might be the same in the developing countries now. However, under the situations where land development and city infrastructure are not working well or are incomplete then 'place' becomes where citizens work on future aspirations and tackle local issues; it is much more than just administrative boundaries.

A Smart City needs to explore this wider idea of 'place' since it is this that should guide the purpose of any Smart City project.

When a city simply divides the plots of land into administrative areas and takes a purely business approach to cities it will be unable to take a 'systems perspective' across economic, social and environmental domains and it is unlikely to grow into a Smart City. The risk in these circumstances is that it becomes just a large construction project with a large number of unintended consequences.

The "place " is the area where the parties do the project. So Smart City projects can be defined as a business project, but the existence of this idea of "place" makes a big difference from other regular business projects. Sometimes this "place" can mean a virtual district or a collection of collaborating organizations. For instance, in the City of New York, they distributed the handheld terminals to connect citizens to fire fighters. The terminals enabled them to share vital property information about layout, the position of water hydrants, vehicle access and vulnerable people. This enables fire fighters to know in detail about the place they entering. This was an important lesson from the tragedy of 911. This project covered the whole of New York City but was limited only to the domain of firefighters.

In this way a city can have many Smart City projects, enabling people and organisations with a common purpose to work together to make improvements. Today with the Internet, smartphones and cloud computing this idea can be shared with other first-responder organisations such as police and medical to create even more value from the collaboration.

2.4 When are City Projects not 'Smart'

Cities are dynamic places with a wide range of new developments, areas of decline and constant change of use. However, these changes often go ahead without a systems perspective leading to unintended consequences that make the city less than smart.

Before the second war, the city of Tokyo was designed with major zones. One area for work and the other was for living. The working area was focused around Tokyo station and connected to living areas by several railways. In addition, many private train services connected to the center of Tokyo and the living areas directly. Because of the sheer size of Tokyo, one of the problems was the large distance between where people lived and the downtown where they worked. The distance from the living areas to the downtown is about 25km, 16 miles. This fundamental design of the city of Tokyo was drawn before the Second World War but it has been continued for 75 years. The average commute from home to the office became about 75 minutes. Imagine how it is hard to go to commute pressed into packed railway carriages working at about 200% normal seating capacity for 75 minutes every morning. The common pattern for travellers is to get into the central area with 45 minutes, then change to the subway network for another 30 minutes before they reach the office. In this post-war era, we could not see how the population of Tokyo would increase and how everything would be gathered into Tokyo area because every big city up until then was set apart and grown up independently. In 1964 the long distant commute using

"Shinkansen; Bullet train" began connected Tokyo and Osaka. It took 3 hours and made Tokyo and Osaka neighboring cities. This is called "Shinkansen effect".

Tokyo and Osaka were now connected directly so people and business from many large cities surrounding them moved into the connected cities. The third biggest city Nagoya started to be skipped and to be isolated because of this effect. So the population then increased significantly in Tokyo. Due to the Shinkansen effect, people thought that a city with functions set apart was the new style of the city. My father who worked in that era used to talk about the bullet train with pride and the famous buzzword on TV was "Being big is Good!" said by Naozumi Yamamoto, a famous composer. We were all expecting the new transportation systems with cars, railways and subways to happen without traffic congestion. This appeared like a 'Smart' idea to cope with city growth after the Second World War.

By contrast, Osaka is designed as a compact city. For hundreds of years Osaka has been a very active trading city, its design evolved to meet this business need with and extensive network of waterways. This tight-knit city has many districts for living inside the central downtown area of Osaka making it a very convenient place to live and work.

Tokyo is the city area that has the largest footprint in Japan. Because the city lost many buildings to fire it was possible to re-design things in a way that separated living places from working places. However, because this project was undertaken with a focus on infrastructure the unintended consequences of travel time and cost on citizens were not revealed until later.

Under the occupation of USA, Japan had a slogan "Create and increase". So the infrastructure industries such as steel, heavy manufacturing, highway and building construction began to lead the design of society. The basic strategy of those industries and the affected nations was to make everything "Large". So the railroad and road extended far away and the city was expanded physically. This is the reason why people now need to sacrifice their time and quality of life to serve the needs of transportation in Tokyo. The lesson here is that just because something is new and big does not mean that it will turn out to be 'Smart'. By taking a systems perspective a city can better match the solutions to the needs of its citizens.

Many cities around the world have been developed with this zoning approach where the thing that is being optimized is the zone at the expense of the citizen. The design of a Smart City from the group business viewpoint is based on the relationship and collaboration. Not from the viewpoint of zones and areas but from the convenience, prosperity and wellbeing of citizens.

In the simple example of the city commuting patterns factors such as time, quality and access need to form part of the transport system design. Innovations like whole system ticketing need to be introduced to make the service both easy and efficient. The location of business districts, living spaces and cultural locations need to be considered as a whole system.

By taking this whole system design approach to city development a city will step up the first rung of the ladder "Discovering the purpose of Smart Cities"; something that is achieved by engaging all the people who have a stake in the city. From that viewpoint, the history of the city construction in Tokyo didn't have a suitable purpose with the needs of the citizens at its heart. Before they knew it the purpose of the city reconstruction became simply 'Make it Big'.

2.5 The shift towards CO2 reduction

After the COP3 Kyoto meetings, the first wave of Smart City projects began work discussing CO2 reduction. The second wave of projects was more practical; now delivering products and service that actually reduced CO2 as a catalyst for cities reducing cost and improving the quality of life.

The business model for C02 reduction has now moved on to a third stage. This business model might be called as 'G2G', Group to Group. This is similar in shape to Smart Cities moving towards B2S, business to the society business model. CO2 projects in business or in cities are no longer just about reducing energy consumption and CO2 production. These projects are beginning to transform cities to make them better places to live and do business. Importantly they also make a significant contribution to global society by delivering innovations for CO2 reduction that can be applied in other locations. This is just an example but when a city has a clear goal, the experience can be easily used by others.

The challenge of reducing CO2 in cities is providing the backdrop to enable cities to discover their new purpose moving forward. Let us dig deeper for understanding G2G more practically.

There is a city of Kitakyushu on the south island of Japan. The city was very famous for the coalmines and the steel plants. From the early 20th century to 2008, the New Nippon steel company and the Kitakyushu city had developed this area. After the Second Word War, the development of a steel-making area grew with vast support from Government. This resulted in a city of pollution. The steel production was considered as a symbol of the Japan reconstruction era. The industry funding supported by the city, Central Government, and private companies meant a rapid increase in the construction of the river levees, roads and buildings.

In 2008, METI (Ministry of Economy, Trading, and Industry) started a project called 2050 workshop in which several industry leaders and I participated. The purpose of the workshop was to make Smart Cities that contributed towards stopping global warming and to make the life of the city people better by 2050. Out of 3 contenders, METI selected Kitakyushu city as the city to focus upon.

The practical strategy of that Smart City was to make electricity smarter by controlling the balance between electricity delivery and consumption by citizens. Then they stop the electricity supply from the power company and switched it to be supplied by the New Nippon Steel own power plant nearby. The purpose explained to the citizen was that it would make electricity supply less expensive. However, the total investment budget was estimated to be $150M. It was not realistic that city hall or companies to make such a large investment just to drive future city development.

Then the city began to explore the model of G2G Group-to-Group engagement. If there would be the possibility of gaining continuous economic benefit after the project completion, then perhaps investment could be viable. The Executive of the city, the General Manager of New Nippon steel, pulled together a team, which included myself, to considering a real plan designed with this philosophy in mind.

We considered Smart City as a business model, we listed the business areas one by one with the aim that every activity must have stable economic profit. The items on the list started not only from the power supply perspective, but also from the demand side in the citizen's apartments, the shopping malls, museums, rental EV (Electric Vehicles), EV taxis, rental bikes, in the extended university, and a wide variety of businesses. We then established a new power company as the first. It provides power generated by the New Nippon steel plant to the district that has a regional energy saving center that shows both the regional power supply and the consumption for all members of the group. Together with the citizens, this group includes over 30 major private companies. This diverse group became the people who implemented the ideas of the Smart City and together they represented the 'place'

As a result, a special power delivery platform was provided to the newly built apartments, the new shopping mall, the museums, and business properties. The EVs were leased to a local taxi company for the EV taxi business. This then encouraged other businesses to join the group to make use of this new power source.

- Rapidly all kinds of new smart city collaborations developed:
- A city bike rental business team.
- Nippon steel company provided important land near the train station.
- City hall workers moved to new rented office space using the new power source.
- An IT company developed the software and the system to manage the energy equipment that in turn was designed by other electronics companies.
- Some of the companies sold equipment to the group and some earned profit from rental fees.

This is the essence of the G2G team, the Group makes the business, it is the Group that makes the decisions, and the group will be the consumers. This G2G Smart City organization model as a business was very success for Smart City projects. This model is very valuable but in terms of the goal making, it is sometimes very hard bring all the different members together to agree on a single common idea. It is good model for managing the project process but difficult for goal setting.

In a similar way in Austria, there are many wooden biomasses based power and heat supply facilities established by groups. One town above Glaz has several rehabilitation facilities. The facilities are used by people living within 700 meters. The local owner of the facility, the local people and the small companies around talked and decided to build a small wooden bio gas plant to provide electricity and the heat. Over a hundred of independent woodcutters were registered along with the immediate neighbours.

- First, they defined the users, the buyers of the powers, and the facilities.
- Second, they defined the wood, the fuel suppliers, and the contracted neighbours.
- Third they established a company for generation the electricity and heat.
- Fourth they designed how they continuously plant new trees by themselves.

It is complete closed energy model for citizens as a smart city. In the limited area, people cut timbers and sell them to the local energy plant. Locals then operate the plant. This creates new jobs. The plant sells electricity and heat back to the rehabilitation facilities. People go stay the facilities and pay the charge for use. People then re-plant the tree. This significantly reduces CO_2 emission and creates lots of benefit to the local society.

Austrian biomass association says in 'Basisdaten 2015', there are almost 3,000 biomass plants nation wide. These types of self-sufficient power project have developed very rapidly in last 2 years. In January 2017, I also visited 6 of the sites myself. I think this model will be spread out into Japan shortly because we also have an energy problem due to the 52 nuclear plants shut down out of 54.

The facility can turns wood to burnable gas and heat will be distributed to the society and the gas will be used to generate the power for them.

The point is that the facilities were built by local companies; collaborating with funding. Neighbors cut, aggregate, deliver and sell the timbers to the facility.

The G2G team both buys and use the heat and power. Neighbors will then replant the trees again. In this way, the energy and its consumption enable significant reductions in emissions. This is a new sustainable G2G smart city model that has started just recently.

3.   STEP 2: EXPLORING THE FOCUS OF MEASUREMENT

3.1 A smart city can mean many different things

In 2008 when IBM announced the smarter planet strategy, the word "smart city" already existed. At that time I was running the environment related business unit named 'Team Green Innovation' in Japan, and IBM in the US was preparing its strategy for helping to create smart cities prior to its marketing announcement. It was at this time when society began to talk a lot about intelligent infrastructures like smart grid and renewable energy.

In December of 2008, IBM announced the smarter planet initiative and developed a 'smarter city' focus about 6 months later. I still remember that at that time the 'smart' or 'smarter' city meant a city with high-tech or IT systems highly implemented.

At this early stage, many people had high aspirations for significant business growth in the provision of Smarter Cities. We soon discovered IBM smarter city projects did grow quickly to over 2000 globally within 2 years.

People who were watching the activity of IBM were surprised with the high number of projects, partly based on the mental image of the smart city as one with a skyline filled with skyscrapers.

In reality, for IBM, the smarter city projects could be applied to any type of city from ancient cities to developing cities to mega-cities. It was even possible to apply the ideas effectively to small towns and university campuses.

One example in Europe, the Stockholm traffic congestion tax system, the smart city project didn't have any high-tech skyscraper buildings at all, it was all about the Information Technology system.

Smart city projects being reported from the US were also far from uniform. From 2008 through 2011, IBM 'smarter city' in the US had a wide variety of meanings. This could range from a tiny project for citizens using smartphones to huge city scale projects. Often the projects centered on the physical infrastructure of cities, however, there were also smarter city projects that were only focusing on the city operations. I had the pleasure of participating in one such project in New Orleans.

In 2011, City of New Orleans, Louisiana USA seemed very calm. It was 6 years after hurricane Katrina attacked and destroyed the city. The levee that surrounded and protected the city from the high water levels of the big lake beside the city was broken at 25 locations. This had allowed 3-meters of water to linger in town for 9 months.

The IBM foundation arranged to support the city by sending 6 IBM consultants, including myself, for a voluntary assignment to directly support the Mayor in his requirements.

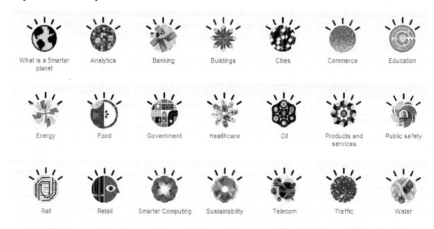

Figure 5 IBM Corporation Smarter Planet 2008

IBM staff had several months to prepare plus a 3-week intensive on site assignment to tackle on of the Mayors biggest problems. To be able to recover as quickly as possible the Mayor needed to know what was going on in the damaged city in near real-time.

By 2011 over 120 km of new levee had been built, but now the problem was inside the city hall itself. Due to that disaster, many house owners abandoned properties and never come back again. Even if the city wanted to demolish the ruined buildings, it was impossible to do that without the permission of the owners. So, there was a huge amount of work needed to identify the owner and to get their permission. This situation challenged not only the budget but also the time that the few people in city hall could spend on this issue. In addition, there were a large number of administrative tasks that were incomplete, especially immediately after the disaster. Our aim was to help by making a wide variety of hidden facts visible so that this evidence could speed up the city recovery.

The city hall employed almost 3,000 employees after the disaster but most of them had changed from the original employees. They came from many cities over the United States to help, however, this generated a big communication problem among the many sections of city administration especially involving the newcomers. Because people wanted to deliver results quickly, each section in city hall tried to work independently in the best way their experienced suggested. As a result, the use of technology increased sharply, for example the number of computer servers used by city hall increased enormously, by about 180 machines, in a very short space of time.

By working independently business processes were struggling. An indication of the challenge was that it now took 1.5 years to complete the cities' annual report so even data for this vital governance and public relations report was disjointed and outdated.

Our team therefor looked into how good timely data could be used to speed up the city recovery. Our aim was to improve the way reporting and open data was used to overcome the internal organizational issues. We designed new systems to improve internal communication, how the voice of citizen could be correctly aggregated, how quickly the data on documents could be transferred from one section to the next and the quality of the data upon which city hall was making decisions. Our recommendations, submitted after three weeks of intensive work, clearly identified the issues that the city hall needed to address and proposed practical ways forward. Because we were able to take a systems perspective to the problems the city faced our solutions did not add to the confusion and fragmentation that was happening when we first arrived. The systems perspective changed the way the city used its data and its technology enabling it to focus on the needs of both the citizen and the city hall. It could make better decisions because of timely shared data meaning they could move from 'guessing to knowing'. This small but urgent example shows how a city can become smarter by using a systems perspective.

Outside of the IBM smarter city initiatives, in general in the US, smart city mean the use of a high-tech facility, in particular city control centers designed to manage operations. This image of this smart city in the US seems to be very common now. In these operation centres, the measurement criteria are often focused on citizen's satisfaction of a particular sub system e.g. the city transport or some metrics about traffic congestions. In another operations centre it could be about city crime rates and police response times.

3.2 Measurement of Smart City Projects in China are designed to fit the purpose of the international bank investors

In 2011, China announced there were over 400 smart city projects in the country. The meaning of the smart city was new and unexpected in this context. At this time China wanted to develop the country very quickly, so the answer became a series of the smart city project. In 2012 China, the Ministry of Housing and Urban Rural Development (MOHURD) announced 90 cities or towns to be the first batch of smart city pilot.

Prior to this expansion, people living in the country regions were not allowed to live in the city areas, historically cities would be defined by a walled boundary restricting urban sprawl.

On March 16th 2014, the Chinese government announced, "National New Urbanization Plan (2014-2020)" (hereinafter referred to as "New

Urbanization Project"). It radically changed the definition of the city that Chinese Government was looking for. Simultaneously the Hukou system was started, a Hukou being a record in a government system of household registration, required by law in Mainland China, and determines where citizens are allowed to live. With this kind of population balance manipulation, a total city coordination plan can work successfully. The defined city diameter changed from 400km down to 50km and people who lived in the countryside were then allowed to live in the city. At this time many high-density tall buildings were developed and cities started being connected to each other with the fast bullet trains.

In April 2015, the third batch of cities was announced by MOHURD. MOHURD and the Ministry of Science and Technology were work together on Smart City promotion. It was reported that that the total number of pilot cities were between 300 and 400.

The idea of a Smart City in China was definitely the city with high skyscrapers. This rapid dense growth of buildings became the measure of success, so much so that it became the misguided purpose of the Smart City.

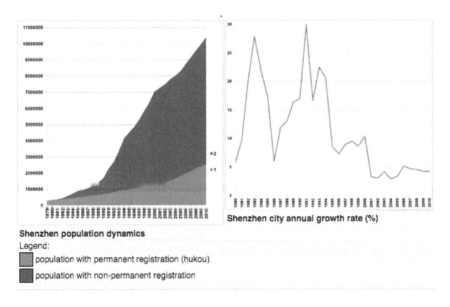

Shenzhen population dynamics
Legend:
■ population with permanent registration (hukou)
■ population with non-permanent registration

Figure 6 Shenzhen Growth
(https://en.wikipedia.org/wiki/Shenzhen, 2016)

3.3 Exporting Smart Cities changed the measurement

After the Smart City project boom in Mainland China, around 2013, many developing countries in Asia and the Middle East started to build to the Chinese model of a Smart City. To enable this, China rapidly established, with the AIIB, Asian Infrastructure Investment Bank, to make the China's currency an official part of the international money system. Once this was done the China Government can then paid construction companies in the Chinese dollar and China can easily send the construction companies to any country in the region that will accept the Chinese dollar directly. One reason for this move was to aggregate the foreign currency in Mainland China ahead of for investing in the city construction projects in foreign developing countries.

The result is that now there are many Chinese construction companies working on Smart City projects all across Asia. Before AIIB was established, China had difficulty constructing smart cities in Asia and Africa. Even though China had enough money to invest, they had no exchange mechanism for Chinese dollar to US dollar. Now China can invest and pay the construction companies in the Chinese dollar.

In this case, the Smart City business becomes an export business in its own right. The exact shape of the business model can be varied. This is a business model of investment. That is why the goal for people or cities is hard to find.

Often it is just a construction business, however, sometimes it is about gaining a foothold in providing services to developing countries. For example in one project in the Philippines, the Chinese investors sponsored the project by providing labour for city construction almost free of charge. This had the effect of excluding local labour ensuring that future projects had little local competition.

In these cases the return on investment becomes a vital part of the measurement system for Chinese Smart City projects, often this comes above the measures of satisfaction from a citizen perspective or the local economy.

The original purpose of the Smart City is that the citizens or organizations team up to solve the issue of the city or industries. However, projects now happening in Asian countries are different from this original purpose.

Rather than focus upon local issue, goals and solutions, they focus on the products that the investing countries or organizations want to sell. Even when poverty is a major problem, where many children living among the city garbage, or the city has other critical issues for its citizens like transport, the projects proposed are high tech, super city monitor software.

Local people may learn about these high-tech solutions if they are employed within the Smart City project as part of the city team. But investors are now sending more to cities than finance. They send experts, construction workers, service companies and even the common currencies.

There is almost no way for the local people to develop their country by themselves. The continuous profit for services that results after the completion of the Smart City will be also transferred to the external investors. Smart City projects in Asia may be a good profitable business model but developing countries should not be the target of investors from the developed countries. This phenomenon reminds me the Tokyo case after the Second World War where the purpose became 'growth' at all cost and the needs of the city were lost.

The purpose of the Smart City is always tied up with the way the city is measured. The diagram below shows how the difference between: developed, emerging and developing countries. There start point is different, however they are all trying to move in a common direction.

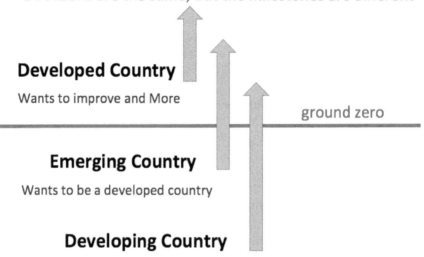

Figure 7 Differing Smart City Goals Across the World

The word "smart" in Smart City can often have a simple meaning of 'good' or "better" in many countries. However many cities want to go much further. It means that every smart city must have a goal to guide them. In practice, the idea of a Smart City is definitely more about moving toward a goal than it is about reaching a specific end point. This constant aspiration is what makes the difference over a city that is just aiming to be a 'good' city.

3.4 Developing country measurement

Developing countries know that the lifestyles cannot be changed instantly even if the rest of the world is talking about aspirations like self-driving vehicles. They have poverty, crime, pollution and many other stark realities. So the only realistic goal that the developing countries can set, as their purpose for their smart city, is to make the basic city infrastructure work for

236

citizens. Obviously, developing countries are looking beyond this to improve all aspects of the city – the economy, the society and the environment. So the measurement for developing countries is usually focused on infrastructure improvement.

For developing countries, most of them have another serious need for the smart city development. That relates to the political issue of how satisfied citizens are with the current Government. Not all cities are like this, but often it is the countries that facing to the risk of being invaded or those that have unstable internal political changes. As propaganda, some Governments intentionally put new names on development projects often labeling them as 'smart city projects'. By doing so people may feel that there will be some 'smart' image of the future under current Government. It is of course very important to keep the country stable. In these cases, measurement is announced only partially, or not announced with specific numbers. It is not uncommon for the measurements in developing country Smart City projects to be manipulated to some extent to make things look good.

3.5 The emerging countries look to measurement standards of the developed countries

Most of emerging countries like countries in South East Asia, Eastern Europe, mid and South America are trading extensively with the developed countries. Some host factories for them and some send their workers to work in the developed countries. The emerging countries can see the future they are trying to reach, the goal of their Smart City projects is therefore to get closer to the developed countries and create the lifestyles that they see are possible. In order to move in that direction, they often use similar measures to those of developed countries.

The purpose or goal of the emerging countries undertaking a Smart City project can be put simply as 'We want to be like the developed countries', but there is one problem with this strategy – the economy. Most of the emerging countries rely on developed countries from an economic viewpoint and domestically they do not have enough money to invest in Smart City projects independently. Funding is a real problem. Even if a city of an emerging country wants to be smart, the developed countries that they trade with do not have a strong incentive to invest in the city. So if the city wants to be smarter, and they do not have any money, and there is no local investor, then the purpose for the Smart City shifts to whatever is attractive to the developed country so that it might be attracted to invest.

Examples of strategies for external investment include: making super resorts for European tourists, creating super cheap but comfortable office blocks for Japanese semiconductor designers or developing secure high-class family living districts for foreigner worker. These "attractive" ideas are sometimes included in the Smart City goals of the emerging countries.

Of course, outside of the Smart City projects, emerging countries expect their own lives to get closer and closer to the standards of developed countries. Ever-closer communications links, better flight routes and international trade help this. This means that as emerging countries become smarter they will start to resemble the countries they take inspiration from.

After the second war, Japan recovered from chaos but one effect was that Japan has got very close, perhaps too close to the US. Not only the design of the physical structures but also the economic structures. When the US is going well, Japan does well too. But if the US is not doing well, this influences directly upon Japan. The most significant impact is on the currency exchange rate. No matter how Japanese companies tried to become more profitable from the products, the currency exchange rate changes rapidly and makes global trading difficult.

Certainly, Japan is not an emerging country, but it shares the dependency that emerging countries experience overdependence of one country on another.

3.6 Developed country measures

In most developed countries they have enough power to improving the cities by themselves with their own budget. The United States, European countries, Japan and other developed countries have their own unique problems but have enough independence to be able to govern themselves. So the Smart City developments can also be designed independently, often working with their own industries.

3.7 The Definition of the Smart City changes the way they are measured

In the table below, I highlight my experience of the differing meanings of Smart City. There are, however, many other meanings of 'Smart' when applied to smaller regions, towns and communities. I will not be able to explain all of those variants here however it is worth noting that there should always be a purpose to a Smart City project. If the Smart City project doesn't have a stated purpose, then the project cannot be defined as smart, instead it becomes just a construction project.

The table below illustrates the many interpretations of Smart City I have seen around the world:

Table 1 Differing Meaning of Smart City Across the World

Location	Meaning of Smart City
US	High tech city with with lots of Information Technology Improvement of the city with support of Information Technology IT
China (**Mainland Cities**)	A city with sky scrapers connected with super fast railways
China (**Constructing in Asia**)	Investment targeted at supporting Chinese companies working abroad
India, Indonesia & parts of Asia	Growing city infrastructure aspiring to be like developed countries
Eastern Europe	The city reborn, and the creation of new city development
Europe Developed Countries	Better cities for better quality of life
Japan	It has become a buzz word, something that does not create business

3.8 Smart City in the US:

In the US the term Smart was first applied to business operations taking advantage of the power of information technology. Due to IBM's extensive smarter city promotion, the word 'Smarter' now has a special meaning in the US. The word 'Smart' already implies 'better', but the term 'Smarter' takes the aspiration a stage further. It is about designing city systems with the feeling of hope. For example: "We want the city to fix the water leaks we want more frequent community buses, we want more energy efficient homes." These are tangible things about becoming 'smarter', where people hope to solve real problems with life in their city.

In 2009, when IBM in the US held the first smarter city conference, the idea of a smarter city was part of the wider strategy of a 'Smarter Planet'. The essence of a Smarter Planet was responding to a world that was becoming more:

Instrumented, Interconnected and Intelligent

This meant that every part of business and society could think of new ways of operating that used data and technology to change the world economically, socially and environmentally.

For example Smarter Grids delivering energy in new and more efficient ways, Smarter Transport improving congestion and public services, Smarter Water reducing pollution and increasing resilience to extreme weather and floods. In 2010, Smarter Planet had 21 areas of focus with the idea of smarter city as an overarching concept that knitted these together.

In the early days (2009 and 2010) there was little talk of measurement or evaluation of projects. I feel that IBM has announced Smarter Planet and Smarter City but at this stage did not have mature products or services. There was a period of exploration where both the clients and IBM were trying to understand the problems ahead of designing technology-enabled solutions.

3.9 Smart Cities supported by developed countries:

There are a lot of countries being helped by Chinese money, from Indonesia to Africa. This process of helping countries to get closer to China, through using its system and its financial activities, feels similar to the encampment game where city resource are placed beyond the city to extend its sphere of influence.

In countries like Indonesia, India, Thailand and Vietnam their populations have grown rapidly. Many developed countries have brought to these places new industries and settled with new business activities. Cities were therefore developed with the needs of those foreigners' in mind with many foreign invested and owned plants. What's happening is an attempt to making those countries as similar as possible for those who are operating and investing those facilities.

There are many Japanese companies running businesses in Thailand. In order to maintain standards of cleanness, not only the plant but also the city environment, the supported city should be smart as Japan. For instance, the roads and railways must be flat and smooth as Japan to prevent damage the products like trucks and trains. So supporting countries are always looking closely and getting involved in infrastructure projects since they open up opportunities for trade. On the other hand, city development for citizens, not relating to the business that has foreign investment, progresses very slowly. In practice there are many un-developed villages without electricity exist all over these Asian countries that have well-developed industrial infrastructure.

Foreign companies often build a factory set apart from the city. This enables them to benefit from low land price. So the city model becomes an old style design. The old design is not a compact city. The city is divided into many separate areas. Living zone can be developed hundreds of kilometers away from factory areas. Living areas are often zoned into the area for factory workers and others that are not. Then there are the slum areas of the city.

In those Emerging countries, cities have a different status depending on whether the city is supported by business with foreign countries or the city is only for local people to live.

If we want to apply city measurement standards (e.g. ISO 3712x) to the two types of cities this will be quite difficult. That is because there are two different purposes at work.

3.10 Japanese experience

In the Asian region the experience of Japan is quite different from countries. One of the reasons is that English words are sometimes translated uniquely in Japanese. The word 'smart' has already been a Japanese word for 40 years. The meaning used to be 'Slim or Skinny' but it has changed to 'clever' in the past 5 years. In 2008, the term smarter city was announced by IBM Japan and used 'clever' as the meaning.

However, a big problem in this non-English speaking country is always "To translate one English word to one Japanese word". Very quickly this idea of clever equated to a city with high buildings. This translation has unfortunately become settled and fixed in the society.

As years go by, the meaning of Smart City has been changing widely in the world but the meaning in Japan has remained fixed as a city of skyscrapers. In 2016, many countries are chasing the Smart City projects but most of the Japanese industries are not interested in that business. When projects do happen in Indonesia or some other place where the relationship with Japan is good, Japanese companies consider that the project must be just high-rise building construction so nobody goes to win the business.

This is perhaps the main reason why Japanese companies are not participating into Smart City projects at this time.

4. STEP 3: HOW ARE WE MEASURING THE SMART CITY?

To be able to measure something effectively we need to know clearly why it is being measured and take care over the units of measurement.

4.1 The paradox of brown water for drinking and clean water for flushing the toilet

When I was working on JAPAN ODA (Official Development Assistance) project for India, our team was assigned to one city of India. As the investment was supported by Japan central government, we primarily started by requesting the analysis based on the survey done by a ministry. The main concern in this region was to do with the quality of the water.

The official report sent back to Japan from India was written by a group of Japanese government officers. It said that the color of the tap water in that area was almost always brown. It also reported that people living there are all drinking this brown water with the exception of several hotels for European business people who purify the water themselves. So the difference in the water quality between the locals and the visitors is huge. The most demanded request is to make some improvements in the city drinking water supply and that is what the report focused upon.

When our team visited the area to understand in detail the nature of the problem by measuring level of the brown color by district and mapping this against the water distribution supply map we found to our surprise that the situation was somewhat different when we talked with the locals.

Locals don't seem to need any improvements in clean water supply, even though the water was indeed brown. They said that if they were planning to drink it they simply boiled it first; they purify it as necessary. Local people questioned us about strange practice of using clean water to flush toilets in Japan! The local hotels used by European business visitors also did not require the purifying system because they are quite satisfied with their own system and the low water price of clean water. So by exploring a little deeper we found that the measurement of the color level of water didn't really mean anything in practice in that location.

When locals were asked what improvement would be of most use to them, most people asked use to invest in more toilets. They needed toilets because there are so few houses with toilets. People often have to use the street, the rivers, the ponds, and almost anywhere else because there is no proper toilet. No toilet means many mosquitos that spread disease. Therefore measuring the portion of the houses without toilets became our new purpose.

Smart City measurement needs to follow this pattern
of exploring what is really important on the ground
with the local people, to discover
the real purpose that the city needs to be 'Smart' about.

From this Step 1 of purpose, there is then a better chance of choosing the right thing to measure. In this case in India, the purpose was not to purify the water, i.e. trying to solve the problem with a Japanese perspective, but the real purpose was to help local people with more toilets. After the selection of the measuring target, we can reach easily design the unit of the measuring. In this case, it became about the number of houses with and without toilets.

All Smart City measurement should therefore only be designed to support a verified purpose.

When we consider the measurement of Smart City, I think the most important point is ROI, Return On Investment. This RETURN must be the financial return for business but also it must solve local issues that are of value to citizens. Japanese people and Japanese companies have an especially strong interest in technology and new products that are used in Smart City project, so there is a clear business interest. China, as described above, is however looking at only the financial return, a market for their exported products, and growth in employment for Chinese companies outside of China. Major US security companies also keep a close eye on ROI for of Smart City project.

The measurement of Smart City is being written, based on ISO regulations. Certainly, there is any value to compare different countries but we need to understand that the context is different and the issues are often highly local. Looking at the case insights from other Smart City projects one by one is an important way of seeing 'the art of the possible' and enables cities to learn fast. But just comparing the numbers is unlikely to help design an appropriate way forward...

On the other hand, we should have comparable, common world standards for focus areas in the measurement of Smart City, for example, about transportation, about water, about security and others independent factors. Measurement of Smart City works well when they are describing the benefits that result in the country's local issue being achieved, its goals, the way it of approach an issue, the required investment and return, time durations vs. estimated durations, and other measurements that are commonly used in the business world, for example BS (balance sheet), ROI (return on investment), and ROE (return on equity). These economic indicators and measurement are used very commonly, however, we don't compare company numbers around questions like: What the company sells, What they buy, How many they buy, What kind of machines they use, How many machines they bought".

Measurement and standardization of Smart City that are often considered and discussed at the moment all look very similar to me. I have many questions when cities take standard measurement too far; much care is needed to match measurement with purpose.

5. STEP 4: JUDGING THE SMART

5.1 Take care when applying standards

There is a strong movement across the world to judging and evaluating Smart Cities using standards. Those standards are very effective to reveal the most important subjects to address in a city. However, because every city is different these standards cannot be used to judge and evaluate the city. Instead, standards are just a tool to allow the city to explore the art of the possible.

When you walk down the street of Vienna Austria, there are so many beautiful old buildings with colorful sculptures. Although they are old buildings they will have up to date information technology to enable them to work in the modern world e.g. lighting, communications, air conditioning, security etc. By contrast buildings in the central area of Tokyo, are often very new designed not to look grand but rather to be resilient to earthquakes. This shows that Smart City standards need to be applied to the local context. What is smart for one city may not be relevant for another.

5.2 Standards can be useful when there is common purpose

For example, it can be relevant for places like Italy and Japan to compare themselves using standard based measurements for earth quake resilience. They can each learn from the other and understand how they are performing and discover new ways to improve. The key thing to keep in mind is that the standards need to be relevant to the purpose of the Smart City Project

This applies to all kinds of Smart City, even those whose purpose is simply a return on investment

5.3 Evaluation of the cities

There have been, over centuries, many ways, magazine articles, academic methods, and organizations to evaluate cities. They are often titled 'The ABC cities rankings' or something similar. All of those city rankings have a clear purpose for the evaluation. This makes for easy comparison, but it has little regard to how the citizens live. At best the rankings give mayors, politicians and companies something to talk about. They rarely make a positive impact on the lives of citizens or make the city 'Smarter' in practical terms.

5.4 What is important when evaluating a Smart City?

The most important way to evaluate and judge the value of the city or its projects is to take a combination of the citizen view and the economic view.

In order to keep citizens happy, the city must enable them to lead a good life and have some level of satisfaction. Taking care of citizens continuously needs the foundation of 'money' to make the economy work. To gain sufficient money continuously, the only thing required is to for the city to constantly develop a healthy business environment.

These two things: satisfaction for citizens and gaining the money through business, look quite different and often compete, however, they need to work hand-in-hand to serve the people continuously.

In the early days of Smart City projects people were just talking about technology, focusing on things like smart grids or some other high-tech dreams. But this created problems because it lacked the realism that recognized discussion of the economics.

Even now looking around at the standards for Smart Cities, there is little city economy. To make Smart City projects work the standards must consider more about the city economy and the life of citizens.

Only by combining citizen satisfaction and economic understanding can cities build an effective way to evaluate what is important when creating a Smart City.

REFERENCES

IBM corporation (2008) Smarter Planet http://www-03.ibm.com/ibm/history/ibm100/us/en/icons/smarterplanet/impacts/

Figure 6 Shenzhen Growth https://en.wikipedia.org/wiki/Shenzhen

Other charts are my original work.

CHAPTER 11

WHAT DOES IT TAKE?

Modelling the transformation of the Hammarby Sjöstad energy systems, exploring potentials for increased efficiency and reduced impacts

Örjan Svane

Abstract: What does it take to reduce energy use and its impacts in the recently built Hammarby Sjöstad, Stockholm by 15 per cent till 2025?

This is the aim of the local initiative ElectriCITY and it could initiate and coordinate the transformation, but it has no direct influence over energy use. Residents have that influence in their flats, and enterprises have it in their premises. Real estate owners can improve the buildings' energy systems and reduce energy use in its common spaces. These are the primary agents of change. In this article, we explore what other organizations and enterprises need to be involved in order to bridge the gap between the primary agents of change and the ElectriCITY initiative. We use a soft systems approach, modelling the transformation of the energy systems and their use as a socio-technical system.

1.   INTRODUCTION AND PURPOSE

Given the magnitude and urgency of mitigating climate change, it is vital to explore how feasible it is to reduce energy use and its impact in recently constructed buildings. Even in a two-generation perspective, energy efficient construction and refurbishment are insufficient to improve the energy performance of the whole built environment in high-income countries such as Sweden (Svane, 2008). Experience shows that transformation does not happen on its own, and unlike in construction and refurbishment there is no established organization to combat inertia. Thus, there is a need for a transformation agent, initiating and coordinating efforts, informing and persuading the primary agents of change. The agent must also network, identifying other transformation agents and bringing the actors together to form a transformative organization. Here we explore this issue based on the case of Hammarby Sjöstad, Stockholm and the local initiative ElectriCITY.

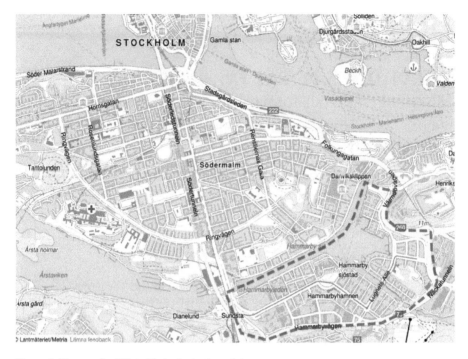

Figure 1: Hammarby Sjöstad is in the bottom right,
the Old Town of Stockholm (Gamla stan) in the top middle.

Two assumptions form the article's departure point:

- *Local actors can reduce total energy use and climate impacts in the* Hammarby *Sjöstad by 15 per cent, and*
- *System transformation is allowed to take 10 years*

We then ask:

- *What measures need to be taken,*
- *Which actors have to be involved, and*
- *How demanding is the transformation?*

These issues are studied in an on-going research project at the Royal Institute of Technology in Stockholm, and preliminary findings are reported in this article. The project's research strategy is the case study (Flyvbjerg, 2006; Stake, 1995), and its methodological framework comes from the futures studies' research tradition. Its findings will be presented as a scenario generated through backcasting (Börjesson et al., 2006; List, 2004). From this it follows that there is little of prognosis. Instead, the scenario is explorative and normative.

The case was selected because it is unique, information rich and informative (ibid.). It is unique in what the initiators want to achieve and in there being citizens with persuasive powers as the main asset. It is information rich since the initiators give us free access to what they are doing. From this it follows that there is great potential to learn from it; as in any case study, generalization is limited but fully possible.

248

With the soft systems approach of this article, the scenario is a model representing the energy systems in a conceptual, and in part, quantitative way. Its features are chosen to explore transformation upstream, from user towards producer. Its focus is on end use and the energy systems inside the Hammarby Sjöstad buildings. A key element is its *energy usage systems* (Jonsson et al., 2011; Nørgård, 2000). In them, energy is transformed, providing services for the end user, e.g. dust removal in the vacuum cleaner or comfortable indoor temperature from the radiator. To reduce energy use, the end user or system owner could use it less or more efficiently, they could monitor it better through ICT or replace it with a more efficient one.

System transformation is intentional change, and intentions are always someone's. To explore this feature of transformation, the model represents the energy systems as socio-technical, including residents and enterprises as the *end users of energy* and real estate owners as the *managers of the local energy system*. The gap between these and the *transformation's initiator* ElectriCITY is the organization being explored, I have called this the *'intervention chain'* which is made up from *intermediate transformation agents*. Forging the chain calls for *arenas* where these actors meet. These could for example be done face-to-face or ICT based.

Being socio-technical, the system is complex, perhaps doubly so since social and technical systems have different dynamics. The modelling of such a system does not enable prediction and little of generalization, but it indicates how the system can be monitored and feedback can be arranged. ICT can provide arenas for conveying information between people, making the system 'smarter'. People using and managing the energy system with the intention to reduce energy use and its impacts should also (at least in a metaphorical sense) make it smarter.

In the main project, the socio-technical changes are understood through Strategic Niche Management (SNM) and the Multi-Level Perspective (MLP). SNM provides a 'theoretical framework that informs policy makers about their choice of instruments, while also recognizing the open-ended character of the induced change processes' (Jørgensen, 2012). The MLP explores transformations as 'non-linear processes that result from the interplay of multiple developments at three analytical levels: niches (the locus for radical innovations), socio-technical regimes (the locus of established practices and associated rules) and an exogenous socio-technical landscape' (Rip and Kemp, 1998; Geels, 2002, 2005, in ibid.). In this article, there are findings stemming from SNM analysis, but little of MLP.

2.   ON HAMMARBY SJÖSTAD AND ELECTRICITY

Hammarby Sjöstad is a large brownfield development in Stockholm, Sweden (Figure 1). It is to be completed in 2017 and was initiated in the early 1990s with the aim to transform an old industrial and harbour area to a modern city district (City of Stockholm, 2014). The planning process was highly ordinary until branding of the district as an environmental spearhead became central in order for Stockholm to apply for the Olympic Games 2004. This branding involved establishing a special project organisation and developing an environmental programme. In it, land use, energy, water, waste and transport as well as the contribution of residents' lifestyle were given specific targets (Svane et al., 2011; Wangel, 2012; Pandis Iveroth et al., 2013). However, evaluations indicate that the environmental performance of Hammarby Sjöstad today is comparable to other urban developments of the same time (Pandis Iveroth & Brandt, 2011).

A key feature of the Hammarby Sjöstad development is its integrated infrastructure for energy, water, sewage and waste. From an international perspective, the level of integration is unusual, but it does not differ greatly from the infrastructure in other parts of Stockholm. The built environment gets its energy from electricity and via the city-wide district heating system. There are solar panels and photovoltaics, but their share of the total is negligible. The district heating is provided from a waste incineration plant and a sewage water heat pump. The electricity is supplied via the national grid, with roughly equal shares of nuclear and hydroelectric power. See Figure 2 for details of the Hammarby model..

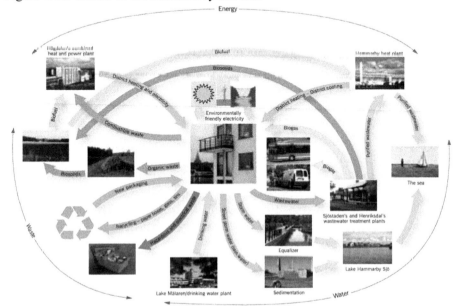

Figure 2: The Hammarby model of integrated infrastructure illustrates a number of attempts to close loops of energy and material flows. It is largely similar to the infrastructure of all Stockholm.

2.1 From persuasive citizen initiative to established local actor

The citizen initiative HS2020 was established in 2011 with the overarching aim of developing a new way of thinking concerning urban sustainable development. This aim was articulated as 'Renewing a New City'. It has established projects on e.g. transport, energy in the built environment, recycling and ICT/Media. All projects are to be realized by 2020. In 2016 its organisation was formalised as 'ElectriCITY', it has stable funding and an extensive network of public and private organizations to realize the projects' visions and programmes (Evliati et al., 2014). In the energy project the target is to reduce energy use to under 100 kWh/m^{2}yr. This would mean a 15 per cent reduction in the residential buildings' energy use. In the on-going research project the transition time frame is extended till 2025 and the aim of reducing climate impacts by 15 per cent is emphasized in parallel.

In current urban development practice in Sweden and other high-income countries, the environmental performance of urban areas is addressed mainly at two stages of the area's service life: when it is planned, designed and constructed, and when it is in need of substantial renovation (the latter typically occurring four to five decades after construction ended). Between these two stages, the area and its infrastructure systems are generally left as constructed, no matter how urgent the need to decrease environmental impact and despite the possibilities provided by technological and social innovation.

Going beyond this practice, the HS2020 initiative aims at exploring how an urban area can be developed outside the windows of opportunity of construction and refurbishment. Ultimately, the initiators are seeking to develop an innovative model for city district management, one that supports a process for continuous improvement, similar to the management and maintenance practices in real estate. Such a management model however calls for an actor constellation that is different from the project organizations of new development or refurbishment. Both have established routines and project type organisations, which the concept of 'Renewing a New City' totally lacks. Therefore, the task of ElectriCITY is complex: To define what could and should be done, and in parallel iteratively to build a suitable network organisation. In late 2016, this task is under way, especially for the transport and ICT/Media projects, but also concerning energy use in the buildings.

2.2 Energy use in 2015 in the Hammarby Sjöstad – a baseline

To model the transition of the Hammarby Sjöstad energy systems, there is a need to baseline present energy use, to estimate the end users' reduction potentials and to operationalize the 15 per cent aims accordingly. Starting with the baseline, we note that in late 2015, the Hammarby Sjöstad had some 8 000 lived-in flats with 18-19 000 residents, about 75 real estates and approximately 100 local enterprises. Total heated area was 737 000 m², of which three quarters was in the flats. For further details, see Table 1.

Baseline for energy use – Sjöstad residential buildings

Areas as of 2015:	1 000 m²	Share, per cent
Flats, total	551	75
Businesses, rentals	40	5
Heated garage, rentals	37	5
Remaining	109	15
Heated total	**737**	**100**

2015 energy use, key ratios and total:	MWh/yr	Share, per cent
Heating + hot water 103 kWh/m²yr	76 000	68
Common electricity 15 kWh/m²yr	11 000	10
Garage electricity 15 kWh/m²yr	500+	≈0
Household electricity 40 kWh/m²yr	22 000	20
Businesses electricity 50 kWh/m²yr	2 000	2
TOTAL	**111 000**	**100**

Source: Author's ongoing research, Owners' Energy Declarations, Experts' Rules of Thumb

Table 1 Baseline for energy use

Two thirds of the Hammarby Sjöstad built environment's total energy use is for heating and hot tap water. This energy is provided via the city-wide district heating system and normally paid for via the rent. The household's cost is based on flat size rather than actual use. The other energy source is electricity, individually measured and billed for each household and each enterprise. The real estate owner pays for the building's common electricity use. The households' use of electricity constitutes another fifth of the district's total.

There is no feasible way to directly measure the climate impacts from energy use. Instead, conversion factors are used. This is a contested area among researchers, consultants, enterprises and authorities alike. For this article, conversion factors based on 'Swedish electric energy mix' and from the district heating company were used (Klimatkompassen, 2016; Fortum värme, 2014). The former indicates that 1 kWh of electric energy results in 20 g of CO_2 emissions, the corresponding factor for district heating is 35 g. Table 2 presents the resulting CO_2 emissions in tons per year. Stockholm City's political majority has adopted conversion factors that result in much higher emissions. If we were to use these, CO_2 emissions would be three times higher, which illustrates the magnitude of the contestation.

Baseline for climate impacts – Sjöstad residential buildings

TOTAL	MWh/yr
Electricity use	35 000
District heating use	76 000

CO_2 per kWh – assumptions
Swedish elmix 15-25 g/kWh (Here we use 20 g/kWh)
District heating, greenhouse gas emissions (Here we use 35,1 g/kWh)

Calculating total CO_2 emissions	Tons
CO_2 El: 35 000 MWh*0,02 kg/kWh	700
CO_2 District heating: 76 000 MWh*0,035kg/kWh	2 700
Total CO_2	**3 400**

Sources: Authors' calculations, Klimatkompassen (2016); Fortum värme, (2017)

Table 2 Baseline for climate impacts

2.3 What can change, what needs to change – potentials for system improvement

How wide is the freedom of action of the energy end users and local system managers, in a ten-year perspective? Their potentials for reducing energy use and its impacts must obviously be greater than the reduction aim if realization is to be at all possible. In the on-going project, potentials are based on literature and experts' assessments, separately for households, enterprises and real estate owners. Here, preliminary findings are presented.

Project estimates indicate that the average Hammarby Sjöstad household could reduce energy use by 5-15 per cent. The wide span stems from a generally valid observation: The difference between high and low users in similar flats can be a factor of two or more, even if you take into account the difference in household size and composition (Gram-Hanssen 2004).

In part, residents could save energy through technical measures such as exchanging bulbs for LED lighting or buying a more efficient fridge/freezer. In the main, however, their field of influence is in changed everyday activities such as keeping the indoor temperature at 20°C, using less hot water or turning off electric equipment standby functions. In the unlikely event that all 8 000 households would realize their full reduction potential, total energy use in the Hammarby Sjöstad's built environment would go down by 5-8 per cent.

As mentioned, there are about 100 enterprises in the Hammarby Sjöstad, and they are very diverse in the goods and services they provide as well as in their energy use: Prewashing in the restaurant kitchen uses lots of hot water and its ventilation hood exhausts lots of heat, while an office uses electricity for computers, copiers etc. Even though reduction measures vary widely between different kinds of enterprise, the research project findings indicate that the average energy savings potential is similar. At 5-15 per cent, it is about the same as that of the households, but together the enterprises occupy only about 5 per cent of the total building area. Even if all of them utilized their full savings potential, reductions in energy use in the district as a whole would be within the margin of error.

The district's about 75 real estate owners on the other hand have an average reduction potential of around 20 per cent through optimizing their buildings' energy systems and another 20 per cent through efficiency measures that are technically and economically feasible within ten years. Optimizations improve the buildings' energy system performance without technical change, through better monitoring and control. Efficiency measures are technical improvements that are feasible investments within the ten-year period. These potentials were estimated through inspections by an energy consultant in around 35 of the estates (concerning the methodology see Willys CT, 2017). If all owners were to realize their full potential, energy use in the Sjöstad's built environment would go down by some 25 per cent. Furthermore, unlike the households' changes in everyday activities, the owners' optimizing the buildings' energy systems and increasing their efficiency are long lasting improvements, sustained by ordinary maintenance.

3.   TRANSFORMATION'S AGENTS OF CHANGE

Assuming that all end users were to fully utilize their estimated potential, the resulting energy savings would be roughly twice of the 15 per cent aim. In that case they, on the average, needed to utilize only half of their respective potentials to reach the aim. If on the other hand half of each category were to utilize their full savings potential, this should also result in 15 per cent reductions. How demanding, then, is transformation? How likely are these extremes as compared to intermediate alternatives?

Reduction Potentials

If all actors do all they can, use their full reduction potential:		
WHOSE potentials	Energy, per cent	CO_2, per cent
All ca. 8 000 households	5-8	4-7
All ca. 100 businesses etc.	≈ 1	≈ 1
All ca. 75 real estate owners	≈ 25	≈ 30
Three actor categories together	≈30	≈35
Transformation aims	15	15

The reduction potential was more than twice the reduction aim, so it could easily be done...

Table 3: Summary of reduction potentials

Together, the Hammarby Sjöstad's 75 real estate owners could in principle realize the energy savings aim without involving the residents or enterprises. The enterprises' contributions to the total is negligible even if all 100 participate, so what is their role in the whole? At most, with all 8 000 households participating, the residents could contribute with one third to half of the savings aim. Furthermore, the residents' contribution mainly takes the form of changed everyday activities, which are less stable than the owners' improvements of the technical system. These observations form the background of the transformation strategy and also indicates its organizational features, the system's transformation agents proper.

3.1 Intermediate Transformation Agents

Given the system boundaries used in this article, only the residents, the enterprises and the real estate owners can directly reduce energy use and its impacts; they are the primary agents of change. ElectriCITY is also inside the system boundaries, with its aim of reducing energy use by 15 percent, but unable to directly intervene. Factual change calls for an organized connection between the two, here called an 'intervention chain'. This in its turn consists of intermediate transformation agents. Some of them participate only in the temporary transformation organization, others are needed to support and manage the energy system also after transformation.

3.2 Strengthening the Savings End of an Intervention Chain

The residents are essentially on their own when saving energy. Being laymen in energy matters, they need to learn from others, and to be persuaded to act. Suppliers can provide them with new energy efficient home equipment, LED lamps etc. As mentioned, the household's visible cost for energy is restricted to electricity use. Heating and hot water are charged for on the rent, making their cost invisible to the end user. It also prevents the provider from using the economic incentive to persuade Hammarby Sjöstad residents and enterprises to save energy.

If an intermediate transformation agent were to provide real-time information on the individual household's energy use, this could be a strong incentive for reductions in use. Literature also indicates that comparison with other households or an element of competition with averages might have the same effect. In both cases ICT could be the means of communication.

Just as the residents, the enterprise's people are laymen in energy issues, and would benefit from intermediate transformation agents' expert advice to facilitate change. In the ten-year perspective, it is feasible to exchange freezers, fridges and other energy usage systems for more energy efficient ones. Suppliers of such goods are therefore needed as intermediate transformation agents for the enterprises. The enterprises' local association might also be involved, for example providing a face-to-face arena for mutual learning.

Around 60 out of the 75 real estate owners are housing cooperatives, which in the Swedish setting means that the owner is a laymen in the association. There are also public and private professional owners. The cooperatives already need to purchase management services from accountants, caretakers, and technical maintenance staff. Specialized energy consultants or energy managers could be contracted as intermediate transformation agents to optimize the energy systems and introduce further efficiency measures. Suppliers could provide ICT, improving the monitoring and automation of the energy systems. Even installing a heat exchanger on the exhaust ventilation could be feasible in some cases. For laymen acting as real estate owners, there is great benefit in learning from others in a similar role. Arenas for this could be face-to-face and ICT based.

The remaining real estate owners are professionals. If their untapped energy reduction potential is similar to that of the cooperatives, they too need the aid of specialized energy consultants and managers. They could also benefit from common arenas for mutual learning.

3.3 Initiating and Coordinating Transformation – the ElectriCITY end of the intervention chain

The residents, enterprises and real estate owners are found at the direct-action end of the intervention chain, where energy use and its impacts are reduced. At the other end is ElectriCITY with its 15 per cent reduction aim but without direct influence on energy use. Bridging the gap between action and aim begins with an analysis such as the one in the previous paragraphs, to identify the necessary intermediate transformation agents. Forging an intervention chain means bringing relevant actors together to identify benefits of contact. Since it is not happening on its own, forging this chain must be initiated from one end by ElectriCITY (Figure 3).

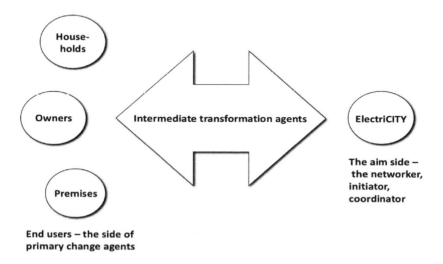

Figure 3: The transformation model has at one end three primary agents of change – the local households, premises and real estate owners – that can directly reduce energy use. At the other end is ElectriCITY – the initiator, coordinator and network builder – bringing the aim to the process and forging the intervention chain of intermediate transformation agents that connects the model's two ends.

Residents, enterprises and owners each need their own combination of intermediate transformation agents, their unique intervention chain. Often, the contact between the primary agent of change and the intermediate agents needs to be formalized in a contract as, for example, between the real estate owner and the new energy manager. But it begins with informal contacts during which the parties can identify the benefits and mutually learn. (Figure 4). As mentioned, the individual residents, enterprises or owners also benefit from coming together for mutual learning among equals. Initiating, supporting and coordinating these contacts is ElectriCITY's "match-making" role. It calls for a set of common arenas, one or two of which are already established. Contact could be face-to-face, ICT-based or take place on the energy market.

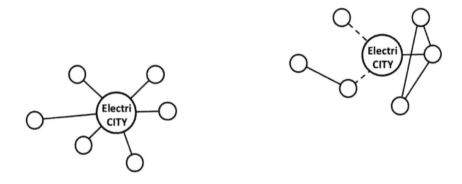

Figure 4: In the beginning, ElectriCITY is the spider of the web, contacts are informal and mediated through the initiator cum coordinator (left). The aim is to formalize direct contact between end user and intermediate transformation agent, ultimately making Electricity superfluous (right).

ElectriCITY's energy project has already established an arena of regular information meetings where board members from different housing cooperatives can mutually learn. Local authorities, energy managers and consultants have introduced their services at such meetings, adding potential actors to the intervention chain. More than half of the cooperatives have had energy inspections, provided by ElectriCITY and the local authorities. The inspector is another valuable transformation agent, especially at the formative stage.

The main connection between the residents and ElectriCITY takes the form of information and persuasion; the desired outcome being less energy demand in the everyday activities without loss of convenience or comfort. The arena here could be an ICT platform, e.g. a cell phone App, introducing the possibility for large numbers of residents to directly interact. The transformation agent cum app provider should also be active, commenting, informing and persuading.

If there is little of cause-effect relations in the uni-directional intervention chain or face-to-face meetings, the multiple influences in an ICT based network totally defy that type of explanation. All the same it could be monitored on a day-to-day basis to function as an informative and persuasive tool of change. In the role as mass informant and persuader, ElectriCITY needs support from professional marketers and also from local authorities that could introduce new policy instruments.

In the main, the Hammarby Sjöstad's primary agents of change do not at present fit into the established professional providers' business models. The research team, for example, found this to be the case concerning energy managers vs. housing cooperatives. However, when a number of cooperatives come together through ElectriCITY's matchmaking, new business models and a potential market might result; bringing together this new demand and the new supplier. In similar ways, ElectriCITY could identify other potential participants in the intervention chain and explore appropriate approaches to involving them.

The findings from the energy inspections could be used to persuade the boards of individual housing cooperatives but also for comparison between them with the same purpose. Here too, the message could be that the energy systems in the buildings can use less energy without reduced quality of services provided to the residents. Face-to-face meetings among board members is feasible as an arena because of the smaller number of representatives, but ICT could also be used.

In the model, it is therefore assumed that information and persuasion uses a wide array of media, including information meetings, marketing's ordinary channels and local authorities' policy instruments. This is of course costly, so ElectriCITY needs to raise funds and to convince the consultants, energy managers, etc. that there is profit in participating. In this, they have already shown that they are perfectly competent through building the present organization.

4.   WHICH IS THE PATH OF LEAST RESISTANCE?

How will the transformation process evolve over time? The system is complex, cause-effect relations rare, and uncertainties abound. Although the theoretical potential is twice the aim, transformation is demanding, success far from obvious. The model should represent these uncertainties through being open to alternative development paths rather than prescribing a single one. For monitoring and development, the system will anyhow need continuous feedback, so the model should illustrate how the actors could prepare for the unexpected rather than provide a strict plan. However, from the article's previous sections, the path of least resistance at transformation's early stages can be outlined, leaving what follows more open.

As has been shown, it is in principle enough for the real estate owners to realize their potentials to reach the 15 per cent reduction aim. However, it is still an extensive undertaking to persuade a majority of them to purchase energy management services that reduce their energy use by an average of 40 per cent, even if given ten years. ElectriCITY could therefore as a first step focus on involving those real estate owners that both have a great technical potential and show an active interest. In practice, they can be found among those housing cooperatives that have done an energy inspection and that have shown up at ElectriCITY's information meetings. Once these pioneers start optimizing their energy systems, the target group can be widened, first to other cooperatives, later perhaps also towards the other real estate owners.

ElectriCITY is already involved in developing a cell phone platform for locals to receive and share local information. The plans are to also include persuasion concerning energy targeted towards residents. This could be an arena on which to test the residents' susceptibility. Enterprises could be approached face-to-face via their local association, also testing their interest of participating. Here, too, the ICT platform could be put to use.

The path of least resistance towards attaining the 15 per cent aim could be quantified in diverse ways, In the full project's report, the intention is to illustrate at least two contrasting such paths. Here we give a preliminary one, presented as an assumptive scenario looking back from 2025:

> *Initially, 30 housing cooperatives pioneered in the transformation with the aim of reducing energy use by 30 per cent. This resulted in 8 per cent reductions in the Sjöstad's built environment. In a second batch, another 25 followed, aiming at 25 per cent reductions in their estates. This added another 5 per cent to the total. Thus, in total 55 owners out of the 75 utilized half or more of their theoretical potential for energy reductions. The missing 2 per cent of the total aim was handled by residents, a small third batch of real estate owners and through further reductions among a few of the first two batches. Enterprises were also gradually involved to support the persuasive argument that 'all are contributing'.*

As can be seen, even this simple calculation illustrates that the aim is demanding although the theoretical potential is twice of the aim.

4.1 From Energy Savings to Climate Impacts

As indicated initially, transformation's aim includes also 15 per cent reduced climate impacts. Experts debate how to recalculate energy use into climate impacts, in Sweden and world-wide. In this article, we assume that electricity use is converted into climate impacts using the "Swedish mix", and that the district heating company's specifications are valid (Klimatkompassen, 2016; Fortum värme, 2014). Then climate impacts are reduced by approximately the same amount as energy use. From this follows a strategically fundamental observation: No extra measures for impact reductions are needed; the climate aim is realized through reducing energy use. If instead Stockholm City's conversion factors are used (Stockholms Stad 2016), climate impacts are still reduced by 15 per cent, but from a much higher total. After transformation, the district's emissions are still around 9 800 tons, which might be insufficient given the magnitude and urgency of climate mitigation. If that is the case, there is a need for a separate strategy for reducing climate impacts, and that strategy must obviously add energy sources with lower climate impacts than the present ones for electricity and district heating

Less obvious but perhaps more fundamental is that this profoundly changes the social side of system transformation, from the end user side, via the intermediate transformation agents to the initiator and coordinator.

The Hammarby Sjöstad's real estate owners could in principle reduce climate impacts through supplementing the large-scale energy systems with local geothermal energy, solar panels and photovoltaics. In the model we so far assumed that this investment, if needed, comes after optimization and increased efficiency, beyond 2025. But given the urgency of climate mitigation, this is too late. Furthermore, local production is probably not enough, also the large system owners and managers need to be included in this mode of system transformation.

Changing the energy sources of large-scale electricity production or district heating has great inertia, technically as well as institutionally (Hughes 1987). Under these conditions, transforming the Hammarby Sjöstad's local energy systems calls for a number of new actors and additional forms of intervention chains besides those previously outlined. Exploring this in more detail lies outside the scope of the article; realizing it within ten years would profoundly increase the demands on the persuasive and organisational powers of ElectriCITY.

4.2 What Can Be Learned from the Hammarby Sjöstad Case?

By definition, a case study is primarily about that individual case. Generalization is often limited, sometimes not even strived for. Still, in many professions case-based knowledge is the norm and learning from one case to others routine (Flyvbjerg, 2006, Johansson, 2005). In this article the Hammarby Sjöstad case is discussed as a socio-technical energy system, the What (technical) and the Who (social) of transformation described in a conceptual model. The model's concepts are in themselves more general than the case description proper and merged to a model even more so. The conceptual model should therefore be applicable to a number of similar cases, more or less as they stand depending on the characteristics of that other case. This illustrates how the researcher can describe a specific case and in parallel generalize to a conceptual model that can be used to analyse other, similar cases.

Such an analysis of other cases can of course also have an openly normative, transformative purpose, asking for example: How could this transformation occur also in other recently built city districts? A tentative first answer is given in the following.

Stockholm has a number of brownfield developments on former industrial and harbour sites, most recently the Royal Seaport (Seaport, 2016). In general, buildings of the early 2000s share many of the Hammarby Sjöstad buildings' technical characteristics and have similar energy systems with similar savings potentials. A large share is housing cooperatives, and the residents are medium and high incomers. Thus, the primary agents of change are also similar. From this it follows that the intermediate transformation agents, the energy consultants and managers, etc. also could be similar.

The main difference between the Hammarby Sjöstad and other city districts lies at the other end of the intervention chain: ElectriCITY and its predecessor the citizen initiative are certainly unique. So, in other recently constructed city districts there is a need for some other actor to take the roles of networker, initiator and coordinator, informer and persuader. Could the local authorities take on a totally new role? Or could market actors initiate parts of transformation on their own? Once the energy consultants, managers and other market based enterprises have established new business models targeted at the Sjöstad situation, the transformation gap is smaller: These new business models need a new, larger market outside the Hammarby Sjöstad, and will certainly look for one.

The model could be applied also to other growing urban areas in Sweden. However, only the very basics of the model could be applied outside the Swedish context of energy system technology, institutional setup and ownership, management culture etc. In particular, the model's social side must by needs vary widely between countries. Differences in local

262

authorities, planning practice, real estate ownership, tenure forms, availability of energy managers and consultants etc. must all be considered when developing a transformation model of a city district outside Sweden.

One issue remains: Are the potentials of reducing energy use and its impacts the same in other city districts, in Sweden and beyond? If they are considerably smaller, the model is not applicable. We have not studied this in the on-going project, so the answer must rely on an assumption. From a few years before construction began, Hammarby Sjöstad has been a showcase of urban sustainable development. If technical and social potentials for optimizing and increasing efficiency in such a prestigious project are in the order of magnitude of 30 per cent, it can be assumed that the owners and managers of less prestigious projects have at least similar potentials at hand. The same line of reasoning could be applied also to the residents and enterprises as primary agents of change.

In other high-income countries, per capita energy is often as high as in Sweden, and in for example the United States significantly higher (Nationmaster, 2017). It seems probable that the potentials for reducing energy use in recently constructed buildings are in the same order of magnitude also in these countries. Based on that assumption, inspections can be made, potentials assessed and the necessary actors in an intervention chain identified. Hopefully the general principles of the model outlined in this paper can facilitate the process.

4.3 The Soft Systems Perspective of the Hammarby Sjöstad's Energy Transition

The conceptual transformation model of the Sjöstad's energy system is hierarchical, with the *social* and *technical* as top level sub systems. The Who and the What of system transformation are iteratively developed to form an integrated whole where there are no technical measures that its actors cannot undertake, and no actors are redundant. This corresponds to Churchman's (1968) long-standing definition of a soft system. See Figure 5.

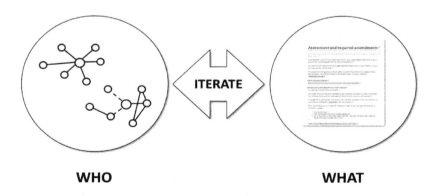

WHO   WHAT

Figure 5: When developing the model of a case such as ElectriCITY in the Sjöstad, the *What* and the *Who* of transformation mutually define one another in an iterative process. The What is the measures initially assumed to be necessary. This indicates the Who – which actors to include. But the actor network thus identified in its turn defines what measures are possible, back and forth.

In its turn, the transition model has two technical sub systems, those of electricity and of district heating. Both end "downstream" in *energy usage systems* (Jonsson et al., 2011). Upstream, only those parts that are influenced by the primary agents of change are in the model. Thus, unlike in normal representations of a city's energy systems, distribution and production beyond the real estate boundaries are outside the system boundaries, and instead of becoming less detailed in the end use part, this is where the model has its focus.

Energy is provided via the production and distribution systems to the flats and premises, for the end users' convenience of comfort. In other words, the systems deliver a set of *services* to the users, such as good indoor climate, artificial light or hot water for personal hygiene. Energy is transformed to services in the aforementioned energy usage systems, for example the radiators, the laptop or the water tap (ibid.). To reduce energy use these energy usage systems can be exchanged for more efficient ones, they can be more efficiently used, or ICT could monitor at least some of them better.

The model also includes the energy distribution systems within the buildings. Energy use in the building's common areas can be reduced and at least the district heating part of the building's energy system can become more efficient. Here, too, novel applications of ICT could automate and monitor energy use better than today.

The energy usage systems form an interface between the technical and the social part of the model. Its social part first represents the different actors that can directly change the local system and its performance. Only the *end users* – the households, the real estate owners and the local enterprises – have direct influence over energy use. Thus, they are the model's *primary agents of change*. If the households are essentially on their own when changing their everyday activities, the owners as already argued for need lasting professional support. The transformation model also needs a catalyst and a series of *intermediate transformation agents*. Together, they form the *intervention chain*. The Hammarby Sjöstad specific model has ElectriCITY at the opposite end of the chain, as *networker, initiator and coordinator*. In other cases, some other actor must take that role.

To bridge the gap between powerless initiator and primary agents of change, the intervention chain needs active collaboration from intermediate transformation agents such as consultants, contractors, marketing specialists, energy managers, local authorities etc. Their influence over energy use is indirect, instead providing expertise, and monitoring and optimizing system performance. To build the bridge, the individual agents of change benefit

264

from coming together, and for this to happen the initiator and coordinator needs to provide an *arena*, be it virtual and ICT based, or real and face-to-face. ElectriCITY and some of the intermediate transformation agents form a *temporary project organization*, while the energy managers/consultants must form *long-lasting partnerships* with the real estate owners. The primary agents of change as well as some of the intermediate actors might benefit from access to common arenas beyond 2025. Just as the intervention chain must grow and develop over the ten transformation years, it is in part dismantled afterwards without totally disappearing.

5. TO CONCLUDE

This conceptual, socio-technical model of the transformation of the Hammarby Sjöstad's energy systems is certainly not a prognosis of what ElectriCITY will achieve until 2025. Instead, if not counterfactual, it certainly has strong elements of futures studies' explorative backcasting, exploring what *could* happen. It is also a scenario of transformation, indicating what *must* happen to realise the initial aim. Thus, it could also be seen as a consequence analysis of the 15 per cent aims.

Modelling starts with an assumption: Our assumption is that energy use and climate impacts in the Hammarby Sjöstad buildings need to be reduced by 15 per cent in ten years from now. Then it explores what it takes in terms of measures taken, and which organization is needed. So far, the transition is illustrated by only one transformation path of least resistance. Ideally this should be replaced by at least two contrasting scenarios. This would better illustrate the openness of the future, the freedom of action of the actors, the indeterminism of future developments and the need for constant monitoring with the 15 per cent aim as a guide.

The model itself could be a persuasive element as well as a practical aid in a transformation process. It could also be part of generalizing findings, to be used for analysis of other cases as well as for introducing transformation in these places. As argued in the beginning of the article, urban sustainable development certainly needs the strategy of gradual improvement in addition to those of construction and refurbishment, given the urgency and magnitude of that challenge.

If realization of the 15 per cent aims also makes the city district smarter is a matter of definition. Reducing energy use is certainly in itself a smart thing to do, and the people involved will learn. Hopefully the initiative could inspire others. ICT is important as an information and persuasion medium and as an arena for actors to engage in multi-directional interaction. It can also monitor and automate the energy systems better than today, increasing system efficiency. Thus, we argue that in the socio-technical model of the Hammarby Sjöstad energy system in transformation, smartness is both an outcome and a transformative tool.

REFERENCES

Börjeson L., Höjer M., Dreborg K-H., Ekvall T. & Finnveden G. (2006) Scenario types and techniques: Towards a user's guide; Futures, vol 38, pp. 723–739.

Checkland P. B. (1999) Systems Thinking, Systems Practice; Wiley.

Churchman C. W. (1968) The Systems Approach; Delacorte Press.

Dreborg K. H. (1996) Essence of Backcasting; Futures, vol 28, pp 813-828.

ElectriCITY (2017) http://www.electricitystockholm.se/ (In Swedish), Visited 2017 01 09.

Evliati M. A., Svane Ö. & Wangel J. (2015) How to "Renew a New City District"? The citizens' initiative HS2020 in Hammarby Sjöstad, Stockholm; Proceedings ENHR conference, jun -15, Lisbon.

Fortum värme (2017) https://www.fortum.com/countries/se/kampanjer/appnyheter-energikonto-varme/pages/miljoredovisning.aspx (In Swedish), Visited Jan 2017.

Flyvbjerg B. (2006) Five Misunderstandings About Case-Study Research; Qualitative Enquiry, vol 12 (2) pp 219-245.

Geels, F. W. (2002) Technological transitions as evolutionary reconfiguration processes: A multi-level perspective and a case-study; Research Policy, 31.8 (9), pp. 1257-1274.

Geels, F. W. (2005) Technological Transitions, A co-evolutionary and socio-technical analysis; Edward Elgar.

Hughes T. P. (1987) The evolution of large technological systems. In W. E. Bijker, T. P. Hughes, & T. Pinch (Eds.), The social construction of technological systems; (pp. 51–82), The MIT Press.

Johansson R. (2005) Case Study Methodology; In Vestbro D. U., Hürol Y. & Wilkinsson N. (Eds): Methodologies in Housing Research; Urban International Press.

Jonsson D. K., Gustafsson S., Wangel J., Höjer M., Lundqvist P. & Svane Ö. (2011) Energy at your service: highlighting energy usage systems in the context of energy efficiency analysis; Energy Efficiency, (2011) 4:355–369.

Klimatkompassen (2016) http://www.klimatkompassen.se/index.php?id=348257 (In Swedish), Visited Nov 2016.

List D. (2004) Multiple pasts, converging presents, and alternative futures; Futures, vol 36, pp 23–43.

Nationmaster (2017) http://www.nationmaster.com/country-info/stats/Energy, Visited Feb 2017.

Nørgård, J. S. (2000) Models of energy saving systems: The battlefield of environmental planning; International Journal of Global Energy Issues, 13 (1–3), 102–122.

Pandis Iveroth, S., Brandt, N. (2011) The development of a sustainable urban district in Hammarby Sjöstad, Stockholm, Sweden; Environment, Development and Sustainability, 13(6), pp. 1043-1064.

Pandis Iveroth, S., Johansson, S. & Brandt, N. (2013) The potential of the infrastructural system of Hammarby Sjöstad in Stockholm, Sweden; In Energy Policy 59 pp. 716-726.

Rip, A. & Kemp, R. (1998) Technological Change, in S. Rayner and L. Malone (Eds.), Human Choice and Climate Change, Vol 2 Resources and Technology, Batelle Press, Washington D.C., 327-399.

Seaport (2016) http://international.stockholm.se/city-development/the-royal-seaport/ Visited Dec 2016.

Stake, R. E. (1995) The Art of Case Study Research, Sage.

Stockholms Stad (2016) § 14 Rapportering av energianvändning och växthusgasutsläpp 2016 Dnr 2016-12427, Utdrag ur protokoll, fört vid Miljö- och hälsoskyddsnämndens sammanträde 2016-10-25.

Svane Ö. (2005) Useful Concepts or Eternal Truths? Reflections on generalisation based on experience from a case study; In Vestbro D. U., Hürol Y. & Wilkinsson N. (Eds): Methodologies in Housing Research; Urban International Press.

Svane Ö. (2008) ...but most buildings are already there Basic starting points for environmental management in the housing sector; In Columbus F. Housing: Socioeconomic, Availability, and Development Issues; Nova Science Publishers.

Svane Ö., Wangel J., Engberg L. A. & Palm J. (2011) Compromise and Learning when Negotiating Sustainabilities – the brownfield development of Hammarby Sjöstad, Stockholm; International Journal of Urban Sustainable Development; DOI:10.1080/19463138.2011.620959.

Wangel, J. (2012) Hur hållbara är Hammarby Sjöstad och Norra Djurgårdsstaden?, in: H. Teleman, (Eds.), Hållbarhetens villkor, Arena.

Wangel J., Gustafsson S. & Svane Ö. (2013) Goal-based socio-technical scenarios: Greening the mobility practices in the Stockholm City District of Bromma, Sweden; Futures, Vol 47, pp. 79-92.

Willys CT (2017): http://www.wctab.se/ (In Swedish), Visited Jan 2017.

CHAPTER 12

PORTLAND, OREGON: A SMART CITY PROTOTYPE

Charles Kelley, AIA, NCARB, LEED BD+C
Principal: ZGF Architects, LLP, Portland Oregon.

Abstract: While automation can be measured by the technologies and systems used in neighborhoods, the real test for enduring success is if the system provides meaningful community benefit and improvement in one's life. This includes connecting appliances in the Internet of Things to networked transportation systems to districts that share energy and open spaces. Smart Cities is a strategy to leverage tools and policies to create healthier and better performing communities.

In Portland, the setting for activities is an important consideration. And, the ability to move around the city to different services and amenities is equally important, preferably by public transportation, by foot, or by bike, especially in this city that pioneered bicycle infrastructure. Portland's history of open source culture, from the early days of software development and Linux to developing interfaces for proprietary systems, informs its approach to enhancing civic life and urban forms. The transformation of community lifestyles has been dependent on supporting urban places and their ease of access to exchange services and civic activities. Urban form is increasingly dependent on access to information technology communication and the exchange of ideas and interests. In Portland, we have found that meaningful value in the community incites collective action to achieve public space, clean air and water, lower carbon emissions, and more efficient energy. Ultimately, improvements create better places that encourage occupants to make wiser lifestyle choices within a smart city.

Through strong community activism and local policy, the City of Portland has innovated an urban configuration and usage indicative of a prototypical Smart City. Three main aspects have emerged: 1) Ecodistricts, in which buildings in neighbourhoods add value beyond their footprint; 2) Placemaking that leverages open space and multimodal transportation system improvements to support community settings; and, 3) Small Interventions in lifestyles that improve overall human health and wellbeing.

Portland has evolved these notions of healthy communities over the last 40 years by working together as a community to successfully realize bike lanes, parks, and clean energy. In so doing, the community has strengthened its resolve to achieve their own interests in cooperation with others, as in the Pearl District neighbourhood. Portland radically changed how citizens use the city in order to achieve open space with cleaner water and air. The community's active participation in city planning and policies improved choices that led to the adoption of the first local climate action plan in 1994. As a result, Portland illustrates a Smart City that leverages policy, politics, and

269

participation to produce better places that amplify health, community cohesion, and wellbeing.

The Portland prototype provides important lessons that are being applied to districts in cities internationally. One of the more recent is Kashiwa-no-ha in Japan. While the district is technologically very advanced, integrated by multiple modes of transit, and supported by an advanced community governance system that integrates business and community interests, these tools were not coordinated to provide a meaningful purpose supporting the evolving interests in the community. The district, using itself as a test site, is implementing Portland's prototype principles to enhance their urban fabric and open spaces in coordination with Smart City technologies. The process shows the principles of the Smart City are adaptable when they are meaningful in shaping spaces that people desire and want to cultivate.

1. INTRODUCTION

Smart Cities is a strategy that leverages tools and policies to create healthier and better-performing communities. Automation of neighborhood functions through technological applications increases efficiency and performance within smart cities. This includes integrating appliances into the Internet of Things and connecting networked transportation systems to districts that share energy and open spaces. For communities to thrive, benefits derived from these applied systems must be purposeful within shared living spaces. Visibly connecting the spaces between buildings is a crucial component because places form along these connections where community benefits may be cultivated and expressed through the quality of experience within each neighborhood. Two case studies illustrate the role of the commons as an integral part of neighborhood design, where the spaces between buildings—open to the sky or weather-protected—create a network of areas contributing to an active and useful public realm, thanks, in part, to information and communication technology.

Portland, Oregon and Kashiwa-no-ha, Japan share a similar approach to cultivating Smart Cities within the public realm. Each has a goal to establish service-rich neighborhoods catering to grass roots initiatives and larger regional policies.

1.1 The City of Portland

The City of Portland, Oregon's public realm straddles the Willamette River and connects large forests and park areas across the region's metropolitan area.

Portland's healthy watershed and air quality today would have been unimaginable in the 1960s. Since then, improving water and air quality have been consistent themes throughout Portland's planning and are now integral to the quality of life within its neighborhoods. The catalytic change in Portland's evolution began when its water and air quality were deemed out of compliance with state and federal regulations for ozone and carbon monoxide emissions, after rules for monitoring pollution in the air and water were instituted in the 1970s. When Portland was threatened with losing its federal community development block grants—combined with State Wide Planning Law requirements passed in 1969 with Senate Bill 10—the city, its business interests, and the wider local community configured new policies and strategies to change the form of the city, aiming to make Portland a healthier place to live. This paradigm shift in policy aligned with business interests to add vitality in districts once exclusively accessed via car. A transition to enhanced public transit required investment in public spaces where transit rider trips were to be encouraged, to make the trip experience competitive with driving. Evolving Internet-based, trip-planning technologies now help people use multiple modes through the city with certitude and confidence.

Forty years of bike and pedestrian improvements have enabled an advanced multi-modal transportation system. Portland has innovated bus, light rail, and streetcar systems and, most importantly, fostered the creation of places that encourage walking and bike riding. Today, Portland's public realm is a smart one because it conveys transportation movements, shares responsibility to manage stormwater through the city's Green Street program, and creates vibrant settings for the local community and its visitors where the outdoors becomes an integrated part of daily life. Physical improvements and changes in the community's awareness and behavior in the public realm have helped organize natural and financial resources across the city and region. Information and Communication Technology (ICT) is now optimizing how the public realm connects building occupants across the city to enable them to live in more sustainable ways.

Once an industrial-dominated city devoid of activity in the evening, and an unhealthy place to live and work during the day, the community has converted lifeless streets into multimodal active and vital places. Source: Evolution of SW 6th Avenue 1970 to Transit Mall 2009 ZGF Architects LLP

1.2 Kashiwa-no-ha Smart City, Japan

The Kashiwa-no-ha Smart City Campus in Japan is a model of an advanced digital district that is responsive to national initiatives.

Once a simple transit-oriented development, Kashiwa-no-ha has been transformed—through green planning technology adapted from Portland—into a place with an active and vital public realm. It features an Area Energy Management System (AEMS) that shaves energy use as normal practice and provides emergency power during times of disaster. This system intentionally layers energy, power, and occupant activity systems—connecting interval data collected from occupant space use with a mixture of automated switches that transfer energy and power in concert with notifications to community members about ways to decrease their energy consumption. While the existing neighborhood information and communication technology system could provide for the community during a disaster, during normal times it did not support aspirations for communal life in the open spaces between buildings. The Kashiwa-no-ha community looked to Portland's approach for a new system to organize neighborhood investments that supported a more robust outdoor community commons experience, including organizing buildings and improvements in the public right of way to form a continuity of experiences in connective spaces. By implementing some simple principles from Portland, Kashiwa-no-ha is now the largest LEED Neighborhood Development (ND) Plan Platinum-certified smart city in the world, and is a model and laboratory for understanding the connections between technology and livability.

Kashiwa-no-ha was initially a simple transit-oriented development but has evolved over time, adapting to become a model of resilience and sustainability in a new 2030 planning concept by ZGF Architects LLP. Source: Mitsui Fudosan Co. LTD, Image by Nikken Sekkei

2.   THE PORTLAND, OREGON BACKDROP

Oregon is unique in the way it organizes growth around cities and requires local jurisdictions to ensure compliance with Statewide Planning Goals. It changes its human movement patterns by reinforcing new public transportation systems, by foot or bike rather than by car (especially relevant in Portland, as it pioneered adaptation of city bicycle infrastructure). The aim is to create measurable value that helps the city achieve its larger livability goals, as required by the State of Oregon. It may be that Oregon's free expression laws, which are the most liberal in the United States, attract a certain kind of person to Oregon and Portland, its largest city. Those who have migrated to Portland and who are now long-term residents seem to understand the connection between setting goals and achieving them collectively as a community. During the 1960s there was a heightened awareness of the environment. For example, the entire state formed a new initiative under then-Governor Tom McCall, approved through Senate Bill 10 in 1969 (then reaffirmed with Senate Bill 100 in 1973), to protect farmland and natural resources from development encroachment, and establish livability as a primary benefit of collective public and private

273

actions coordinated across the state. This was the foundation for Oregon's unique and innovative Statewide Planning Goals. These goals are a manifestation of the open dialogue, resulting in innovative city policy, and are the means for the city to achieve important aspirations. One policy achievement places the onus on applicants during the permit process to demonstrate how they meet or exceed the 19 Statewide Planning Goals. As a result, all jurisdictions tend to support decisions that align with their own and the larger community's goals.

Oregon's unique goal-based planning is a model when studying public-realm improvements. People drawn to the Portland area also tend to embrace open-source culture, from the early days of software development for Linux, to incubating new software businesses based on using Application Program Interfaces (APIs). There is an overall ethic manifest in the community's approach that places a value on enhancing civic life through improvement in urban form and establishes goals to achieve a desirable future. Most importantly, there is recognition that the transformation of community lifestyles has been dependent on supportive urban places to enable the exchange of services and ideas, and civic activities. Downtown Portland's physical organization exemplifies these forces.

The successes of statewide policy changes in the 1970s also led to new thinking about downtown's organization in terms of reducing air pollution. Portland's 1972 Downtown Plan assigned new responsibilities for downtown districts, and the city implemented policies and improvements intended to foster more housing development in the area.

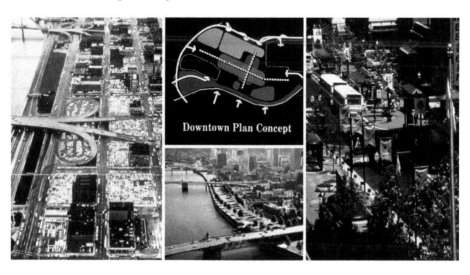

Downtown Plan Concept

The 1972 Central City Plan assigned a new responsibility to each area of the Downtown and identified a transit spine along the downtown Transit Mall and new Waterfront Park to encourage transit-supported, mixed-use development as a means to access the area apart from single occupant vehicles. Source: ZGF Architects LLP

274

In Portland, when the larger community finds meaningful value in pursuing health and livability initiatives, it incites collective action to achieve quality public space, clean air and water, lower carbon emissions, and more efficient energy. Sustaining this new urban environment depends on engaging communication systems to promote the exchange of ideas and connect shared interests. Information and communication technology connects people across the city who are not typically expected to be allied partners and who may support larger community initiatives, such as changing urban neighborhoods to influence the decisions of its individual occupants. Prior to widespread use of APIs, Portland's metropolitan regional government, Metro, generated support for and approved a regional vision called the 2040 Growth Concept. It included a data-driven, goal-based idea for neighborhoods across three counties considering their capacity, and interest, to receive development where transportation improvements and environmental protections could be reasonably planned. It modeled travel time, safety, and transit ridership in radial corridors connecting regions to downtown Portland in order to prioritize and make improvements across the transportation system. Metro used this framework tool to assess and reinforce decisions about land use, transportation, and environmental plans along these corridors. Because of the transparency during the making of Metro's 2040 Growth Concept and the resulting plan, community members are able to understand the underlying planning principles and intended improvements to make their own decisions about where to live and how to get to work, and therefore of which community they are a member. APIs that reveal the behavior of people living in the city give each occupant the ability to compare multi-modal trips dynamically with real-time information. Prior to this technology, efficiency was planned for, or made possible by, the city's design through the imagined capacity of amalgamated buildings, open spaces, streets, water, energy, and other services. Ultimately, both sustained improvements in city capacity and real-time performance feedback is what creates a Smart City. This encourages occupants to make wiser lifestyle choices within a better place.

Pedestrian-Oriented Development

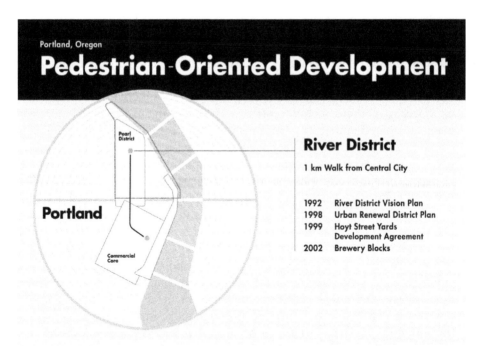

River District

1 km Walk from Central City

1992	River District Vision Plan
1998	Urban Renewal District Plan
1999	Hoyt Street Yards Development Agreement
2002	Brewery Blocks

Portland

The Pearl District is located north of Portland's downtown commercial core. Source: ZGF Architects LLP

During the mid-1990s, the city established a new meaning and purpose for an antiquated rail intermodal distribution and industrial area as a place designated for housing—both market rate and affordable—that would reduce commuter trips to the downtown commercial area. The Willamette River, Interstate 405, SW Broadway Avenue, and north of SW Burnside Street loosely bound the area known today as the Pearl District. A consortium of developers opened a dialogue with the community living in the area's abandoned warehouses and surrounding neighborhoods about how to achieve its goals and exceed the city's expectations for the area. City council directed city and agency bureaus to support the new vision and created a development agreement that coordinated public and private development over the entire district.

The initial public-private partnership that coalesced to advance projects in Portland's Pearl District disbanded once the development had gained momentum. After approximately 10 years, the River District Steering Committee and Coordinating Committee stopped representing private and community interests to plan the district. That role transferred to the Pearl District Neighborhood Association. Both the neighborhood association and downtown business improvement district worked with the city to assume part of the burden of reviewing and approving building projects and maintaining surrounding open space systems. Because of this balance of both public and private investments, it was able to yield a livable compact community with a service-rich, walkable, and vital public realm. Here 27% of housing units are affordable and developed with a net-positive financial outcome on tax revenue. The result is that the Pearl District is now highly regarded nationally and internationally. For example, China Development Bank Capital Corporation (CDBC) published "An Urban Development Case Study of the Pearl District and Brewery Blocks in Portland, Oregon" in 2015. Both Portland's Pearl District and Hammarby Sjöstad in Stockholm are cited as the foundation for CDBC's "Green and Smart Urban Development Guidelines" as a framework for sustainable development applicable across China.

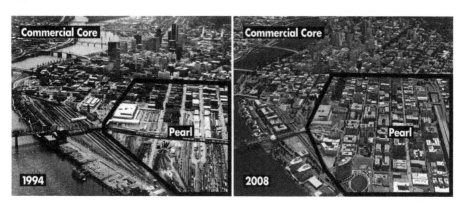

The Pearl District's evolution from a rail yard to a vital, mixed-use district, 1994 to 2008. Source: ZGF Architects LLP and Google Earth (Gray Buildings @2008 Sanborn)

Portland's Pearl District is a prototype mixed-use neighborhood with active and vital streets that accommodate the activities and intensity of uses as an attractive benefit to residents and tenants within a Smart City. Source: ZGF Architects LLP

277

3. PORTLAND SMART CITY: 382% INCREASE IN GDP AND A 21% DECLINE IN CARBON EMISSIONS

The community's active participation in city planning and policies that created the context for the Pearl District was parallel to the adoption of the first local climate action plan in 1994. The resulting deliberations on the Pearl District illustrated how larger initiatives, such as the reduction of carbon and other emissions, are contained in a new type of urban form. One of the basic ingredients of a Smart City is the ability to leverage abstract ideas generated from policy, politics, and participation to produce better places that amplify health, community cohesion, and well-being in a tangible and experiential way. In this process, Portland radically changed how citizens use the city to regenerate cleaner water and air, and to measure other important indicators of healthful urban living. Portland has innovated a unique urban configuration that delivers performance indicative of a model Smart City. Since 1994, the Portland Metropolitan Region has achieved a 382% increase in GDP while Portland and Multnomah County have achieved a 21% decline in carbon emissions. Urban enthusiasts from all over the world visit Portland to learn from its approaches and experience. Four key strategies have driven Portland's success:

1) Configuring open space and multi-modal transportation system improvements to support community settings through placemaking;
2) Designing 20-minute neighborhoods—where various uses in a given neighborhood are within a 20-minute bike ride or walk from where the community lives and works;
3) Creating connections between different places in the city that have a continuity of experience with a pedestrian scale and enjoyable activity; and
4) Empowering community-scaled governance structures, temporary and enduring, that organize neighborhood aspirations and interventions to improve overall occupant human health and well-being.

Portland has evolved notions of healthy neighborhoods over the last 50 years through engagement with the community and improvements that have retrofitted the city with an updated pedestrian realm, bike lanes, parks, stormwater management, and clean energy. In so doing, the community has strengthened its resolve to achieve its own interests through cooperative partnerships between public and private sectors. These partnerships form unsolicited private sector initiatives, development agreements, neighborhood associations, and business improvement districts that support community and business goals.

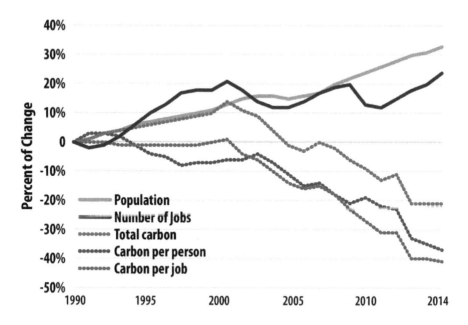

Population and Jobs Up, Carbon Emissions Down

Legend:
- Population
- Number of Jobs
- Total carbon
- Carbon per person
- Carbon per job

"Since 1990, Portland has welcomed 33 percent more people and 24 percent more jobs while carbon emissions have fallen 41 percent on a per person basis. This trajectory demonstrates that it is possible to achieve significant carbon emission reductions while growing the economy and population." Source: City of Portland and Multnomah County, City of Portland, Climate Action Plan Progress Report, April 2017

4.   ECODISTRICT INNOVATION

The initial notion of ecodistricts recognized that at the neighborhood (or district) scale, there lies an opportunity to design truly innovative, scalable solutions to some of the biggest challenges citymakers face today. Started in 2009 and led by the Portland Sustainability Institute (PoSI), the City of Portland established a framework for creating EcoDistricts that included collaborative governance to set and attain meaningful sustainability outcomes. The approach drew on best practices from the city and elsewhere with early adopters piloting the method in Portland and a handful of other U.S. cities. Some of the lessons from buildings, open spaces, and community engagement have informed a new approach in urban design that uses placemaking to create measurable and experiential outcomes with transformational benefits for communities in urban neighborhoods.

BICYCLING	OPEN AIR STREET CAFES	SAFE STREETS FOR CHILDREN	WALKABILITY	STRONG RETAIL BASE	STORMWATER MANAGEMENT	PUBLIC TRANSIT

Ecodistrict systems conserve water, reduce energy, and reduce waste, transforming neighborhood settings with stormwater management supporting community activities and services. Source: Living Future Competition Entry: Portland Symbiotic Districts Towards a Balanced City. ZGF Architects LLP/Portland Oregon Sustainability Institute, 2011

More recently, EcoDistricts (the new nonprofit entity grown from the PoSI) evolved to address national and international demand with a framework that addresses equity, resilience, and climate protection. It takes a collaborative, holistic, neighborhood-scale approach to community design to achieve meaningful performance outcomes that matter to people and the planet. The EcoDistricts Protocol and EcoDistricts Certified provide a rigorous approach for citymakers and project teams. Certification is a flexible performance framework that recognizes that every community has the ability and need to advance a place-based sustainability agenda. District teams tailor the Protocol to local circumstances; they set performance targets, and measure progress over time.

Like the planning of the Pearl District, EcoDistricts Protocol values holistic design and performance at the district scale through meaningful public-private partnerships and other creative governance structures and agreements. The Ecodistrict idea helps municipal communities implement broad initiatives that embrace equity, function more resiliently, and reduce resource use. It is a new tool for communities to build their own capacity. This helps develop projects and programs in their neighborhoods that create tangible benefits. The tool has evolved from a locally created framework, tested in Japan and elsewhere, to an international standard with the purpose of building a cohort of exemplar projects from which to model and test best practices to achieve global imperatives. EcoDistricts Certified is a global verification standard to measure and accelerate innovation using the Ecodistrict Protocol.

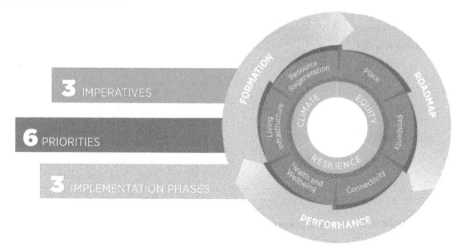

EcoDistrict Protocol includes climate, equity, and resilience imperatives at its center, plus six priorities: Place, Prosperity, Health and Well-being, Connectivity, Living Infrastructure, and Resource Regeneration. The imperatives and priorities work together in three implementation phases: Formation (of a community), Roadmap (a new kind of plan), and Performance (measuring success). Source: Ecodistricts

EcoDistrict ideas were incubated in the Pearl District, a part of Portland's downtown that was revitalized by the **formation** and coordination of residential, employment, and development interests to create a mixed-use residential neighborhood. The River District Urban Renewal Plan provided a **roadmap** that included projects and operational support from city commissioner resolutions, city staff leadership, community engagement, private business interests, and public-private partnerships. The **performance** of a potentially smart development is understood from studying this area. Here there is a balanced mix of uses in an interconnected grid. A predictor of daytime and nighttime activities in the neighborhood, as exemplified in the design of the district's Brewery Blocks, found a strong correlation between a desirable number of people on streets and the associated activity, based on the mix of uses in nearby development. Where areas of the Pearl District include a ratio of three jobs for every resident, there is a relationship between a balance of energy exchange between daytime and nighttime activities and the vitality of the street experience. While bringing an important equilibrium to energy use and generation, this ratio supports the viability of ground-level services, as there is an approximately equal population occupying the buildings during daytime and evening hours. A critical mass of occupant activities, over 18 hours, contributes to street vitality and energy use. This was an important feature missing in traditional urban development patterns and specifically valued in Japan as a means to achieve national priorities through smart city placemaking.

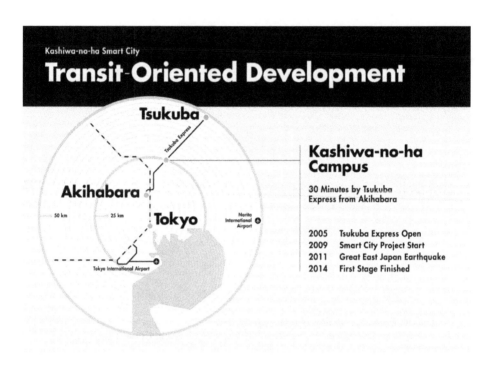

Location of Kashiwa-no-ha relative to downtown Tokyo, as shown above.
Caption: Kashiwa-no-ha, Japan's signature smart city, is located along the Tsukuba
Express line within Japan's High Tech Corridor. Source: ZGF Architects LLP

5.   LEARNING FROM THE PORTLAND EXPERIENCE: KASHIWA-NO-HA, CHIBA PREFECTURE, JAPAN

The Kashiwa-no-ha project started as a transit-oriented development along the Tsukuba Express train line, which opened in 2005 and spurred the Kashiwa-no-ha Campus Station development.

Located on the site of an abandoned golf course, the initial development plan included a commercial mall, LaLaport, and a large multi-block housing community. Part of Kashiwa-no-ha Campus Station's organization is formed by a unique governance structure led by the Urban Design Center Kashiwa-no-ha (UDCK). UDCK is a consortium of public, private, and academic entities working together to make a place that is attractive to both community residents, and commercial tenants and technology industry employees. As people moved into the prototype district and used the spaces, an ever-greater interest emerged in how the neighborhood supported community interests. Residents and businesses found that all of the development's elements and the innovative area energy management system (AEMS)—including other prototyped information and communication technologies—did not, by themselves, improve the public realm and its use between buildings. Commencing in 2006, the UDCK began to serve the communities who were moving into the Campus Station by organizing and adapting development for new residents and businesses in new ways. Over the next 10 years, UDCK helped the community shape the neighborhood, including implementing significant societal changes in response to national disasters and advances in technology.

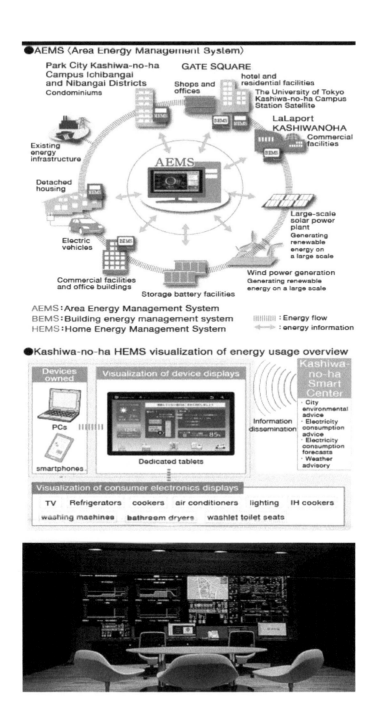

●AEMS 〈Area Energy Management System〉

Park City Kashiwa-no-ha Campus Ichibangai and Nibangai Districts — Condominiums

GATE SQUARE — hotel and residential facilities

Shops and offices

The University of Tokyo Kashiwa-no-ha Campus Station Satellite

LaLaport KASHIWANOHA — Commercial facilities

Existing energy infrastructure

Detached housing

AEMS

Large-scale solar power plant — Generating renewable energy on a large scale

Electric vehicles

Commercial facilities and office buildings

Storage battery facilities

Wind power generation — Generating renewable energy on a large scale

AEMS : Area Energy Management System
BEMS : Building energy management system
HEMS : Home Energy Management System

||||||||| : Energy flow
◄───► : energy information

●Kashiwa-no-ha HEMS visualization of energy usage overview

Devices owned

Visualization of device displays

Kashiwa-no-ha Smart Center
· City environmental advice
· Electricity consumption advice
· Electricity consumption forecasts
· Weather advisory

PCs

smartphones

Dedicated tablets

Information dissemination

Visualization of consumer electronics displays

| TV | Refrigerators | cookers | air conditioners | lighting | IH cookers |

washing machines | bathroom dryers | washlet toilet seats

The AEMS connects with an API to provide real-time display of occupant activities during normal operations, and then supports community recovery after an unplanned disaster. Source: Mitsui Fudosan Co. LTD.

Established in 2009, Smart City Project was an international consortium composed of major Japanese and global firms including NTT, Shimizu

Corporation, Sekisui House, Hewlett-Packard, Hitachi, and Mitsui Fudosan. These companies fully supported the Kashiwa-no-ha Smart City project through the coordinating efforts of Smart City Planning Inc. With support from the Smart City Project, UDCK developed Kashiwa-no-ha as a laboratory to incubate technology across many of Japan's advanced industries to model a new kind of urban development at a neighborhood scale.

In 2011, following Japan's Tohoku earthquake, tsunami, and Fukushima Power Plant disaster, an emphasis on developing a new urban design paradigm to integrate resilience, promote energy independence, support super-aging populations, and improve birth rates emerged as a national priority to achieve at the neighborhood scale. The national government's Cabinet Office encompassed Kashiwa-no-ha Campus Station into this FutureCity Initiative as a demonstration project. UDCK helped Kashiwa-no-ha became an even more advanced standard to test the programs and physical neighborhood improvements to support sustainable lifestyles within increasingly resilient communities. After the earthquake, Kashiwa-no-ha amended its AEMS to include battery storage, an aerobic digester, and the ability to transfer heat between buildings at Gate Square, the development's commercial center, so residents and businesses can operate off the grid during a disaster until regional power and water are restored.

In 2014, Kashiwa-no-ha Smart City Planning signed a Memo of Understanding with the Portland Development Commission (PDC) as part of Portland's We Build Green Cities (WBGC) initiative—an element of the PDC's economic development strategy to export green planning technology from Portland directly to international communities. With a group of local consultant team members who have collectively spent more than four decades working with PDC and transforming Portland into a sustainability showcase, WBGC offered advice on placemaking through public-private partnerships. Representatives from ZGF Architects LLP's Portland office, along with other WBGC members including the PDC, Glumac, Murase Associates, and EcoNorthwest, entered into an agreement with Japanese real estate development company Mitsui Fudosan to design and develop Kashiwa-no-ha's Innovation Campus in collaboration with UDCK to fully realize environmental harmony, healthy lifestyles, innovation, and economic sustainability. The Innovation Campus is located just north of the Campus Station around an existing large stormwater detention pond. WBGC's charge was to analyze and propose methods to create more active and vital community spaces using Portland's proven strategy themes and ecodistrict ideas to unify the Campus Station and

5.1 Innovation Campus

By 2014, Kashiwa-no-ha was implementing UDCK's Campus Town Initiative. This established a planning context for the proposed Innovation Campus. The initiative recognized the need to allow a mix of uses and connect the district with other users in nearby communities to amplify public realm activities in both the Campus Station and the Innovation Campus. The intent included a new public realm experience to satisfy prospective high-tech business desires to attract and retain top employee talent while serving the aspirations of the local business and resident community.

Around the Kashiwa-no-ha Campus Station there was a lack of daytime activity. While there were facilities for biking and walking between the Tsukuba Express station and nearby neighborhoods and institutions, there were not enough facilities for workers, who might linger or use services that contribute to the perception of daytime activity or warrant systemic open-space systems improvements shared with residents. With this as a starting point for WBGC, the Portland team conducted an EcoDistrict Vision Plan by looking holistically at the existing Campus Station and Innovation Campus designs to establish measurable progress toward business goals, resident goals, and national initiatives in a vitalized district. Through a series of role-playing exercises with stakeholders, the WBGC team identified ideas for the neighborhood's configuration to increase the district's population during the day and night.

A new link connects the Kashiwa-no-ha Campus station to a developing employment center within a new Innovation Campus located around a park reclaimed from a fenced-off stormwater detention basin, a place where emerging and established businesses contribute to the activity and vitality of the public realm. Source: ZGF Architects LLP

Working with the WBGC team, the business and resident community identified the value of supporting new connections in an expanded public realm. The places along the proposed connections would be attractive settings to tech companies who might leverage proximity to University of Tokyo, Chiba University, National Cancer Center, as well as other residents and businesses nearby. Programing the mix of uses so there was an equal number of occupants during the day as at night expanded the use of the streets and pathways with activities that would support emerging, established, and growing business services along the ground floor of new buildings. Adopted guidelines organizing building improvements support the desired street character and activity. The resulting open-space system and its potential to be active is important to high-tech tenants, who know employees appreciate active and vital places distinguished by unique environmental character. Existing Kashiwa-no-ha businesses and residents are embracing the needs of those future tenants and their employees, who will ultimately help finance and activate the public realm.

By configuring public spaces around buildings with higher density employment and ground level services, local residents and businesses benefit from the creation of new streets, pathways, and publically accessible spaces, as amenities are shared between the existing and new Kashiwa-no-ha occupants. Improvements planned across the Station and Innovation Campuses included:

1. Establishing a mix of uses to balance evening and daytime activities to better share byproducts of daytime cooling (heat byproduct) and evening heating (cooling byproduct) between daytime workers and nighttime residents;
2. Organizing buildings' ground floors with active uses to enliven the experience along streets and pathways;
3. Using information and communication technology to engage residents and visitors with programmed outdoor events and new civic functions; and
4. Adapting the neighborhood form to manage stormwater in natural settings for programmed activities.

These outcomes were transformative as a means to achieve the activity and vitality the UDCK imagined and the community desired. UDCK continues to plan for development. This local control at a neighborhood level is a significant step forward in area development and regeneration, and a distinct advantage for UDCK. Had it not been for UDCK, the agreements required for coordinated development would not have been possible. And many of the credits applicable for the site's LEED ND Plan Platinum certification would not have been achieved without ideas from Portland about community engagement, mixed-use programing, and placemaking with stormwater management in mind.

6. CONCLUSION

The Portland Smart City prototype provides important lessons that are applicable to districts and other cities worldwide—like Kashiwa-no-ha, which illustrates how Portland's cultivation of the public realm was a model for Japan's signature Smart City project. Engaging connections between unusual partners endured in both projects, guiding and financing community-desired development. While Kashiwa-no-ha is technologically sophisticated, integrated by multiple modes of transit, and supported by an advanced community governance system that merges business and community interests, these tools were not initially coordinated. Only by harmonizing these facets have we provided a meaningful purpose, supporting settings, and activities to respond to evolving community interests. Kashiwa-no-ha has become a smart city test bed, implementing Portland's principles to enhance its urban fabric and open spaces to expand the boundary of its health, resilience, and economic initiatives. The process shows that smart city tenets are adaptable when they are meaningful in shaping the spaces people desire and want to cultivate.

REFERENCES

Carl Abbott, Portland Planning, Politics, and Growth in a Twentieth-Century City. University of Nebraska Press, 1983,Oregon State Wide Planning Laws, Page 250-251Portland's Downtown Plan 1972, Page 215, Department of Land Conservation and Development, Oregon's Statewide Planning Goals and Guidelines, State of Oregon, March 12, 2010, http://www.oregon.gov/LCD/docs/goals/compilation_of_statewide_planning_goals.pdf

Metro Council, Metro 2040 Growth Concept, 1995, http://www.oregonmetro.gov/sites/default/files/2040GrowthConcept.pdf, Portland Development Commission River District Urban Renewal Plan, September 25, 1998, https://scholarsbank.uoregon.edu/xmlui/bitstream/handle/1794/8564/Portland_River_District_URP_1998.pdf?sequence=1&isAllowed=y

Johanna Brickman, Author (Charles Kelley, Illustrator), Ecodistricts: An Opportunity for a More Comprehensive Approach to Sustainable Planning, Trim Tab, Quarterly Publication, Cascade Green Building Council, Winter 2009/2010 pp 27-32, https://issuu.com/ecotone/docs/trim_tabv1_winter2010/19

Japan National Government's Cabinet Office, "Future City" Initiative (FCI), 2011, http://www.japanfs.org/en/projects/future_city/index.html, Smart City Project, Smart City Planning Inc. ,Established as Joint Venture Company to lead a consortium of companies to develop and spread state-of-the-art next generation environmentally conscious cities in Japan and globally, http://www.smartcity-planning.co.jp/en/index.html

Mitsui Fudosan, Kashiwa-no-ha Smart City, A New Vision for the Cities of Tomorrow, Kashiwa-no-ha http://www.kashiwanoha-smartcity.com./en/, Kashiwa-no-ha Environmental Initiatives, http://www.kashiwanoha-smartcity.com/en/concept/environment.html , China Development Bank Capital Corporation, Ltd, The Pearl District: An Urban Development Case Study of the Pearl District and Brewery Blocks in Portland, Oregon. CDBC's Green and Smart Urban Development Guidelines, October 2015, Draft for Comment, http://energyinnovation.org/greensmart/ , http://energyinnovation.org/wp-content/uploads/2015/11/Pearl-District-Case-Study.pdf

EcoDistricts.org, Ecodistrict Protocol, 2017,https://ecodistricts.org/get-started/the-ecodistricts-protocol/, Ecodistrict Certified, 2017, https://ecodistricts.org/ecodistricts-certified/,

City of Portland and Multnomah County, City of Portland, Climate Action Plan Progress Report, April 2017, City of Portland https://www.portlandoregon.gov/bps/article/636700, The Portland and Multnomah County 2015 Climate Action Plan charts a path to reduce local carbon emissions 80 percent below 1990 levels by 2050.

Institute of Portland Metropolitan Studies College of Urban and Public Affairs, Portland State University, Progress of a region: the Metropolitan Portland economy in the 1990s Technical Report of the Regional Connections Project, April 1999, Page 2.15, Table 2.8, Portland Metropolitan Area Estimated Gross Domestic Product, 1994 $45,346,144, 000, https://www.pdx.edu/sites/www.pdx.edu.ims/files/ims_neoprogressregion.pdf

Bureau of Economic Analysis, U.S. Department of Commerce, Gross Domestic Product by Metropolitan Area, 2015, ,Table 1. Current-Dollar Gross Domestic Product (GDP) by Metropolitan Area 2015, Portland-Vancouver-Hillsboro, OR-WA $158,770 200,000, https://www.bea.gov/newsreleases/regional/gdp_metro/2016/pdf/gdp_metro0916.pdf

CHAPTER 13

SEVEN IDEAS THAT MATTER FOR CREATING AND SUSTAINING SMART CITIES

Ian Abbott-Donnelly

Abstract   For cities to be able to thrive in a constantly changing environment they need to see the way they work with new eyes. These seven ideas will provide a diverse set of perspectives that reveal how the city systems functions as a system and presents a set of powerful ways to help practitioners, leaders and policy makers see how to improve the way cities work.

By seeing the city with a systems perspective we can understand why the city does what it does and how it can be guided towards a better future. In times of rapid economic, social and environmental chance one of the things that distinguishes a Smart City is its ability to adapt and evolve.

These ideas have been gathered while developing systems for businesses, new ways of working for governments and while restoring and enhancing the natural environment. Cities are pivotal places where all of these systems coincide so need a range of perspectives to be able to understand the system dynamics. Each idea explores how a city can become smarter by looking at what it does from a systems perspective.

1. Requisite Variety
2. T-Shaped City People
3. The Natural Environment of Cities
4. City Agility
5. Cities Tuning to the Edge of Chaos
6. Working with the Domains of Complexity
7. Information Friction in City Systems

For a city to become Smart it needs more than just technology. For me 'Smart' is about understanding more, thereby enabling better decisions.

1. INTRODUCTION

This set of 7 ideas illustrates that to take a systems perspective is not just a simple recipe. It is about exploring a situation, such as the development of Smart Cities, with insights from many different disciplines.

Cities are certainly complex, the people in cities have a huge part to play in its systems, the infrastructure has evolved from the needs of earlier times and the future needs new and often untried ways of working. There is no one right answer for a city, it needs all of the players: it's leaders, it's policy makers, it's operators and it's citizens to continuously evolve effective ways of interacting with the city systems to make them viable.

These ideas are based on a career of applying information technology to improve systems in business, government and nature. They are highly relevant to Smart Cities because this is where the domains of business, government and nature overlap the most. Cities are where most of the people live on the planet and are the systems that have the most impact on society, economy, climate change and biodiversity.

If you can use these ideas as systems perspectives to help you understand the world they will then help you design interventions at an individual level, at a business level or at a society level that are more likely to succeed and less likely to be surprised by unintended consequences.

The ideas should be viewed as a network of related insights that can be used in many combinations to develop your understanding of Smart City systems and as catalysts to design new Smart interventions.

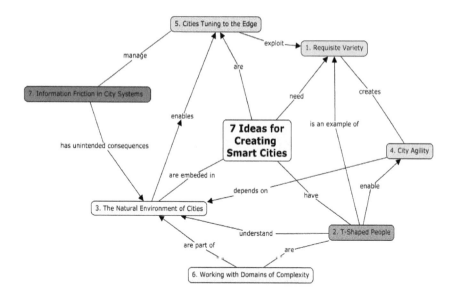

There are many routes through this network. My aim is to provide you with something like a Lego set of ideas and examples that you can then apply to your own situation.

Every city is in a different state of maturity and the same idea will not produce the same effect if done at a different time and in a different place. Part of the reason for trying to isolate these ideas is that they can be applied to all cities from these rich in technology with long established systems to emerging cities that have little exposure to technology. City Smartness is not a direct result of technology, it is more about the way a city uses technology. The poor use of technology can quickly make the most advanced city a 'Dumb' place to live.

My recommendation is that you explore the ideas, initially with no aim in mind. Then consider applying them to your own unique situation by focusing on the biggest threat or opportunity in your city. From this initial idea you can link to adjacent ideas that that will suggest change the way the city systems can operate. Each of the ideas will open up the search space for 'Smart' ways in which systems can be improved.

Creating a Smart City is a collaborative venture, it always has been. The difference today is that we now have insights from rich sources of city information and an increasing array of technology enabled tools to help us make cities that are worth living in and enhance the natural environment in which they reside

2.   REQUISITE VARIETY

Requisite variety describes what it takes to be able to create an effective system.

2.1 Context

When creating and operating any system it is vital that the available options to control the system are well understood and are well suited to the task in hand. For cities that are both complicated and complex in nature it helps to explain why it is so difficult to make them Smart.

If a city system is to work well and be stable, the number of states, of its control mechanism, must be greater than or equal to the number of states in the system being controlled. This is achievable for many complicated parts of a Smart City, but also impossible when systems display highly complex behaviours. Good control systems can cope with highly complicated systems, way beyond the capabilities of people. However when systems are complex in nature there is an important place for people-in-the system to be able to make judgements about how to work with the complexity. This chapter's focus is on the systems that are controllable and what it takes to do this. Idea number 6 'Working with Domains of Complexity' looks beyond this at systems that are inherently uncontrollable.

The usefulness of Requisite Variety comes from the ability to see when there is a mismatch between the system and its controls. Once this is understood, a systems designer can either vary how complicated or how simple, the control system is, in order to achieve a better match. Using the idea of Requisite Variety enables systems designers to design systems that are more likely to work and be more reliable in operation. Without it, systems are likely to suffer from poor control and generate frequent surprise.

The originator of the idea of Requisite Variety is W. Ross Ashby 1903-1972. (Ross Ashby Digital Archive, 2016) A British pioneer in the field of cybernetics and the development of systems theory (cybernetics being the science of communication and control). He first developed the **Law of Requisite Variety** in the domain of biological systems but it quickly started being used across many domains of science, including human and machine-based systems where it became a practical tool for good design.

If we look at any system, whether it is a biological organism, a mechanical infrastructure, a human organisation or a digital system, we can

294

see that it is constantly confronted by many events from the environment in which it works.

The insight underlying the idea of Requisite Variety is that to be able to cope well with the environment in which it is working, a system needs to be able to match the variety of the environmental system.

- Too little variety in the system and it is unable to exert effective control or has inappropriate responses that result in unintended consequences.
- Too much variety and the system becomes costly and inefficient.

2.2 Examples of Requisite Variety

Perhaps one of the best examples of a control system that is in balance is the humble light switch. If the aim of the system is to be able to provide light or no light then the simple switch is all that is needed.

ON/OFF switch controlling the on/off system of a light

However, there are many situations where this simple control is insufficient. To be able to cope with the needs of the environment in which the light operates it may need to control many additional aspects. For instance:

- when the light comes on
- how bright the light is
- how rapidly the light needs to change from on to off
- how much power the light consumes
- the colour of the light
- the direction of the light.

A theatre lighting system shows Requisite Variety working at a much more complicated level.

It needs to create atmosphere, to direct attention and illuminate the moving performers, it needs a control desk with thousands of options, faders and timers, plus the skill of a creative lighting engineer. A lot of the operations can be recorded and automated. However, for a live performance, this complicated application shows the need for 'people in the system'. The control desk alone cannot cope with the uncertainty and nuance needed to respond to the interactions of performers and audience that make live theatre so special.

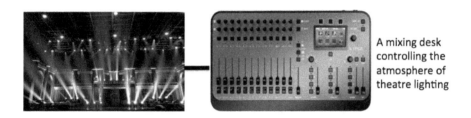

A mixing desk controlling the atmosphere of theatre lighting

Moving up the scale to a city lighting system, this shows Requisite Variety working at a far more complicated level.

To be able to cope with the incredibly varied needs of lighting from buildings to transport systems, from fibre optic communications to laser surgery the idea of creating a bigger, more complicated control desk will not come anywhere close to achieving Requisite Variety.

Complicated communications technology, the internet-of-things and data standards do, of course, enable cities to do far more in terms of controlling lighting systems. However, at this scale the system has become complex in the scientific sense; it is a complex adaptive system. In this situation, the 'people in the system' and how they collaborate are the way Requisite Variety is created. People design the systems, the policy, the feedback loops and the governance. The more the city can use its own data the more it can create a distributed collaborative intelligence from which can emerge the essence of Requisite Variety.

People collaborating across city systems:
- Governance
- Business
- Culture
- Construction
- Infrastructure
- Policy
- Standards
- etc.

Cities themselves are obviously complex places. Through the intertwined nature of history, geography, culture, economics and technology cities have emerged as places that attract: people, construction and trade. However is often very difficult to see what is going across the city systems; few people have a good picture of the whole system. The systems are designed and optimised in isolation and there is constant and rapid change being imposed at every point.

All cities are constantly confronted by events across the spectrum of the economy, society and the natural environment. To be able to thrive in its context the city develops a wide range of systems to be able to respond to past events and optimise current events and design capability for future events. Therefore city systems need to be in constant flux in the search for Requisite Variety.

In a place as complex as cities, the chances of perfection in terms of 'Requisite Variety ' are very low. Even if a city were close to perfection, the world around the city would be changing again and again.

This suggests that systems need to be designed with this incompleteness in mind; constantly searching for the right amount of variety yet leaving space to adapt in new directions.

This idea of leaving space to adapt is an important part of infrastructure design. Infrastructure can become very fragile if it is designed with only efficiency in mind. Conduits built for electricity or water and other services need to mindful of an unpredictable future. For example replacing cast iron water pipes with plastic, replacing copper communications with fibre optics or replacing centralised electricity generation with distributed generation. The quest for efficient in the short term can quickly result in a city being constrained by its past. Urban design is not just about the current - it needs to design in requisite variety to be able to be resilient to a different future.

One of the best ways of increasing the ability to cope with variety in a city is to ensure there are **'people in the system'**. A city system that has fixed infrastructure and is highly automated runs the risk of becoming fossilised and brittle - unable to cope with the unexpected and unable to evolve.

A lot of the Smartness of a city comes from its ability to respond in an efficient way to the problems it faces.

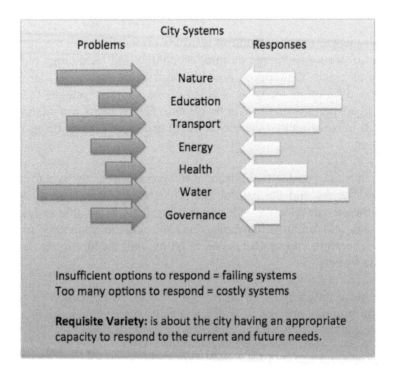

"*Every good regulator of a system must be
a model of that system.*"
(Ashby & Conant, 1970)

In the city context what this means to me is that it is only the city itself, the people and the systems working together, that has any hope of guiding, controlling and developing the city systems in a healthy direction.

If a city is dominated by one system it has no chance of working well. This can be seen when a city is taken over by just one domain. This could be a military dictatorship, a religious cult a single dominant industry or when it is hit by the impact of some natural system such as a flood or an earthquake.

When one system dominates, the other subsystems just do not have the Requisite Variety to respond well to the unfolding challenges the city faces. When dominated by just one system the city will always degrade. Over-consuming resources, eroding social good will, slowing down innovation and struggling with inflexible systems that cannot cope with the needs of the real world.

Cyber Security is an important topic to enable a city to become smart. It is important to develop a sufficient level of requisite variety to protect against the threats to good governance: Trust, Identity, Privacy, Protection, Safety and Security. (See Chapter by Florence Hudson & Mark Cather for details of TIPPSS) In this context designing people into the system is a vital strategy.

The idea of Requisite Variety suggests that it is only through extensive collaboration, intense systems thinking and constant growth in diversity of the city, will it be able to work with the current situation, make wise decisions and design a healthy future for citizens.

Requisite Variety helps cities move beyond the commonly found issues:
- **Monocultures** that become fragile to change e.g. old industrial zones or suburban sprawl.
- **Single success economies** that are doomed to decline e.g. ship building, iron & steel manufacture, coal mining.
- **The sameness of culture** that restricts a city's ability to learn e.g. in a closed country such as North Korea.

The key message for a Smart City is that complete control is not possible. Instead, it is necessary to create sufficient complexity so that the city can self-organise. Understanding Requisite Variety is a vital insight towards creating the conditions for city self-organisation.

The huge threats of climate change, the velocity of technological change and shrinking world dynamics as people realise that we all live on one tiny blue marble spinning in space, all suggest that the pace of change will not slow down in the future. By constantly seeking Requisite Variety a city can hope to adapt to the changing world in which it finds itself.

3.   T-SHAPED CITY PEOPLE: SEEING PEOPLE AS A VITAL ENABLER OF CITY SYSTEMS.

T-shaped people have both depth AND breadth to their knowledge, skills and experience.
These characteristics are increasingly necessary for a city to be able to ride the constant waves of change.

3.1 Context

T-shaped people are what innovative organisations are looking for to be able to create high capability teams. T-shaped city people take this idea to the wider population and to the heart of its' education system.

The 'Smartness' in a smart city comes from the creative combination of people and their use of technology. To be T-shaped, a city needs to enable its people to learn, developing both a breadth of understanding across many disciplines and some specific specialism where people can create value.

In a Smart City, it is vital to see beyond the foundation of the hard, fixed infrastructure - the buildings, the bridges, the roads, the pipes, the pumps and the concrete, that forms the visible artifacts of the city. To become smart, cities need to see themselves as systems. With this systems perspective, the people in the city can see how the system works and thereby open up the possibility that it could be improved.

To be able to see the systems perspective people who live and work in the city need to grow in two directions. Deeper learning is certainly an advantage, and there are many good examples of cities becoming specialists 'I' shaped so that they are able to compete well in the global market for goods and services. However, on its own, depth is not sufficient. The advantage at a city scale is that through collaboration people can develop much deeper levels of specialism, thereby creating innovation and new sources of value. However without some people in the city looking after the broad perspectives cities can grow themselves into a fragile cul-de-sac. Cities that can combine and re-combine specialists significantly increase their chances of success in a changing world.

Learning is not just about schools and the city having a good university, it is about the whole population constantly learning how to live well in the current situation and contributing creatively to the process of designing and building the future city.

The city needs to see itself as a learning machine able to cope change. Cities appear to be changing faster and faster: it is probably a function of the 'Super Linear Growth' idea from Professor Geoffrey West combined with advances in technology enabling cities to be more connected at the global scale.

The thing that great organisations recognise, be they businesses, governments or social movements, is that they are at their heart a people based system. Certainly, they do have complex systems of technology supporting their operations, everything from, financial accounting, to governance, to marketing and much more. But it is the people that make the whole system possible.

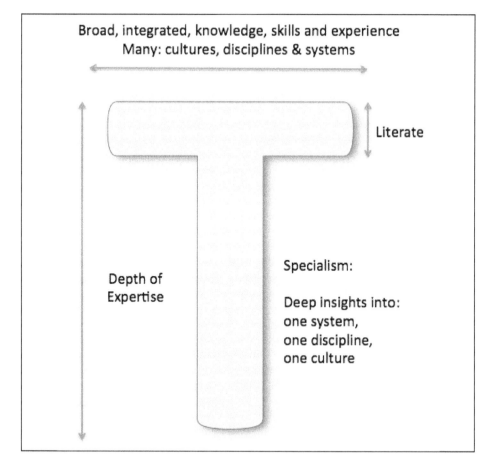

The idea of a T-shaped person appears to have been first used in the early 1990s as a metaphor to describe the abilities of a person in the context of recruitment. The aim being to find people that could work well in interdisciplinary teams. This breadth of experience to be able to collaborate covers many aspects including culture, domain knowledge, and understanding of systems.

T -shaped people are all about combining two types of skill. The cross bar or the T represents a breadth of education and experience, whereas the vertical bar of the T represents the depth of knowledge and tenacity to apply themselves to create innovation that matters. A wide range of industries from technology to engineering to design are using the idea of T-Shaped people to recruit develop their workforce.

The idea of T-shaped citizens needs to start in schools but be well understood by the wider city. The value of T-shaped city people is that by working together they can develop collective intelligence that works well with and in city systems.
In business this ideas has been termed 'Collaborative Advantage' by Hansen and Nohria

In school, it's all about individual performance...but there's more to being T-shaped than just having breadth and depth. It's also about having balance and the agility to pick and choose from a set of knowledge and skills as they are needed."
Jim Spohrer, IBM University Relations
(Spohrer, 2016)

Cities need to go beyond the curriculum focus of schools. The curriculum is not the target for education; rather education is about creating capacity within people to develop their individual talents and the capacity for collaboration to create a society with collective intelligence.

Businesses are finding that the higher education system isn't geared up to create T-shaped people. They focus just on the specialisms (vertical bar) and leave the students to work out for themselves the value that is embedded in the horizontal bar.

Like businesses, cities can also benefit from having T-shaped people as citizens. It is exactly the skills, knowledge and experience of T-shaped people that drives innovation, collaboration and openness to new ideas that are the foundations that drive a prosperous city. For a city to be 'Smart' the people in the system also need to be 'Smart'. My assertion is that the more T-shaped citizens translate directly into Smarter Cities.

302

3.2 What happens when a city does not enable T-shaped People?

If you look around at cities that grew up in the industrial age of Iron & Steel they often find that now in the knowledge era their underlying fabric of economic, environmental and social systems just cannot adapt quickly enough to the new realities. The city rapidly declines because it has developed a specialism that is no longer relevant or in demand.

The decline may also be because a city is too general purpose. The reason for existing has become unclear; there is little sense of place or a compelling reason to make it special. Sometimes it has simply has lost the will to be the best in the world at something... anything. Instead, the city just exists; living off the proceeds of past success.

A city may struggle because it cannot integrate across many of its systems and domains. Some parts of the city attract all the economic activity, capture the best environmental locations and create a disconnected privileged society, while other parts of the city become second-class, disadvantaged both economically and socially. This lopsided shape of city success then sows the seeds of further decline. A city that does not integrate well limits prosperity to a few and drives social unrest in the many. It becomes a place where no one rich or poor wants to live because of the high crime rate, poor culture and damaged environment. Young people increasingly move away at the earliest opportunity and the cycle of decline picks up pace. This exodus of the youth means that the city skills become fossilised in the needs of the past, limiting the ability to adapt to the inevitable changes of the future that need fresh, new, open thinking.

This picture of 'Un-Smart' cities is especially important when you observe the acceleration of technology adoption.

Technology adoption is becoming easier, faster and less expensive. This plot, illustrates the pace of change well, since it is easy to see this change in the physical devices around us.

Technological Acceleration

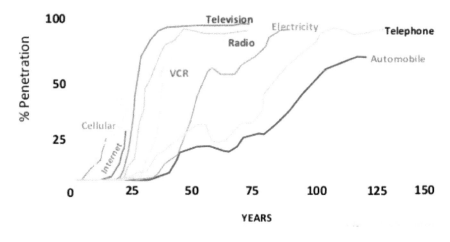

(What's UP at IBM, 2013)

Many other city technologies are also coming into play in cities at a very rapid rate:

- LED lighting is transforming domestic, industrial and public lighting by being easy to swap out, far more efficient and needing less maintenance
- Solar power is popping up on homes, warehouses and in agricultural landscapes as the materials and efficiency undergo constant improvement.
- The ethics of autonomous vehicles are being talked about a lot at the moment - while many of the most valuable technology features are being installed piecemeal and used on a large scale, e.g. Start/Stop engines, Self parking, Lane control, crash prevention, internet connection, emergency assistance.

However, the real message is that this trend is happening in the softer systems of cities, the city data the city services and the interconnectedness of people and things. The technologies plotted on the graph are not just fashions in consumer goods; these technologies have changed the very fabric of cities and how they work. Here are a few examples:

- Access to city information has exploded in recent years. For the developed world it centres on the Internet, however even in the developing world where the Internet is weak, the mobile phone is revolutionising access to information.
- Mobility and the ability to connect to people, has changed the very nature of work, social life and culture
- The city economy has made a massive shift from the physical industries to knowledge working and services

The Internet-of-Things (IoT) is the latest trend. By combining sensors, communications and compute power technology can now be embedded in a vast diversity of real world objects. This will transform our awareness of what is actually happening in the real world and if used well will enable a new kind of Smart City.

These technology trends are just in their infancy and we are only just learning how to use them to create value. Much of the IoT is just at the stage of producing data, it is in great need of being transformed into useful information and analysed for valuable insight.

These shifts in technology are affecting the very nature of work. Many of the jobs that are emerging in cities did not even exist a few years ago e.g. Smartphone App developer, social network manager, cloud infrastructure designer, distributed renewable energy operator, 3D additive manufacturer are a few examples. These might start as specialised skills but you can already see how they are changing the nature of even very physical jobs.

To be able to cope with a vast array of new and unusual jobs the people employed in cities need increasingly to become T-shaped in order to both collaborate well and to add sufficient value with their specialist skills. Without this level of skill, jobs become commodities with little job satisfaction and are rewarded by low wages.

It is estimated that 85% of the jobs that today's learner will be doing haven't yet been invented,
they'll be using technologies that don't exist to solve problems we don't yet know are problems"
Jim Spohrer, IBM University Relations (Spohrer, 2013)

One of the big shifts that is taking place is that information - the new natural resource for cities - has become super-abundant. This means that instead of the value a worker in a city coming from what they know it moves to what they can do with knowledge. In this context, domain expertise is still necessary, but no longer sufficient. It needs to be combined with the ability to integrate across several domains and systems.

On a city scale, the art and science of driving prosperity is also changing. In the industrial age, it was all about exploiting the city resources - water, transport, minerals and labour. Now it is about to create value using information and technology.

Cities need to take care of citizens that are struggling with technology and the ability to make effective use of information. The WWW is only 28 years old so there is a large part of the population for whom the information age is not where they grew up.

Simply exploiting resources is no longer where the potential for growth lies for cities. As Professor Geoffrey West has shown when a city grows, it not only benefits from the network effect of growth but also suffers. The bad things in city systems also grow - the pollution is worse, the crime is worse, and the city resilience is worse.

Prosperity in cities going forward will not be about simply consuming resources, it will be a function of better resource use, being able to adapt more quickly and creating value from integrated services.

Luis Bettencourt [53] of the Santa Fe Institute describes a city as being made up of the interaction of Matter-Energy-Information. People living in cities with T-shaped skills enable the matter of cities to be designed better, the energy in cities to be used more efficiently, driven by the effective use of information.

Instead of exploiting resources, the potential for prosperous and sustainable city growth lies in the new systems of the knowledge economy. These actively decouple value-creation from resource use. Using data, knowledge and systems means a city can generate rapid economic benefits simply by being more efficient with energy, time and materials. It can diversify the economy without high infrastructure changes; quickly respond to new needs and increasingly it can move from a product-focused economy to a more flexible service based economy.

"None of us is as smart as all of us".

(Rogers, 2015)

The 'T-Shaped' Populations of Cities

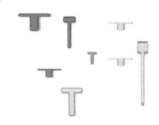

A Smart City:
- Is where citizens have the opportunity to develop their talents and have a broad education and experience.
- Diversity of expertise is everywhere
- Collaboration is pervasive.

A Struggling City:
- Is were citizens have few opportunities to develop talents
- People see the world in very narrow ways
- Populations are polarized

In this emerging knowledge economy of cities T-shaped people are needed in abundance. Cities need people who are skilled in collaboration, not just collaborating with others with different T-shaped skills but also with technology to amplify their skills. The term Kevin Kelly (Senior Maverick at *Wired* magazine) uses is - 'artificial smartness' - the ability of technology to do (some) things exceptionally well. When T-shaped people work with this technology it opens up huge opportunities to make cities better.

The city first transformed when industrial development added horsepower to its systems - increasing the capability of everything from pumps to trains to communications. The current era is about augmenting smartness of people to amplify the personal smartness, making cities more efficient, more resilient, and more innovative. Artificial intelligence is not about robots taking over the world - it is about people working with technology

Although it does need to be recognised that technology is a double-edged sword. On its own, it is neither smart nor dumb. With poor governance, it can certainly bring many negative consequences and lead to a decline of civilisation. The mark of a Smart City is not how much technology it has but what value it creates with these new tools. A Smart City needs to move on from the simplistic dynamics of growth and develop a real sense of what the city should be optimising. My hope is that by careful use of technology we can understand more, move from guessing to knowing and thereby make better decisions.

My personal experience of two global business organisations that have lasted over 100 years (Thomas Cook the travel specialists and IBM the technology company) has shown me that when they are at their best, most dynamic and most innovative the people in these companies are making full use of their T-shaped capabilities. In effect the whole company becomes T-shaped, they are designed not just as a single specialised business, they have breadth and a series of interconnected businesses that are constantly learning.

My assertion is that all citizens in a Smart City need to become more T-shaped, it is not just about the professionals and the elite, it needs every citizen to develop their talents and to be effective collaborators. Being T-shaped is also not just about the world of work - it also applies to leisure and culture. It is especially important where city work is repetitive manual labour that people have the opportunity in other aspects of life to follow more deep interests. Though not easy at the scale of a large city, it is a vital part of becoming a Smart City.

There are some businesses that are taking this idea one step further as a way of enabling innovation. The idea is for people to develop ore than one area of expertise. Taking the idea from T shaped to Pi shaped

$$\pi$$

Pi shaped people combine expertise in more than one discipline to enable innovation.

Although this looks a very attractive idea for dynamic businesses striving to invent new solutions products and services, cities would do well to reach a high degree of T-shaped people since many of the benefits of Pi shaped people can come through collaboration.

To close this chapter, this quote illustrates to me the importance cities striving to climb out of ignorance.

"The evil that is in the world almost always comes of ignorance, and good intentions may do as much harm as malevolence if they lack understanding."

(Camus, 1947)

4.   THE NATURAL ENVIRONMENT OF CITIES

The city does not stand alone as a system, it is,
a 'wholly owned subsidiary' of the natural environment.

4.1 Context

It is increasingly easy to live our life disconnected from the natural systems that surround us. We live many hours a day living and working indoors, engrossed in the digital world. We need to remind ourselves that every aspect of a city is built on the resources of the natural systems. The city is completely embedded in the natural world.

City systems rely one hundred percent on the natural systems to provide water, energy, food, materials and waste management. Most cities developed in a specific place because that was where there were convenient local resources combined with a favourable physical geography. As the city grew there was fresh water to hand, the surrounding soil was good for agriculture and the port was practical as a place from which to trade. During the industrial revolution, it was the place to bring together resources from further afield - wool, cotton, iron ore, coal and minerals. This concentration then created new industries and economic prosperity.

Cities are now hugely more complex than in their early beginnings, but the principle still holds that they need good access to clean water, secure food, reliable energy, minerals, construction materials and transport options. These may now come from distant places but the systems of the natural environment are still as the sole supplier.

In the globally connected world, every city is now dependent not just on its' own local environment, but also on systems in the cities with which it trades. This dependency extends across the whole planet when you consider large-scale systemic threats to cities from climate change, extreme weather events, air pollution, sea level rise and resource shortages.

To be 'Smart' today, the city needs to understand and work with the natural systems at all levels: local, regional and global.

One of the first steps a city needs to recognise is that the natural world in which it resides is itself a 'System of Systems'. Often just referred to as ecosystems, nature has evolved into a fantastic interdependent network. In our quest to understand things we separate things into boxes to be able to simplify study. The real world is however not like this. Reality is that we are highly connected to this natural system of systems - even in the most Smart City we would not last long without fresh air, clean water, quality food and an aesthetic environment.

> *"The major problems in the world are the result of*
> *the difference between how nature works*
> *and the way people think."*
>
> (Bateson, 2011)

4.2 Smart City v Resilient City

It is evident that many cities are falling behind in their resilience as they lose connection with their natural systems. When cities are small there is a large amount of capacity to change and adapt to emerging conditions in the surrounding natural environment. An emerging city has room to manoeuvre.

However, with today's incredibly complex interconnected cities this ability to adapt needs to be designed into the fabric of the city. Instead of adapting, city districts often appear to need to decline to a decrepit near death situation before they can then redesign things to cope with their new realities of a changing world.

A stark example can be found in the tragedy of New Orleans at the time of Hurricane Katrina. Developers grew the city focused on the principles of economic gain but they had little regard to the impact of hurricanes and flooding in a low-lying city. It was only a matter of time before catastrophe would strike as the city grew out of the wetlands.

> *"There is no such thing as a 'Natural Disaster', there are*
> *significant natural event that have disastrous consequences by virtue*
> *of what humans have done or not done"*
>
> (Williams, 2016)

It is possible for New Orleans to cope much better with the risks of extreme weather and the risks from floodwater. But it takes an awareness of the changing risks combined with creativity and investment, to design in resilience. Many cities in the Netherlands are doing an excellent job of designing with water in mind.

UNISDR has been addressing the need for resilience in city systems using it "Ten Essentials" and a detailed assessment using the City Resilience

Scorecard. (R P Williams, (2016) [54]. It has been developed with experience and expertise from government agencies, the engineering company AECOM and Technology company IBM

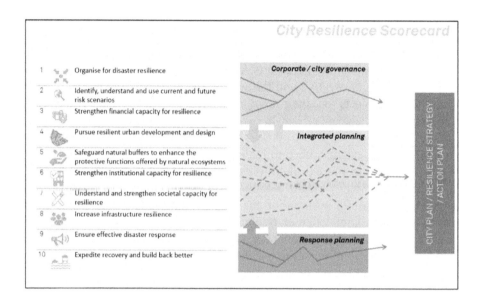

To build Urban Resilience it takes collective intelligence across all the city systems. It is far from easy to do...but in my experience can be both fun and productive because everyone in the process learns huge amounts from each other about a place you thought you knew well. The down-side is that city leaders often fall into the trap of politics; focusing on self-interest, believing only in their own ideas and relying on public relations spin, rather than practical capability, as their measure of city direction and progress.

A Smart City, by contrast, uses evidence to form a realistic view of how it creates value and prosperity. It measures much more than just economics and extensively uses collaboration as the preferred tool for driving change.

It is vital that cities create a connection between its' people and the natural environment.

A city depends entirely on the natural environment for clean drinking water, breathable air, healthy food and even the aesthetic experience of the city landscape. Without well-functioning ecosystem services a city will deteriorate rapidly; suffering economically and culturally.

The connection between a city and its natural systems needs span the whole population. However, children in cities are vulnerable since it is now very easy to grow up with little recognition of the value of nature. One of the problems is that education systems in most cities become fixated on the value of learning the core subjects of language, mathematics and science. These are of course vital parts of a well-rounded education, important building blocks for progress. But they have big problems in the way they break down systems into piece parts. They are weak at the integrated view of the world in which we live and the way the natural environment functions. These core subjects on their own miss out on the essence of systems thinking.

Curriculum designers need to realise the skill of remembering facts is no longer the ticket to success that it once was. The combination of the Internet and mobile technology means that the average primary school pupil now has access to more useful information than a university full of professors. In the Internet enabled knowledge era, education shifts towards the importance of understanding information, connect knowledge, and apply insight to create value, and away from remembering facts.

At the heart of the problem is the design of our current education system; its business model was designed for the industrial age. In the industrial age, fragmentation was a useful strategy, however, in the knowledge economy we need to move beyond this and layer on a more integrated view of the world and add systems thinking to connect fragmented parts.

Take the case of the humble worker that comes to repair a domestic hot water system in the city. Because this is a heating 'system', the industrial age approach is no longer sufficient, the person providing the service now needs an integrated education to be able to cope with the many demands of the system.

Plumbing, is of course, an important part of the city infrastructure, but it is no longer a profession that is just about the pipes.

- Increasingly cities need to take great care of their water.
  Understanding where it comes from and where it goes is a vital part of maintaining the quality of drinking water and effectively managing waste water. With climate change there are great risks of the risks of too little water and too much water.
- The heating boiler is now controlled electronically and digitally, with new boilers being connected to the internet as part of the Internet of Things (IoT)

- A global supply chain now supports the hardware, so now it needs digital skills for Internet ordering and technical support.
- The design specification is increasingly precise, so knowledge of science and engineering is a must to be able to choose the right product to install.
- Heating systems (and air conditioning systems) are a major contributor to the CO_2 footprint of a city. So the plumber needs to know the significance of climate change and how to select products and configure settings that make a positive difference to the environment.
- Added to this technical knowledge is customer service; a vital part of the business model. Insights from social science and the rigour of accurate data management are key to delivering good customer service.

Every job in the city now has this need for a complex, systems perspective.

One example of education using a systemic approach is a groundbreaking project in the UK called 'Natural Connections'. This project has revealed how important it is for children to have the opportunity to learn outside the classroom in the natural environment.

"One of the big challenges for children growing up in cities is that three-quarters of UK children spend less time outside than prison inmates!

This finding is from a recent survey that revealed the extent to which time playing in parks, wood and fields have shrunk. A fifth of the children did not play outside at all on an average day, the poll found.

The new survey questioned a nationally representative sample of 2,000 parents of 5-12 year-olds and found 74% of children spent less than 60 minutes playing outside each day. UN guidelines for prisoners require "at least one hour of suitable exercise in the open air daily".

(Natural Connections, 2016)

The decline of children time in the Natural Environment has a profound effect on many things like physical health, mental health, and engagement with the wider world.

The Natural Connections project tested a series of interventions in the way schools used the idea of 'Learning in the Natural Environment' and measured the positive impact on pupils. It concluded that, along with the specific benefits listed below, this style of learning creates the vital conditions for improving overall education - improving the 'character of children' and increasing the motivation of teachers.

The project found that positive impacts, for pupils, from Learning in the Natural Environment include:

- enjoyment of lessons (95%)
- connection to nature (94 %)
- social skills (93%)
- engagement with learning (92%)
- health and well-being (92%)
- behaviour (85%)
- attainment (57%)

Learning about nature and natural systems was a direct consequence of this style of outdoor learning. The big change was the way in which the core subjects were being learned in a new context, this gave the subjects much more relevance to pupils and started the important process of systems thinking at an early age.

The call to action for cities is that the citizens, the policy makers and the leaders, need to really understand the natural environment in which they are working.

Children need to be connected to the natural environment through play and well-designed learning outside the classroom. It is not just about learning about the natural system, it is about learning core subjects (the mathematics, the science and the language) in the context of the natural system. Taking this perspective will enable the next generation to have some tangible experience of the world in which they are learning to live.

4.3 Revealing the value of connected natural systems to the prosperity of cities.

A lot of innovation is going on to transform our energy systems - e.g. the move away from carbon-intensive fossil fuels that is an essential part of city sustainability. But just tackling individual systems is not enough; we need to look at the other systems at the same time since they are all connected.

Below are a couple of examples of the interconnection of three big natural systems, based on work Jeremy Bentham at Shell in its strategic planning process called 'Scenario Planning" and work done by IBM as part of their 'Smart Planet' theme. There are many more interconnections in the network of city systems, however, we will be wise to ensure that these big ones like food, water and energy work well together since each system feeds back on the others.

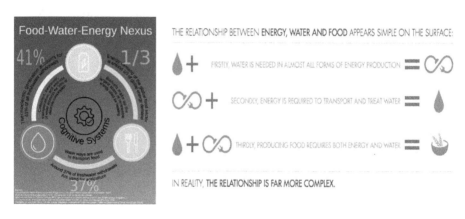

(IBM, 2016) & (Shell, 2012)

Perhaps the most immediate danger to cities is that of clean water for drinking. The catch here is that with fresh water there is no plan B. Fresh water is the only thing we drink. We may be able to transform small amounts of seawater using desalination, but in the scheme of things this is tiny and the energy cost is huge. We have more resilience around food and energy because there are many alternatives.

The threats to fresh water in the city include:

- Pollution from agriculture, city flooding and runoff from roads
- Sewage from citizens
- Waste from fossil fuel production,

- The complications of pharmaceuticals disposed
- Changes land use changes degrading the functioning of watersheds and rivers
- Salt water diffusion into aquifers caused by over-abstraction of groundwater
- And of course, the big one, climate change shifting the patterns and intensity of rainfall.
-

A lot of these issue of city water quality become critical, as the city grows in size and exceeds the local crying capacity of the natural environment.

4.4 Nature and cities work within the limitations of physics

Lastly, in this chapter on exploring the natural systems of cities, there is a cautionary note from Richard Feynman Nobel Prize winning Physicist. In this quote,

"For a successful technology, reality must take precedence over public relations, for Nature cannot be fooled"

(Feynman, 1986)

Cities are in essence, a human made technology. No amount of marketing can fix a city with poor natural systems (though some cities do try!).

This "Nature cannot be fooled' comment from "Richard Feynman" was part of his conclusion about the 'O' ring problems that resulted in the explosion of the US Space Shuttle in 1986 explaining that the physics of a situation cannot be denied.

Cities obey the same laws of physics. We may fool ourselves that we are in control of our cities and that they can grow and grow using the incessant innovation of technology. But we cannot get away from the fact that a city system is a wholly owned subsidiary of the natural environment.

A Smart City is one that realises the strong connections with nature It works with the limitations of the physical world. It teaches its young about the natural systems - locally, regionally and globally.

However, to be sustainable it needs to go further than just understanding from where it gets its water, food and energy. It needs to start to become regenerative. The city must start to improve the natural environment in

316

which it exists: repairing the degradation of the industrial age, building resilience to climate change and creating capacity that enables a prosperous city for future generations.

5. CITY AGILITY

City Agility describes the conditions that are necessary for a city to become 'Smart'

(An image representing agility, 2016)

5.1 Context

'Agility' is having the faculty of moving quickly; to be nimble and active. It's about the capacity to evolve with your changing environment. City systems need to constantly learn and re-learn how to be agile, in order to create and sustain success.

The background problem is however that cities are not designed to collaborate, they are made up of many organisations that are designed to optimise themselves.

The characteristics of an agile city are when it demonstrates these qualities:

- Shared purpose, beyond the immediate task process.
- Fast, effective modification of operations.
- A capacity to deal with unanticipated problems and opportunities.
- The ability to rapidly re-deploy resources and adjust structures
- Speed, grace, dexterity and resourcefulness.
- An attitude of managing the unexpected as a strategic asset.
- A refusal to be trapped by the success of the past.
- Uninhibited dialogue, feedback, and open constructive contention.
- High tolerances of ambiguity.

5.2 To be able to develop agility a city needs to work on these three ideas as part of its city culture:

- Self-organisation
- Heedful Interrelations
- Mental Models.

A note of caution is needed here since the background problem is that cities are not designed to collaborate, they are made up of many organisations that are designed to optimise themselves.

These three ideas around agility explain some of the practical things that help Smart Cities to enable people-in-the -system to operate effectively. Interestingly, cognitive computing and deep-learning systems are starting to provide tools that work with information in the same way as people, opening up the prospect of the People-in-the-system being able to work faster, with more insight and with more rigour.

5.3 Self-organisation.

Self-organisation is possibly the most important idea for enabling agility. In a complex, changing environment where new solutions need to be created this offers a highly intelligent and responsive way of developing.

Self-organisation is visible in many places from molecular chemistry to jazz groups, from flocks of birds to technology networks. However, our tendency is to stifle this natural behaviour by imposing detailed controls in the human organisations we create.

In traditional city organisations, it is common for a select few to dictate strategies, policies and plans that focus the city on some ideal solution that they hope will deliver results. Unfortunately, this top down 'command and control' approach has many serious limitations. The information the leaders are working with is often historical, backward looking and loses much of its insight because it is summarised in simple forms for executives to understand. The amount of brainpower and diversity of views in the leadership team is constrained simply because small numbers of people are involved. When the one solution they have crafted does emerge it is often late, inflexible to a changing world and lacks the resilience. The aspirations of a city designed by top-down command and control repeatedly fail when they encounter changes and shocks in the systems of economy, society and environment.

Self-organisation, by comparison, is about creating the conditions where order can emerge. The aim is to find order that is dynamic, which can respond to current conditions and change rapidly as they unfold.

A single ant, a single brain cell, or a single Internet computer is not very useful on its own. However, a few million connected together with a few simple guiding principles can do amazing things. This self-organising behaviour, known as emergence, is one of the fundamental dynamics driving evolution in the natural world.

The key principle for emergence is:

Interaction of simple parts that are networked together.

By networking, proteins create cells, cells create organs, organs create organisms, organisms create societies and societies create cities.

Most city organisations have too little information flow, too little diversity and too many differentials in power, to enable self-organisation to happen easily. Command and control organisations are simply not fast enough, or flexible enough, to cope with a rapidly changing environment.

An agile human organisation does throw up some issues. Agile city organisations are by nature impossible to control; they can only be led. Instead of giving commands there is the need to give meaning, vision, feedback, purpose and space. This lets self-organisation develop. The important concept for city leaders is that control is replaced by feedback. Feedback is what enables dynamic stability. It is dynamic stability that then creates resilience in changing conditions.

What constitutes a valuable citizen in an agile city is worth highlighting. In a traditional command and control organisation, value is created through holding authority, distributing resources and gathering information. However in agile cities value is about shared resources and shared information, and constructively challenging past authority to find better ways of working.

The 'hyperlinked' citizen – knows how to get things done, where to find knowledge and has a wide range of collaborative relationships. These roles do exist in many cities, though they often operate in the informal organisations of the cities; the voluntary sector, for example, thrives on the energy of these hyperlinked citizens.

As top-down government struggles with funding, using current technology and engaging with the issues that matter to citizens one of the trends that rapidly increases smartness of cities is the growth of bottom up initiatives enables by technology. This can range from crowdfunding, to the maker movement, to the sharing economy. However I feel that there is huge hidden value being created by people sharing how to do things via sites like YouTube. It is now possible to learn about almost anything, at a time that suits you, at very little cost because so many people have uploaded some wonderfully useful content. Of course care needs to be taken, Internet content is very variable in quality, however, this user-generated content enables just-in-time learning on almost any subject.

5.4 Heedful Interrelations.

Heedful interrelations are when people begin to connect with each other on several levels at the same time. In cities that are heedful there is a heightened sense of what is going on, people are listening, observing, sharing and providing constructive feedback. Interactions happen very quickly, trust abounds and there is even the beginning of predictive insights where citizens collaborate to design the future they want. Heedfulness can be viewed as group intelligence - an essential component of the systems in a smart city.

Many field sports, such as football, cricket, hockey or rugby, rely heavily on heedful interrelations. Imagine how poorly a team would play if they were organised with systems commonly used by a business project team!

- The experienced players would spend most of their time in meetings, before passing the ball to other players.

- Instead of looking around at the complex situation on the field of play at that moment, they would exchange numerous emails about how it has been in the past and who should be held responsible.
- Team tactics would be described by a set of PowerPoint bullet points, in small font, at an offsite meeting.

Cities often follow on the coat tails of business, picking up bad habits and poor systems without really understanding the dynamics that create success.

Practical measures to maximise the amount of heedful interrelation in a city include:

- Creating a simple common purpose that is clear to all the cltizens, created with their engagement.
- Enabling people to work together on issues, rather than prescribe fragmented responsibility.
- Sharing stories - both aspirations of success and insights into challenging issues.
- Taking care of newcomers - helping them learn the best of the city and valuing their new perspective.
- Seeking to combine the two worlds of experience and innovation.
- Encouraging distributed leadership at all levels across the city.

Heedful interrelations may, at first, seem like a soft skill possibly even a luxury in the incessantly changing world. Operational studies have shown that it is one of the essential skills in harsh and demanding organisations where high reliability is essential.

Increasingly the basis of heedful interrelations is the use of open data where evidence of how the city is working is flowing to and from citizens, as well as from citizen to citizen.

IBM's work on creating a Smarter Planet describes how to use technology to help create heedful interrelations enabled by technology.

(IBM Smarter Planet Logo)

5.5 Accelerating collaboration in the city through:

Situational Awareness, Analytics and Smart Response

It starts with **Situational Awareness**. Using sensors, the Internet of Things and the increasingly pervasive communications of the Internet.

It then needs some **Analytics.** Real-world data needs a considerable amount of work doing to it to transform it into insight. The data quality is vital to understand, its meaning is often complicated and several data sources needs to be combined to reveal what is going on. Then this data needs to be presented, visualised, in ways that engage people in its meaning.

Lastly, the acid test is **Smart Response**. Making use of new insights is at the heart of creating a Smart City. The timely application of new knowledge is what delivers better outcomes. This is where the challenge is to get the insights into the hand of the right people, enable them to accelerate collaboration and influence the city systems at all stages of planning, design and operations.

5.6 Moving from Horsepower to Mind-power.

The industrial age saw a revolution in the use of energy. This enabled people and cities to multiply their efforts to gain improved outcomes. Engines and electric motors applied tens, hundreds and thousands of horsepower to transform manual tasks allowing so much more to be achieved at all scales from the individual to the city.

In a similar way, the information age is using computing and data to amplify mind-power, enabling people and cities to design new and better ways of working. There is, however, a big difference in scale between horsepower and mind-power.

A Formula 1 racing car has about 1000 horsepower and the largest diesel engine in the world powering a cargo ship has just over 100,000 horsepower and the biggest aircraft carrier has 240,000 horsepower.

Yet the effect of information technology benefiting from Moore's law over the past 50 years, can amplify human capability and outcomes by perhaps a million times, a billion times, or even more. For example, the astronomy project called 'The Square Kilometre Array' will use compute power equivalent to 100,000,000 PCs to process radio images.

Here are just a few examples of this principle touching every aspect of city life:

Search by reading	1 book per day	To Searching millions of books in 1 second
Plan a transport route with a map	1 route in 10 minutes	To all practical routes every second
Monitor energy use with a dial	1 dial per second	To millions of sensors every second
Analyse one medical image	1 issue per minute	To compared with millions of past cases per second

The amplifying effect doesn't just stop with the technology itself. The rapid take-up of mobile technology, smartphones and cloud computing mean that technology is increasingly distributed AND networked. It is becoming possible for almost anyone to apply technology to amplify his or her mind-power. The challenge now is how education can keep up with the pace of improvement in technology.

5.7 Coherent Mental Models

In a human organisation everyone is an individual – free to act in ways that are not predictable. An individual's action changes the context for those around them. This combination of personal mental models, independent actions and dynamic interrelations makes what happens in our cities highly complex. The bobsleigh image illustrates how easy it could be to get into bother by misunderstanding just one part of how a system works.

In cities, individuals operate according to their own mental model of what the city is about - using their own set of rules for interpreting and responding. These rules are not explicit, and may not even look logical to others in the city.

Fortunately, people can share mental models, and learn from each other even if sometimes it is a little inaccurate. This is an important mechanism for cities to learn. It is these shared mental models that allow powerful, coordinated behaviour to emerge and for city systems to work well.

A story from Michael Parkinson, the English chat show host illustrates the way people interpret the world through different mental models.

"At a dinner he was seated next to an American lady who he had never met before; they got on well and began talking about many different subjects. Eventually, they began talking about the sport of cricket, a passion of Michael Parkinson's. Since this was an unfamiliar sport for the American, she asked all kinds of questions that Michael was very happy to explain. They became engrossed in the detail of this quaint English sport: the tactics, the equipment, the language, and the etiquette. The conversation unfolded over about an hour until it was time to leave the table. The American lady added one last comment about her new found interest in cricket: 'Gee... and they do all that on horseback!' "

Mixing up horse riding in the sport of polo with the sport of cricket must have produced some perplexing images in her head. My point is that everyone has a unique perspective on the way the world works and for a city to work well it needs a high degree of interaction and collaboration for the inaccuracies to be resolved safely.

The interconnection of individuals, sharing mental models creates great potential for agility. As new understanding ripples through an organisation a small change in one place can have a significant effect overall.

Shared mental models in city systems are what make cities work in practice.

- How the traffic system works - the rules for safety, the ways to avoid congestion.
- How law and order works - informing what is acceptable behaviour.
- How the city copes with its waste - the rationale for effective refuse disposal and re-cycling.

There is however a paradox. Coherence in mental models is important but so too is diversity. It is the interplay of these two that enables agility.

Individual mental models are the key to personal understanding. Shared mental models are the key to effective collaboration.

In these common illustrations, what do you see? By looking away and then back again or through discussion with others you can reveal more than one view of the world.

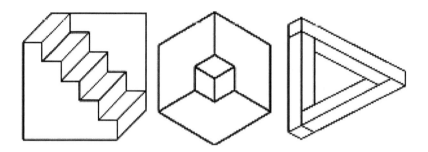

To enable agility, cities need to create high levels of knowledge, a willingness to share, and constant feedback processes. Unfortunately, these are not things that are often found on city organisation charts.

To improve agility a city needs to look beyond its static assets, resources and formal structure, to develop the dynamics of the city. It needs to embrace the ideas of self-organisation, heedful interrelations and constantly sharing mental models to thrive and become a 'Smart City'.

6. CITIES TUNING TO THE EDGE OF CHAOS

Cities are not about 'stability',
they are dynamic living things that thrive close to the edge.

6.1 Context

Rigid approaches to city systems, that focus only on efficiency tend to produce the constrained 'city as machine', with no ability to adapt, little ability to learn and low capacity to fix themselves when things go wrong. In these circumstances one minor change in the cities environment, be it economic, social or natural, and the effects on these rigid cities can be catastrophic to the health of all its systems.

'Tuning to the Edge of Chaos' is about shaping the dynamics of city systems so that it is far from predictable, but not so far that it becomes destructively unstable. Cities are not deterministic machines and we need to remind ourselves of this whenever designing city system.

If cities are static they are on the path to decline, if cities are swamped by frantic change they never thrive. From a system dynamics perspective, a city needs to be at the edge of chaos.

Cities display strong patterns of complex behaviour. They need to constantly adapt and reorganise themselves to respond to an ever-changing social, economic and environmental context. If they change too little they become non-competitive, outdated and ineffective. If they change too much they fall into the instability of chaos where demand exceeds capacity. It takes careful observation across many systems to understand where a city sits.

The phrase **'edge of chaos'** was coined by mathematician Doyne Farmer, to describe the transition phenomenon discovered by computer scientist Christopher Langton. (Understanding Complex Systems, 2014)
55

Cities need to actively tune towards the Edge of Chaos. This is beyond stability, but not so far as chaos. It is about creating capacity in city systems, but avoiding over investment or stagnation. It is about responding to growing demand, but not becoming overwhelmed.

6.2 Capacity and Demand

Below is a diagram based on one by Daryl T. Conner, this illustrates the 'edge' that the city needs to carefully work towards.

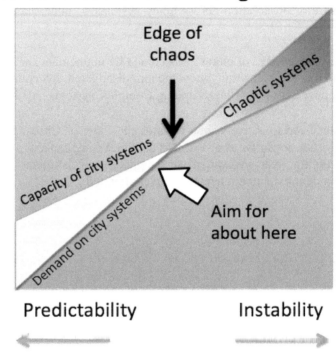

As a city grows it needs to tune towards the edge of chaos

(Conner, 1998)

Conner explains how organisations need to be aware of the challenge between capacity and demand in business to ensure that they stay competitive and innovative. Cities have a similar dynamic. Too much growth or demand in one city system can quickly affect adjacent systems and the wider city.

An obvious example is that as demand for transport exceeds the capacity of roads and public transport then these systems trigger a decline in other systems producing economic inefficiency, air quality pollution, delays in city processes and poor resilience to respond to extreme weather events.

A good measure of how 'Smart' a city is can be seen in how well they manage their waste. Failings in the waste management system often have a delay before the impact is felt. Air pollution, sewage overflow events and maxed-out landfall sites are a sign that the city is going beyond the edge and into chaos.

A smart city has the capacity to be nimble in its response to the context in which it operates. Cities face a constant stream of threats and changes - storm events, population demographics, the viability of its products and services, changes in culture and the accelerating adoption of technology. By taking a systems perspective to these challenges a city can strive to avoid the pitfalls of stability and chaos.

A vibrant city that is living in a healthy position, towards this edge of chaos, is reminiscent of the thrill of sailing a small boat in a strong wind.

'On the Edge'

Placid Lake:	Sailing Boat on the edge of	Crashing Waves:
Stability	**Complexity**	**Chaos**

When sailing in calm water, with no wind, it may be pleasant for a while, but the boat doesn't get very far. Sailing on crashing waves near rocks can be disastrous.

To successfully navigate in a turbulent environment with gusts of wind, flowing tides and rolling waves the sailing boat needs to direct and shape the energy in the system. In a similar way, the city that wants to perform well and have a good quality of life needs constantly to tune its systems to the prevailing conditions.

This is where city scale collaboration becomes vital. As has been seen, a command and control style of city management wouldn't have the requisite variety to be able to constantly change in ways that keep the systems interconnected and healthy - there are just too many moving parts and too much free will in a city to control it.

An important dynamic for city leaders is to understand when it is performing '**on the edge**'. An agile city has a great advantage; it only takes small changes to produce large effects. This non-linear effect is a very valuable tool, but also needs to be handled with care.

In **stable situations,** interactions tend to be predictable and linear. Small changes produce small effects and it is only through huge effort that large effects are produced. You can see this dynamic when you observe a city that has been based on one industry for many decades. Heavy industries of iron & steel, car manufacture, mining, chemical manufacture are often examples. These cities have been stable and successful. They even know what needs to change. But the rate of change and innovation means that they will decline significantly before improvement happens again. This is a real danger to success in city economies that lack diversity.

In **situations of chaos,** the effects of both small and large changes are lost in the turmoil. Huge amounts of effort and energy produce few constructive results when surrounded by chaos. This is often the outlook for cities in a conflict situation. Those during general strikes, experiencing riots and in the midst of war for example. There is just too much going on for the city to begin to recover gradually. It first needs to slow down or be shocked into a serious decline before stable situations can begin to emerge again.
Information friction
By contrast, taking a city towards the **edge of chaos** is very productive, if handled well, with collaboration, good governance and the foresight of emerging changes. It is both a creative and adaptable place to be. The reason why small changes produce big effects, on this edge, is because of the connectivity and interaction. These enable emergent behaviour that feeds back on itself cascading and multiplying throughout the system.

6.3 Top Down Bottom Up

In the U-shaped model of the Smart City the top-down approach delivers stability, but at the cost of the city being dynamic. Some top down management is needed, however, it also needs to be balanced by healthy bottom up and side-to-site systems to generate diverse and dynamic systems and prevent city systems descending into chaos.

Smart cities are "U-Shaped"

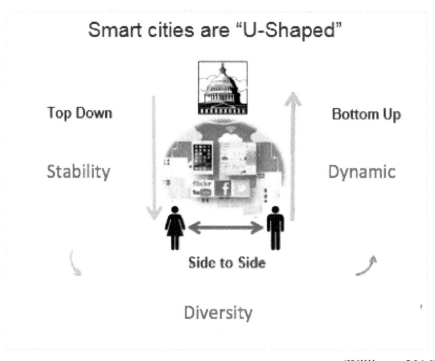

Top Down

Stability

Bottom Up

Dynamic

Side to Side

Diversity

(Williams, 2016)

Perhaps one of the most visible examples of cities Tuning-to-the-Edge is when they hold festivals - these are often based on sport, culture, art, literature or even commerce. During these festivals cities really push for innovation and success is often measured by maximising the use of capacity while managing demand so that people have an excellent experience. Creativity, play and new ideas are the order of the day. These festivals give the city the opportunity to upgrade its infrastructure, try out new technology on a manageable scale and actively encourage people to collaborate in new ways.

It is interesting that one of the ways that the Rockefeller 100 Resilient Cities programme advocates as very practical way to increase a cities resilience is to get the city to work together on festivals. This works from the small neighbourhood scale to enormous projects like hosting the Olympics. I would even go so far as to say that if you wanted to see the worlds best Smart Cities then you need to look closely at cities that can host festivals that are significant all the way from the local community up to world class events; this is where cities learn by doing

7.   WORKING WITH THE DOMAINS OF COMPLEXITY:

*A Smart City has many of its systems operating in scientifically complex
ways, so it needs to understand when to apply the insights of complex
adaptive systems*

7.1 Context

A complex adaptive system is a collection of individual agents who have
the freedom to act in unpredictable ways and whose actions are
interconnected such that one agent's actions changes the context for other
agents.

This definition fits well with the many city systems where people have a
large part to play. The important words from this definition for cities are:

- **Freedom:** to act: because every day a city needs to respond
  in a myriad of new ways to the situation in which it finds
  itself,
- **Unpredictable:** because there is both individual and
  collective intelligence at play in cities,
- **Interconnected:** because this is what creates a network of
  possibilities.

The key point is to affirm that the city is far from being a giant machine.
The nature of the city as a system is that people are a fundamental part of its
fabric it is made from a large number of relatively simple things brought
together in a large network of interactions. The result is that it behaves in
scientifically 'complex ways'.

A complex city has the following attributes:

- A city is made from individual elements that can change
  themselves,
- The emergence of novelty & creativity in the city is a
  natural state,
- Highly complex city behaviours emerge when it use a few
  simple rules, order emerges without central control,
- Non-linearity is everywhere in cities: that is small changes
  in cities have BIG effects,

- City systems are nested, where each system is embedded in another - hence the term systems of systems,
- Cities are inherently not predictable in their detail: forecasting is therefore always inexact, but nevertheless it is useful to explore future possibilities.
- The evolution of cities is a in practice a co-evolution with its context. The city proceeds through constant tension & balance.

(Adapted from a insightful list by McCandless & Plsek, 2009)

7.2 How do you make progress and design prosperity when cities are unpredictably complex?

In a system of systems that is a city, the level of complexity means that there is no option but to do everything all at the same time. A city is not a project with a beginning middle and end. The practicalities mean that for a city to thrive it needs to act, learn and plan in parallel.

To be able to work with this interplay of reality, there is an excellent framework called 'Cynefin'. It enables sense to be made of the complexity found everywhere. It helps explore the patterns in city systems and design appropriate interventions to improve the systems.

Cynefin was developed by Dave Snowden and collaborators and is pronounced : Kih-neh-vihn (/ˈkʌnivɪn/). It is a Welsh word meaning 'usual abode' or 'habitat'. This appears very appropriate for cities.

Although Cynefin is described as a **'5 Domain Framework for sense making'** it can also be described as a landscape that reveals how a system behave. The value in this landscape view is that you can explore how a city system might respond and so design your actions to be more appropriate to the system, at a specific time.

Depending on how a system is designed and how it is operated it can move around this landscape creating interventions that are appropriate to the system. Cities do not just sit in one of these Cynefin domains, they are in constant flux. Interventions to make cities better places need to understand where city systems are today but where it needs to move to. When the city context is constantly changing the systems needs to be constantly guided around this landscape to keep the city healthy.

- If the city system is **simple and obvious** then 'Good Practice' interventions are appropriate. In this state the best solutions from the past are likely to work again.
- If city systems are **complicated** then there will need to be analysis to be able to work out how to manage the system. Data gathering, increased precision and careful analytics can reveal useful insights to improve the system.
- If the city system is **complex**, which many city systems are, then neither established 'good practice' nor in-depth analytics will create the best way to operate the complex system. In this complex domain, the approach needs to work with the insights of emergence. Sensing how the system is performing and then amplifying or damping the things of interest; all the while remembering that the outcome is inherently unpredictable.
- A city system that is in **chaos** needs some kind of a shock to disturb it. The aim of the shock is to disturb it enough to drop back into one of the other systems.
- The black area in the centre represents **disorder**. It describes a place where there is no knowledge of how the city system is working. In this position, the priority is to gather information to begin to make sense of the system.

Transitioning a city system from one domain to another is an important aspect of system design. This is a skill that city leaders and policy makers need to develop. In their HBR article 'A leader's framework for decision making (Snowden & Boone 2007), David Snowden and Mary Boone explain how leaders need to be able to understand the nature of the system they are working on, and use a range of strategies to move the system from one place to another to enable appropriate change.

Often a city system starts out as obvious and simple but then grows into a more complicated system to be able to cope with a variety of situations. For example traffic lights are simple - red, amber, green. However, to work well in the city context they need to be managed as part of the road network, not just in isolation. By taking in data from traffic sensors and understanding flows at different times of the day, the simple traffic light, which worked well in a small town with few cars, becomes a complicated traffic management system. In this complicated city environment, analytics is vital to generate insight to be able to effectively manage and develop the system.

No specific domain is more desirable than the other, with the exception of disorder that is a bad place for a system to be in. The framework brings is a way of observing how a system is working and then designing interventions that are appropriate for the system.

For example if you apply simple solutions to a complex situation it is unlikely to produce the results you expect. Sometimes it is good to move towards chaos. Often systems are more than simple – deterministic solutions might work if something is complicated e.g. the design of a passenger aircraft., but if the system is complex e.g. the emergency evacuation of an airport during a fire, then insights from complexity are needed to design the system and prevent solutions that are chaotic, complicated or overly simple.

There are already many methods for designing interventions when systems are simple, complicated and even chaotic. The main benefit of this framework is how designs emergent interventions in complex situations through the use of the pattern 'Probe-Sense-Respond'

Sometimes systems become overly complicated and it really helps to move them towards the simple domain. This is especially helpful for the people in the system. The citywide 'Oyster Card' single ticket and payment system in London is a good example of making a system better by making it simpler; one standard card that works for all modes of transport.

The direction you choose to move around this landscape needs care. It is easy to think a system is in one domain and wrongly apply systems solutions from another domain, resulting in rapid failure. Perhaps the most common error is for a system designer to think that something is simple when in practice it is much more complicated or even complex. The result will not be the simple solution hoped for. Instead, the system moves through the domain of disorder, that is not knowing what is going on, and quickly drops into chaos.

This 'falling off a cliff' effect is seen often as a system drops unexpectedly into another domain. A good example is when a city suffers an extreme weather event, perhaps a flood or a large snowstorm. The initial response is chaos. As the efforts of the emergency services engage, a complex situation emerges which shows improvement but is still highly unpredictable. As the recovery options and plans are worked out the city transitions into a complicated domain. Finally, as the city systems recover and behave normally as designed its systems can revert back to the 'Obvious' domain.

The city of Newcastle, UK experienced a significant failure when it tried to get ahead of an incoming snowstorm without the insights of complexity. It wanted to help but only applied a simple solution. Broadcasts on the radio and to government workers suggested that everyone should leave work early to avoid the storm. The rush to depart the city meant traffic quickly ground to a halt, that snow ploughs and essential services stopped. The city and then moved rapidly through the domains of simple complicated, complex and into chaos.

The incoming storm was a complex problem and needed complex domain thinking. If the city had recognised this they could have designed a suitable set of interventions in the spirit of Probe-Sense-Respond to provide a complex set of options from which a good solution would emerge:

- Prioritise key exit routes.
- Provide extensive and real-time information about emerging congestion so individuals can make good judgment calls.
- Get fine scale feedback from people on the ground - some places will fair better than others and alternative responses will emerge.
- Specifically design a range of solutions, not just one: some groups might be able to safely not evacuate the city, public transport could become free for a time to maximise its use, cycling to refuge locations might become a safe alternative when key points such as bridges become gridlocked.
- Develop social cohesion ahead of extreme city events so that people already have experience of working together in their neighbourhood. People then know, ahead of a shock to the city, who the vulnerable people are and who has resources that can help.

In this Cynefin model of the world, a city needs to be highly aware of how its systems are operating. To the unaware city, its systems quickly degrade and tend towards chaos.

With good systems design cities can improve performance and prosperity by mindfully moving from one domain to another other, creating systems and interventions that are suitable for the domain in which they operate.

The ability for a city to use collective intelligence to understand what is going on, observe in which domain a system is operating and then navigate an appropriate path through these domains, is a good measure of how 'Smart' the city is.

8.   INFORMATION FRICTION IN CITY SYSTEMS

*To stay 'Smart' a city needs information to flow at an appropriate rate.
We need to reveal the invisible delay in systems and enable the
interconnection of systems and people.*

8.1 Context

The idea of Information Friction has three parts:
Delay:
> Where information is flowing but it is not timely, so it creates
> problems in the system.

Disruption:
> Where information is flowing but it is degraded in some way
> during transit

Failure to connect:
> When information does not flow at all and poor decision making
> results.

8.2 Delay

Delay in city systems is a significant problem well worth worrying about,
especially because it is often difficult to see. It reduces the system's ability to
function well, it costs time, resources and money and it often has significant
side effects.

Although delay can be used with good effect, as part of deliberate system
design, e.g. Creating damping effects, more often than not its' presence
develops unintended consequences that are many and varied. The outward
sign of delay is a simple pause or slowing down of flow in the system.
However, its causes and its effects can be complex and large. Delay in
systems has an impact on resource flow, information flow, and decision
quality. There is often a second loop in play meaning that poor resource
flow, poor information flow and poor decision quality then create further
delays and failures.

(Not all delay is visible, unlike a 3-hour airport delay)

Smart cities actively look for the systemic delay, not just the obvious ones we often see in transport systems but also the hidden delays in every system from healthcare to education to governance.

The issue is not really that delay means systems perform slowly from a time perspective. The more important impact on city systems is that systems become disconnected and time shifted from important feedback loops.

Delay often means that a system can start to behave in strange and unpredictable ways as people in the system try to get it to meet their needs. Even a very simple city system can be thrown into chaos if an invisible delay is introduced.

Imagine trying to drive a car where there is a delay between the steering wheel and the movement of the road wheels (see diagram below). The delay means that the driver's responses oscillate between under-reaction and overreaction. This constant inaccurate adjustment in steering decisions will mean a lot of energy wasted and the quality of driving will be poor. In some circumstances, reactions may be too slow with disastrous results.

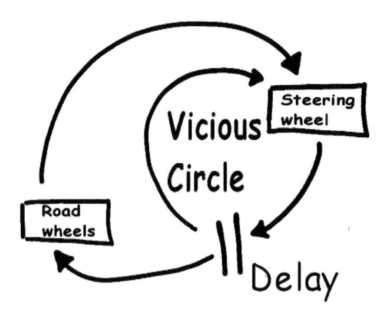

NB: this **\|** is the symbol for a delay in a systems diagram

The classic example of delay in a system is often felt in the domestic shower.

In showers where the hot and cold mixer is positioned a long way from the showerhead the water initially feels cold, so more water is added, but this takes time to have an effect because of the delay in the system introduced by the long pipe to the showerhead. This invariably means too much hot water is added. In reaction, once the scalding hot water gets through, an injection of cold water is added. This oscillation between hot and cold means the system is inefficient and may never get to a comfortable temperature.

Many city systems suffer from being unaware of delay in the system that results in poor decision-making:

- The **energy system** that burns fossil fuels today but doesn't see the catastrophic costs of climate change in the future.

- The **health system** that fails to respond quickly enough to a disease outbreak, the resulting delay making it much more difficult to control the number of people who get infected.

- The **transport system** that does not respond quickly to an approaching storm. Traffic flow grinds to a halt just when it needs to be at its most efficient because everyone wants to leave the city as late as possible before the storm hits.

- The **water system** that pollutes its local drinking water because the effect of agricultural and industrial pollution on groundwater happens over decades. If the pollution had an instant effect on drinking water and hence people's health it would probably get the attention it needed to fix the problem.

The lesson for a city is to look for sources of delay, make them visible and then systematically work to manage the delays. Some delays need to be eliminated. e.g. The time for a first responder to engage in an emergency situation. Whereas some delays have an important damping effect on the system e.g. you don't want everyone to do the same thing at the same time, thereby creating significant unintended consequences in other system.

The aim should be to create timely feedback loops, both within systems and between systems. A smart city uses data and communications as the main tools to create these feedback loops; capturing, propagating and assessing the state of the system. Often common data standard and common data sources are created to correlate insights from analytics.

A great deal of confusion, frustration, misunderstanding, over-reaction and tension in cities can be avoided if delay in a system can be understood. Simply removing delay in the system can make often improvements. However delay is not always a bad thing since it can have an important contribution towards stability. The key is to make the delay visible so that the system can be designed with this in mind.

8.3 Information disruption

Information Disruption has the effect of changing the information as it flows.

As Smart Cities increasingly rely on the flow of information to support their design and operation then information disruption needs to be factored into the design. It is especially important when there is more automation and fewer people-in-the-system who can spot and manage the anomalies.

Information disruption in terms of translation, errors and mistakes is perhaps easy to understand. Indeed, by taking a systems perspective a city can become smarter simply by avoiding many of the problems that currently occur because city is making decisions on the wrong information.

One of the less obvious examples of information disruptions is in the poor use of city data analytics. There is a constant urge to simplify city information in order to make a point or argue a case. This often results in statistics that talk about the average, e.g. the average delay in accident and emergency, the average ridership on public transport, the average water consumption per person. I propose that for a city to be smart it needs to avoid the use of averages wherever possible.

Information analytics and data visualisation can now happily cope with all of the data a city can produce. Technology can present the data in informative, entertaining and often amazing ways that avoid data disruption.

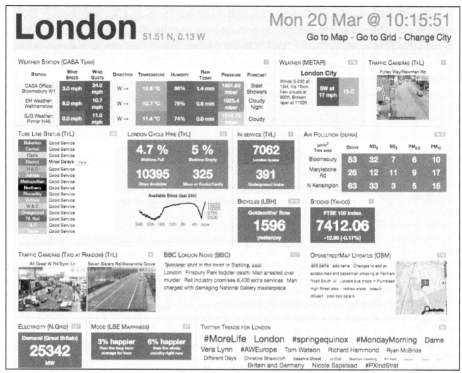

(CASA (2017)

As with delays in the system, Information Disruption has the dangerous dynamic that it can feedback on itself, one translation error generates more errors, averages of averages can be taken and vital information becomes completely lost in the system.

8.4 Failure to connect

Failure to connect is the ultimate delay. It is of particular importance with information flow in city systems. Many systems are not yet designed to share information and the open data movement is only in its infancy. To become 'Smart' a city needs to have a high degree of information sharing to enable autonomous systems to work as if they were part of the bigger city system.

> *"There needs to be a concept of requisite timeliness,*
> *supported by a concept of requisite sharing"*

(Williams, 2016)

By having a rich network of connected systems a city can move from operations that guess what is needed, to systems that know what is needed. Connected system get the right information into the place where better decisions can be made. For example:

- Designing public transport services based on up-to-date origin and destination information.
- Pricing energy use based on demand and supply to avoid wasted energy generation and encourage peak use shifting
- Designing infrastructure that can cope with flood risk.
- Enabling housing development to better meet the needs of demographic changes and shifting availability of work.
- Avoiding damaging changes to environmental quality, society and culture for short-term growth making the city unsustainable.

This connection is certainly about system-to-system interconnection that is growing exponentially. But in addition, it should not diminish the people-to-people cultural interconnection that is one of the fundamental driving forces behind why cities as a social construct have been so successful.

We see the embodiment of the city through its physical infrastructure. Increasingly how smart a city can become will depend more and more on how wisely it uses its information. However, the soul of a city comes from cultural interaction not data exchange. It should be remembered that the infrastructure and information systems in a Smart City are there to support the people and their place in the environment, it is the interaction of all these elements that makes a city truly 'Smart'

9.   SUMMARY

I would propose that a Smart City is not a thing, or a place full of wonderful technology, rather it is about creating the conditions where people can evolve as a society, learning from the past, solving issues with current city systems and designing future city systems that are more viable both at the local scale and in the context of the planet.

A 'Smart City' will always include the principle of 'People in the System' and this still needs to be an important focus. But two of the biggest things affecting cities are the new opportunities that in information technology can bring and the new threats from the natural systems in which they are embedded. My hope is that the seven ideas will reveal new insights into how Smart City systems operate.

The exam question for Smart Cities is 'What are the things that we want to optimise?' By taking a systems perspective it allows people at all levels in the city system to understand what creates value and what destroys it. The insights from a systems perspective will enable the quest for constant improvement in cities.

REFERENCES

Abbott-Donnelly I. (2016) Cynefin Landscape adapted from Dave Snowden diagram

Ashby R. (2016) "The W. Ross Ashby Digital Archive" http://www.rossashby.info/

Bateson G. (2011) An Ecology of Mind http://www.naturearteducation.org/AnEcologyOfMind.htm

Bettencourt L. (2014) Cities as Complex Adaptive Systems https://www.youtube.com/watch?v=vp6eKjQHNl0

Camus A. (1947) The Plague https://en.wikiquote.org/wiki/Albert_Camus

CASA (2017) The Bartlett Centre for Advanced Spatial Analysis: CASA city dashboard
> http://citydashboard.org/london/

CCO (2016) Image representing agility https://pixabay.com/en/athletics-sport-hurdles-648020/

Conner D. (1998) Leading at the edge of Chaos: How to Create the Nimble Organisation

Farmer D. (2014) Chaos Theory in Politics Understanding Complex Systems https://books.google.co.uk/books?id=R-
> VsngEACAAJ&dq=chaos+theory+in+politics&hl=en&sa=X&ved=0ahUKEwisy8WLv9DPAhWEBsAKHRe
> BCu0Q6AEIITAA

Feynman R. (1986) https://en.wikiquote.org/wiki/Richard_Feynman

Hansen and Nohria (2004) How to Build Collaborative advantage http://sloanreview.mit.edu/article/how-to-build-
> collaborative-advantage/

IBM (2009) Smarter Planet Logo https://en.wikipedia.org/wiki/File:IBM_Smarter_Planet.svg

IBM (2016) Cognitive systems manage food-water-energy https://www.ibm.com/blogs/internet-of-things/food-water-
> energy-nexus/

McCandless K. & Plesk P. (2009) Complex system attributes
> http://www.slideshare.net/Schot.Sander/Complexityintrocourse

Natural Connections (2016) Three quarters of UK children spend less time outdoors than prison inmates
> https://www.theguardian.com/environment/2016/mar/25/three-quarters-of-uk-children-spend-less-time-
> outdoors-than-prison-inmates-survey

Conant R. and Ashby W.R. (1970) "Every Good Regulator of a System Must be a Model of that System," International
> Journal of Systems Science, 1970, vol 1., No. 2, 89-97.

Rogers M. (2015) "Myron Rogers Master Class". http://leadershipforchange.org.uk/wp-content/uploads/Myron-Rogers-
> Master-Class-Slides.pdf

Shell (2012) 40 years of Shell Scenarios http://s03.static-shell.com/content/dam/shell/static/future-
> energy/downloads/shell-scenarios/shell-scenarios-40yearsbook061112.pdf

Snowden D. and Boone M. (2007)
> https://www.acu.edu.au/__data/assets/pdf_file/0006/659004/David_Snowden_A_Leaders_Framework_for_De
> cision_Making.pdf

Snowden D. (2010) Cynefin Framework Introduction https://www.youtube.com/watch?v=N7oz366X0-8

Spohrer J. (2013) "What's Up at IBM". http://www.slideshare.net/spohrer/t-shaped-people-20130628-v5

Washington Post (2016) "The myth of the well-rounded student? It's better to be 'T-shaped'"
> https://www.washingtonpost.com/news/grade-point/wp/2016/06/01/the-myth-of-the-well-rounded-student-its-
> better-to-be-t-shaped/

Williams R.P. (2016)
> http://www.unisdr.org/campaign/resilientcities/assets/documents/privatepages/Resilience%20Scorecard%20V
> 2.2%20-%20April%2030th%202015.pdf

About the Authors

Colin Harrison

Dr. Harrison retired from IBM in 2013 as an IBM Distinguished Engineer. He was most recently the inventor of IBM's Smarter Cities technical programme. He was previously Director of Strategic Innovation in IBM Europe and Director of Global Services Research. He is an IBM Master Inventor and a Member of the IBM Academy of Technology.

He spent 1972-77 at CERN developing the SPS accelerator and its distributed, real-time control system. In 1977 at EMI Central Research Laboratories in the UK he led development of the first clinical MRI system. After joining IBM in San Jose, California in 1979 he worked on micromagnetics, medical imaging, parallel computing, mobile computing, intelligent agents, telecommunications, knowledge management, and Smarter Cities. In 2011 he spent several months working in Tohoku, Japan on plans for the region's recovery from the 3/11 earthquake and tsunami and has increasingly focused on Resilient Cities.

He studied at Imperial College, London and the University of Munich, earning a PhD in Materials Science. He is Fellow of the Institution of Engineering and Technology, Senior Life Member of the Institution of Electronic and Electrical Engineers, and Founder Member of the Society for Magnetic Resonance in Medicine. He is an Expert Advisor to the Swiss Academy of Technical Sciences and has been a Visiting Scientist at MIT, Harvard Medical School, and Lawrence Berkeley National Laboratory. He has published some 60 articles and has been awarded some 30 patents. He speaks worldwide on Smart Cities. He is currently affiliated with Arizona State University.

Harold "Bud" Lawson

Professor Emeritus Dr. Harold "Bud" Lawson has been active in the computing and systems arena since 1958 and has broad international experience in private and public organizations as well as academic environments. Bud contributed to several pioneering efforts in hardware, software and system technologies.

He has held professorial appointments at several universities in the USA, Europe and the Far East. A Fellow of the ACM, IEEE and INCOSE. Head of the Swedish Delegation to ISO/ IEC JTC1 SC7 WG7 (1996-2004) and the elected architect of the ISO/IEC 15288 standard. In 2000, he received the prestigious IEEE Computer Pioneer Charles Babbage medal award for his 1964 invention of the pointer variable concept for programming languages.

In 2016 he was awarded the INCOSE Systems Engineering Pioneer award. Harold "Bud" Lawson is an independent consultant operating his own company Lawson Konsult AB and is, as well, a consulting partner of Syntell AB, Stockholm

Dr. Rick Robinson

Dr. Rick Robinson is Director of Technology for Amey, one of the UK's largest providers of public and regulated services and infrastructure. In this role, Rick is responsible for driving advances in digital technology into public services and infrastructure that are used by about 1 in 4 people in the UK every day.

Previously, Rick was Executive Architect for Smarter Cities for IBM. Rick collaborates with a network of technology entrepreneurs, Universities and social institutions to explore innovations in digital technology, and has advised the UK Government and United Nations on their impact on infrastructure, communities and society.

Rick is a Fellow of the British Computer Society, a Fellow of the RSA, a member of the Academy of Urbanism, a member of the Board of Innovation Birmingham and Birmingham Science City Alliance.

He founded and chairs the Birmingham Smart City Alliance. Rick writes about his work at http://theurbantechnologist.com/

Dr. Roland Kupers

Dr. Roland Kupers is an advisor on Complexity, Resilience and Energy Transition, as well as a Visiting Fellow at the Smith School of Enterprise and the Environment at Oxford University.

A theoretical physicist by training, Roland spent a decade each at AT&T and at Shell in various senior executive functions, including Vice President for Sustainable Development and Vice President Global LNG. He has a long running interest in complexity theory and its impacts.

He has published widely, including in HBR, on Project Syndicate and co-authored *Complexity and the art of public policy* (Princeton 2014), *The Essence of scenarios* (Amsterdam 2014), and *Turbulence: A corporate framing of resilience* (Amsterdam 2014). In 2010 Roland was a co-author of a report commissioned by the German Government on a New Growth Path for Europe, applying a complexity lens to climate economics.

Roland is a Dutch national; his travels have made him fluent in five languages.

Hsi Ching

Hsi Ching is a senior researcher with the Institute of Governance and Policy at the Singapore Civil Service College.

Her research interests include the practice of cross-sector collaborations, impact of technology on public policy and complexity thinking in public policy. She holds a Master's degree in Tri-Sector Collaboration from the Singapore Management University.

Chuck Benson

Chuck leads IT strategy & operations, risk management, and information security for Facilities Services, SmartGrid, & building and space automation systems at the University of Washington (UW). He Chairs the Internet2 IoT Systems Risk Management Task Force.

He has Chaired the University's IT Service Management Board, the Task Force on Protection of Industrial Control Systems/Internet of Things, and is currently Co-Chairing the UW Compliance and Risk Services effort on IoT Systems Risk Mitigation. He is also a member of the University's Unmanned Aerial Systems working group where he contributes to the development of drone policy.

He has a bachelor's degree in Electrical Engineering from Vanderbilt University and a master's degree Computer Science from Eastern Washington University and is a former US Marine Corps helicopter pilot. He maintains a blog on managing institutional IoT systems risk at http://longtailrisk.com.

Chair IoT Systems Risk Management Task Force, Internet2
Assistant Director for IT, Facilities Services, University of Washington
cabenson@uw.edu or cabenson361@gmail.com
1-206-221-4001
blog: http://longtailrisk.com, twitter:@cabenson361

Abhik Chaudhuri

Is a Chevening Fellow and Fellow of the Cloud Security Alliance (USA). He has over 14 years of consulting experience and is a Domain Consultant in Cyber Security, Privacy and Policy, working with Tata Consultancy Services in their Global Technology Practice.

As Co-Editor and Rapporteur of ISO/IEC JTC 1/SC27 Abhik is providing thought leadership in developing security and privacy standards for the IoT and smart cities.

He is a member of IEEE's IoT Community and ETAP Forum. Abhik is on the Editorial Boards of EDPACS Journal (Taylor and Francis) and the Journal of Data Protection and Privacy (Henry Stewart Publications).

Florence D. Hudson

Florence Hudson is an aerospace and mechanical engineer educated at Princeton University, with executive business education at Harvard and Columbia Universities. She is Senior Vice President and Chief Innovation Officer at Internet2, working with the Research & Education community in the identification and development of new innovations leveraging the Internet. She leads a Collaborative Innovation Community including Innovation Working Groups for the Internet of Things, end-to-end trust & security, distributed big data & analytics, and smart campuses & cities. Her 2012 TEDx talk presents the idea of a smart city as a system of systems. Prior to Internet2, she was with IBM for 33 years, including Director of Internet of Things business development and Vice President of Corporate Strategy. Prior to IBM she worked for Hewlett Packard, NASA, and Grumman Aerospace Corporation. She was honored as a Top Woman of Machine to Machine in 2014 by Connected World Magazine.

Mark Cather

Mark Cather, Chief Information Security Officer (CISO) at University of Maryland, Baltimore County, has over 20 years of experience in information technology, networking, communications, construction, privacy, and security. He is a Certified Information Systems Security Professional (CISSP) and has a wide range of engineering and management experience, allowing him to work on everything from technical topics to the development of law and policy for technology and information. In addition to his role as CISO, he is co-chair of the Internet2 End-to-End Trust and Security Working Group and co-chair of the Internet2 Innovation Program Advisory Group which leads the Internet2 Collaborative Innovation Community of over 333 research and education individuals representing 135 research and education institutions. Mr. Cather has spoken at national and international events, by groups such as Microsoft and IEEE, and has extensive experience with the Internet of Things and TIPPSS - Trust, Identity, Privacy, Protection, Safety, and Security.

Dr. Francois Coallier

After more than 21 years in industry, François Coallier became professor at the École de technologie supérieure (ÉTS), one of Canada's leading engineering school affiliated to the Université du Québec network.

He was CIO of ÉTS between 2010 and 2016 and the founding chair of ÉTS' Department of Software and IT Engineering from its creation in 2004 till 2010.

Dr. Coallier has been continuously involved in software and systems engineering standards development since 1984. He is the international Chair of the Joint ISO and IEC subcommittee responsible for the elaboration of Software and Systems Engineering Standards (ISO/IEC JTC1/SC7) since 1997, the subcommittee that was also the incubator of JTC1/ SC40 on IT Governance and IT Service Management, and the international Chair of the new JTC1/SC41 on the Internet of Things and related technologies since its creation in 2016.

Lluïsa Marsal

Is an Architect with two Masters and two Doctorates in the fields of urban planning and applied ICT (2008, 2013). She is the founder of Intelligent'ER, an international think tank providing expert advice and counsel on smart and sustainable cities, including innovation on standards, urban policies, planning and regulations. Prior being established as a consultant, she worked for governments in the UK and Spain and she spent fifteen years in the academia developing different research and leadership roles in two different Spanish universities.

Her academic career includes the creation and direction of world's first official scientific master's program in smart cities, several competitive and commercial research projects in the domains of smart and sustainable cities, postdoc scholarships in Germany (2006) and the USA (2011), a US patent on urban planning standards technology and the publication as main author of fifteen papers in top peer-reviewed academic journals of her areas of expertise.

She served as UN Habitat III expert and she currently holds a second mandate as a chair at UN's U4SSC initiative, this time to explore Blockchain applications for cities.

Miguel Reynolds

Miguel Reynolds Brandão, is a father of 4. Curious and independent by nature, he is graduated in engineering and management.

He is a serial entrepreneur who started his first venture in his early twenties.

Today, he mostly works as a business strategist, negotiator, business broker and mentor.

He has authored books and articles on strategic management systems, entrepreneurship, business brokering and teleworking and has participated in several international events as a guest speaker.

Hisakazu Okamura

Professor Hisakazu Okamura from Faculty of Urban Innovation, Asia University in Tokyo Japan has been leading worldwide Smartcity projects in his over 32-year career in IBM Japan and in the new role of teaching Smartcity and Big Data at the newly developed faculty (2016) for Smartcity in Asia University in Tokyo Japan.

From a 350 citizen, snowy small village project to the largest Japanese €1B 340MHz Photovoltaic plant to a project supporting the mayor of New Orleans, the range of his work is highly diverse.

His book "Smartcity" published in 2011 became the guidebook for Smartcity business in Japan.

In 2017, International NPO CSR day awarded him the recognition of one of the "50 most impactful Smartcity leaders of the world". His philosophy for Smartcity thinking is:
"Only healthy business can help people and society be sustainable."

Örjan Svane

Is trained as architect and now Professor Emeritus in Urban Sustainable Development at the Royal Institute of Technology in Stockholm, KTH. After graduating in 1972, he practised doing refurbishments, and later with "green architecture".

Returning to the academia, he got his Ph.D. in 1999, and was appointed Professor ten years later. In that role, he supervised doctoral students and held courses in undergraduate education.

Between 2007 and 2012 he coordinated a cross-disciplinary research project entitled Situations of Opportunity in the Growth and Change of three Stockholm City Districts, involving seniors, Ph.D. and Master students. From 2011 on, he conducts a series of research projects studying a citizen initiative in the brownfield development of city district Hammarby Sjöstad, Stockholm. The citizen initiative aims at "Renewing a new City", and his approach is real-time research with elements of action research.

Charles Kelley

Charles Kelley is a principal architect and senior urban designer in the Portland office of ZGF Architects.

With more than 32 years of experience, he brings an interdisciplinary approach to design that incorporates community aspirations and the use of natural and financial resources to reach balanced solutions for institutions and municipalities.

Charles speaks regularly on the value of integrated design to leverage multiple objectives across mobility, watershed, energy, water, land use, and open space systems, which contribute to resilient neighborhoods.

He is a founding member of the 1% for Green Committee at the City of Portland, a founding member of the non-profit EcoDistricts, and lead designer for Portland's We Build Green Cities export program. Charles has a Bachelor of Arts in Architecture from the University of Washington, Seattle, and a Master of Architecture with a Certificate of Urban Design from the University of Pennsylvania, Philadelphia.

Ian Abbott-Donnelly

Until his retirement in 2015, Ian Abbott-Donnelly was the European Chief Technology Officer for Big Green Innovations and Smarter Cities at IBM. His job involved pushing the boundaries of IBM in the areas of Smarter: water management, carbon management, alternative energy and the application of high performance computing to environmental issues.

Since leaving IBM, he continues to work on Smarter Cities, Sustainability and Resilience projects under the heading of 'innovation that matters'. As an Associate at Cambridge University Centre for Science and Policy (CSaP) he collaborates with a wide range of policy makers.

http://www.csap.cam.ac.uk/network/ian-abbott-donnelly/

He enjoys combining the diverse disciplines of: technology, innovation, change and learning from nature to help him and others make sense of the world.

Prior to taking up his role at IBM Ian was Head of Technology for English Nature (now Natural England), providing stewardship and regulation for over 4000 special protected sites for nature conservation across England.

Lightning Source UK Ltd.
Milton Keynes UK
UKHW021011100822
407108UK00002B/4